Psychology of
Development and History

Perspectives in Developmental Psychology

Series Editor: Michael Lewis
The Infant Laboratory
Institute for Research in Human Development
Educational Testing Service
Princeton, New Jersey

PSYCHOLOGY OF DEVELOPMENT AND HISTORY
Klaus F. Riegel • 1976

Psychology of
Development and History

Klaus F. Riegel
University of Michigan, Ann Arbor

PLENUM PRESS · NEW YORK AND LONDON

Library of Congress Cataloging in Publication Data

Riegel, Klaus F
    Psychology of development and history.

    (Perspectives in developmental psychology)
    Bibliography: p.
    Includes index.
    1. Developmental psychology. 2. Psychology—Methodology. I. Title.
BF713.R53   155   76-26547
ISBN 0-306-30930-0

© 1976 Plenum Press, New York
A Division of Plenum Publishing Corporation
227 West 17th Street, New York, N.Y. 10011

Printed in the United States of America

Preface

This book documents my return to a topic that has always been one of my closest interests: the systematic study of intellectual and political history. I became involved in historical studies while in high school and continued this work during the years that I spent as a metalworker in a shipyard and in a factory. Indeed, I succeeded in being admitted to the University of Hamburg only after submitting a comparative analysis of the history of early Greek and early Western philosophy to the late Professor G. Ralfs. He gave me much encouragement and remained one of my main academic sponsors during the years in Hamburg. Recently, I translated into English the manuscript that had opened the doors of the university for me, and extended it to the history of psychology. The results present the unfolding of an intellectual theme as if it were an historical dialogue. They (chaps. 10 and 11) are, perhaps, controversial achievements, but they are among my proudest.

Before I began my studies in psychology and philosophy, I spent almost two years in physics and mathematics. Subsequently, I began to approach psychology with a natural-science emphasis. Even when I began to shift my attention from general experimental to developmental psychology (especially gerontology), I continued to maintain this orientation and deemphasized my historical interest. This interest did not find any resonance in the developmental research and theory of these years anyhow.

In 1956, while still at the University of Hamburg, I began a rather large-scale investigation of adult development and aging with its focus ranging from perceptual-cognitive to social-personality variables. In the course of the follow-up investigation, five years later, the interdependence between individual and societal changes became increasingly apparent to me. Long before that time, Felix Krüger and Charlotte Bühler, and more recently scholars at the University of Chicago, most notably Ernest Burgess, Robert Havighurst, and Bernice Neugarten, had called attention to this topic. Later, it was especially the work by Warner Schaie and Paul Baltes at the University of West Virginia that brought the topic into focus and provided means for explicating it in a concise manner. Several chapters in the first part of my book reflect this influence (most notably chaps. 2 and 5).

As I began to realize that developmental analysis cannot succeed without an understanding of societal changes, I also began to realize that the study of history might benefit from an application of the concepts and methods of developmental psychology. The immediate outcome was the chapter entitled "Nomothetic Interpretations of History" (chap. 4), as well as several empirical investigations of historical changes that are reported in the third part of the book (chaps. 12 to 15).

In my studies of development and aging I had become especially interested in changes in language and cognitive functions. In these areas of investigation we find not only the thought-provoking interpretations by Piaget, but we also observe that cognitive functions remain quite obscure when we attempt to explain changes during adulthood and aging. Inasmuch as I became aware of the limitations of cognitive interpretations by studying the changes that take place during the later years of life, I became critical of modern linguistic theories and their a-developmental and a-historical conceptions. Several chapters in this book are generalizations from research and theories about language and cognitive development as they relate to the study of societal changes. These chapters are either concerned with systematic interpretations of language acquisition as a general topic of development (chaps. 2 and 3), or with the influence of cognitive and of linguistic theories upon our modern concepts of development (chap. 8 and 9).

When we link the study of development and aging to the study of societal and historical changes, we cannot avoid coming face-to-face with philosophical and ideological questions that form the basis for scientific inquiries, as they form the basis for the changing individual and the changing society that these studies explore. The ideological bases of developmental psychology are examined in two chapters of this book (chaps. 6 and 7).

If we take seriously the concept of the changing individual in a changing world, we are bound to depart from the traditional explorations derived with the aid of formal logic of classical sciences. We are forced to apply a form of thinking more basic than formal logic and more akin to the explorations of development and change, that is, dialectical logic. Explorations founded upon such a basis not only deal resolutely with the interdependence of individual and societal changes, but, for the first time, succeed in assigning a distinct and significant place in scientific theory to the human being, a place that had been abandoned in traditional sciences.

During the past few years, I have become firmly engaged in the exploration of a dialectical psychology, and have published a number of articles and edited some books on this topic (see Riegel, 1973c, 1975e, 1976a, 1976b); thereby I have returned to the area of interest with which I started my academic career. In the present volume these endeavors are described in several chapters, most notably in the concluding chapter of the book (chap. 15).

The chapters for this book are either original contributions (although some of them have been written many years ago), or they are revised versions of articles or chapters prepared during the last 10 years and scattered throughout several journals and volumes. I have been encouraged by friends, students, and/or colleagues to bring them together in a separate publication. While doing so, I too became convinced of the value of the total package. Although the present collection is addressed to students and scholars from various fields of inquiry—psychology, sociology, anthropology, linguistics, philosophy, history, education, political science, economics—it certainly does not exclude the educated layman. The book elaborates a theme that is not only coherent but that also points to new directions for the study of development and history. It represents issues with which I identify myself and with which I hope many others will be ready to identify. It represents a beginning, of course; I hope, an inspiring one.

My preparation of these chapters has been dependent on challenges, guidance, and encouragements from friends, students, and/or colleagues. My thanks, gratitude, and love belong to all of them. Since it would be quite impossible to name each and every one, the following list is a rather arbitrary one: Inge Ahammer, Mary Arnold, Paul Baltes, John Broughton, Susan Buck-Morss, Bobbie Coffman, Nancy Datan, Roy Freedle, Bill Gekoski, Frank Hardesty, Adrienne Harris, Dale Harris, Wilbur Hass, Lynn Liben, Gerhard Lipp, Jack Meacham, Chuck Perfetti, Leon Rappoport, Carol Ryff, Elliot Stern, Rob Wozniak, Marilyn Zivian, and, outside of her alphabetical place, Ruth Riegel.

K. R.

ACKNOWLEDGMENTS

The author and publisher are grateful for permission to reproduce, either partially or in their entirety, articles by the author that had been previously published.

Academic Press, Inc., New York: "Models of growth and development," previously published as part of "Time and change in the development of the individual and society" in H. W. Reese (Ed.), *Advances in child development and behavior* (Vol. 7), 1973; and "Developmental psychology and society," previously published under the same title in J. R. Nesselroade and H. W. Reese (Eds.), *Life-span developmental psychology: Methodological issues*, 1973.

American Psychological Association, Washington: "The ideological bases of developmental psychology," previously published as "Influence of economic and political ideologies on the development of developmental psychology," *Psychological Bulletin*, 1973, 78, 129–141; and "Cross-reference analysis of the history of psychological gerontology," previously published as part of "On the history of psychological gerontology" in C. Eisdorfer and M. P. Lawton (Eds.), *The psychology of adult development and aging*, 1973.

Behavioral Sciences, Health Science Center Library, University of Louisville, Louisville, Kentucky: "The recall of events from the individual and collective past" parts were previously published as "The recall of historical events," 1973, 18, 354–363.

Human Development, S. Karger, Basel, Switzerland: "Ecological interpretations of development," previously published as "Development of Language: Suggestions for a verbal fallout model," 1966, 9, 97–120, and "Structural historical analysis of the Department of Psychology at the University of Michigan," published under the same title in 1970, 13, 269–279.

Journal for Social Issues, Society for the Psychological Study of Social Issues, Ann Arbor, Michigan: "Nomothetic interpretations of history," previously published as part of "History as a nomothetic science: Some generalizations from theory and research in developmental psychology," 1969, 25, 99–127.

John Wiley and Sons, Inc., New York: "Structure and transformation in modern intellectual history," previously published under the same title; and "Historical comparisons of monetary and linguistic systems," previously published as part of "Semantic basis of language: Language as labor." Both chapters appeared in K. F. Riegel and G. C. Rosenwald (Eds.), *Structure and transformation: Developmental and historical aspects*, 1975.

All chapters have been revised and reedited by the author.

Contents

PART I

Theoretical Issues

CHAPTER 1

The Individual and History:
An Introduction

The relationship between the individual and society has long been the concern of philosophers, sociologists, and psychologists. The more sophisticated and appropriate question of the relationship between the individual's development and societal changes is about as old as the first problem but has not been raised with the same persistency. Not all scholars have directed their attention to the growth of the individual and to the growth of society and very few, indeed, to the interactive development of both. Undoubtedly, such disregard restricts their interpretations in a serious manner.

Students of history have traditionally bisected the topic under consideration by either overemphasizing the role of the individual in history or by overemphasizing that of society. This bisection led, on the one hand, to personalistic interpretations in which the generative aspects of the historical figures, the hero, received singular attention; and on the other hand, to the naturalistic interpretations in which the formative influence of social conditions (including the infamous construct of Zeitgeist) and anonymous forces, the masses, were overemphasized. In segregating both interpretations in this manner, scholars either disregarded or rejected the dialectical relationship between the changing individual and the changing society. It is our contention, expressed throughout the following chapters, that only such an interactive interpretation can provide an appropriate conception of the individual, society, and their development. For an explication of this argument I rely, first, on a demonstration of various paradigms of psychological analyses; second, I compare the conceptualization in developmental psychology with that applied in historical studies.

PARADIGMS OF PSYCHOLOGICAL ANALYSES

The complex issue of the individual's development in a changing society can be clearly elaborated in reference to statistical research designs. Table 1 shows a typical condition in which twice the performance of two age groups is compared, once in 1920 and again in 1970. This diagram demonstrates three levels of abstraction or alienation in research and theory.

The first and still rather common orientation represents general-experimental psychology. This approach, by focusing upon a single cell of the matrix shown in Table 1, is the most abstract and alienated form of a scientific inquiry. Both individual and historical changes are eliminated, and thus, the person represents a fictitious point in a developmental–historical vacuum. Using the fanciful expressions of the behavioral scientists, we might say that fixating one's inquiry in such a manner reduces the degree of freedom in the diagram to zero but increases the degree of alienation to its maximum of two. Using common sense, we might say that such an approach represents an academic escape.

Regarding the second approach used by individual-developmental psychologists, the situation is not much better. Although they study developmental differences (and sometimes changes), they eliminate (with a few exceptions in gerontology) any consideration of historical differences and changes. Table 1 shows clearly, however, that 20- and 70-year-olds, tested cross-sectionally in 1970, for example, differ also in respect to the cultural–historical conditions under which they grew up. After all, one group was born in 1900 and the other in 1950. Historical changes in education, health care, nutrition, communication, etc., are likely to account for the greater proportion of variation than differences attributable to individual

Table 1. Years of Birth of Four Cohorts in a
Demonstration of Developmental–Historical
Research Designs

Time of testing	Age	
	20	70
1920	1900	1850
1970	1950	1900

psychological development. In comparison with the general experimental psychologists, the degree of freedom in variation is higher and the degree of alienation is lower in investigations by developmental psychologists; both equal one. Also, students of individual-developmental psychology offend human dignity, but they do so only because of their disrespect for cultural differences and historical changes.

Thus there can be only one proper approach to the study of the individual, an approach that takes account of both individual-developmental and cultural–historical changes. Recent investigations in life-span developmental psychology (Baltes, Baltes, and Reinert, 1970; Nesselroades and Baltes, 1974; Riegel and Riegel, 1972; Schaie and Strother, 1968a, 1968b), related to explorations in the sociology of generational shifts (Bengtson and Black, 1973; Riley, Johnson, and Foner, 1972; Ryder, 1965), have explicated the confounded changes in the individual and in society. These advances, made possible by the elaboration of developmental research designs (Baltes, 1968; Schaie, 1965, 1970), have been limited, however, to formal explorations. They did not focus upon the underlying cultural–historical processes themselves that, in principle, these investigators recognized as influencing the growth of the individual. The sociology of generational shifts, on the other hand, has directed our attention to these cultural–historical processes but did not explore their impact on the development of the individual.

Only dialectical psychology (Riegel, 1975b, 1975e) has fully recognized the interaction between individual and historical development (Meacham, 1972), both of which it traces, in its Marxist's extension, to their inner and outer material foundations. Without necessarily taking this step, we can, nevertheless, agree with Marx that "man creates himself through his own labor; by transforming nature, he transforms himself." Early societies, for example, by inventing a tool, a sign, or linguistic expressions changed, at the same time, the sociophysical conditions under which they lived. These conditions, in the process of history, have in turn changed the individual. Thus, through dialectical interactions, the individual as well as society move forward to new achievements and new structures.

COMPARISON OF DEVELOPMENTAL AND HISTORICAL STUDIES

Traditionally, developmental psychologists have investigated the skills or performances, traits or behaviors of individuals *here and now* (see Table 2). By repeating these observations longitudinally or by comparing different age groups cross-sectionally they thought to extract age changes or age differences without realizing that the former are tied to historical changes and the latter confounded with generational differences. Moreover, the measurement of performance of behavior *here and now* represents a highly artificial selection that hardly captures the developmental status and direction of an individual at any particular time. Does it, indeed, matter for an individual's daily success whether he or she can or cannot abstract some shared features from stimuli, solve some algebraic problems, trace a maze, or reassemble blocks? Granted that these performances and behaviors might be predictive of certain occupational and professional skills, they do not encompass the array of an individual's activities that occupy him or her and reflect lifelong experiences, feelings about one's past, and hopes for one's future. Determinants reflecting these aspects of an individual's well-being have rarely been investigated in developmental psychological research nor do they enter decisively into theoretical accounts.

If we turn to the study of history, represented by another section of Table 2, we find an approach distinctively different from the methodology of developmental psychology. Historical investigations consist in the reconstruction of the past on the basis of collective records and memories. Undoubtedly, these interpretations are not only influenced by the prevailing sociopolitical attitudes of the historians but also by the selective collection and retention of those records that survived the ages. Despite these limitations, historical interpretations capture the experienced and enacted past with which not only society but each individual is confronted at all times. Present-day developmental psychology has barely attained a comparable status; unlike history, it rarely searches for causes and directions of development but consists of descriptive recordings of the individual's activities *here and now*.

In comparing the historical with the developmental psychological paradigm, we have to consider two exceptions. First, the historical para-

Table 2. Paradigms of Developmental and Historical Inquiries

	Past	Present	Future
Individual	Clinical retrospective interpretations.	Developmental performance descriptions.	Prospective analyses of goals.
Societal	Historical retrospective interpretations.	Archival record collections.	Prospective analyses of policies.

digm has been used in clinical case studies. Here the individual's past is retrospectively constructed, for example, through psychoanalytical inquiries. Unfortunately, most of these investigations lack nomothetic rigor, a difficulty that I will try to overcome in the studies reported in part III. Second, the developmental psychological paradigm has been applied for historical purposes in archival collections. Through these efforts significant events *here and now* are recorded and stored for future descriptions. If these efforts are carried out with sufficient foresight and persistence, they should, eventually, produce more systematic objectification of past events than those incidentally retained and recovered through the historians' efforts.

Finally, the comparison of developmental paradigms in Table 2 suggests two other approaches in the study of the individual and of society; both are concerned with the future. These possibilities, as self-evident as they may seem, have neither been realized in psychology nor in the study of history. I shall address this issue in the concluding chapter of this volume.

PREVIEW OF THE BOOK

In part I, I address theoretical issues concerning individual and societal development. I start with a case typical for the social sciences, the case of theoretical linguistics (chap. 2). Scholars in this discipline, most notably de Saussure (1916), pretend to study both synchronic—general and diachronic—historical aspects but on the basis of such dichotomy fail to provide a place for the individual in their analyses. Subsequently, they are unable to promote adequate developmental and historical interpretations.

Continuing the inquiry into language and language development, I discuss next, in chapter 3, the possibility for deterministic explanations of development, and of simulating developmental progression by laboratory studies. In chapter 4, I extend this exploration to the nomothetic analysis of historical progression, and in chapter 5, to the concepts of time and change in the study of the individual and of society. Chapter 5 applies some theoretical models of developmental psychology to the study of history; this chapter represents a transition to the other two parts of the book, which report on traditional idiographic studies of the history of sciences and some nomothetic research explorations.

Part II contains the six major chapters of this book. In chapter 6, I attempt a systematic, prospective construction of cultural—historical changes; this report is based on idiographic material. Chapter 7 discusses the dependence of the development of developmental psychology on political and economic ideologies. Chapter 8, a further extension of this topic, deals with a modern outcome of these movements, i.e., the study of structure and transformation.

For most of us it is inconceivable to propose a transformational analysis unless the structures subject to transformations are specified beforehand. Nevertheless, a reversal of this thinking is possible. Chapter 9 presents a demonstration of such an attempt by comparing different conceptions of language and cognitive development with the history of monetary systems. Finally, chapters 10 and 11 apply some of the nomothetical models presented in chapter 4 so that we can derive systematic interpretations of the history of Greek and European philosophy and of the history of psychology. Without exception, these interpretations rest, however, upon idiographic historical reports.

In contrast to these last two attempts to systematize idiographic histories, part III in general and chapters 12 and 13 in particular rely on empirical research methodologies. Chapter 12 is most restricted in scope; it analyzes, on the basis of the differing composition of dissertation committees, the brief history of the Department of Psychology at the University of Michigan. Chapter 13 reports a crossreference analysis of publications in psychological gerontology. In contrast to that of the preceding chapter, its analysis is performed retrogressively; i.e., it starts with a recent publication and traces the network of its intellectual ancestors backward in historical time.

Finally, chapter 14 and the concluding chapter 15 attempt a transgression of developmental psychological and historical methodologies. These chapters report on the recall of persons and events in the history of the individual and society. By applying the retrospective historical approach in a systematic manner, these attempts enrich the perspectives of developmental psychologists as well as the methodological scrutiny of historical analyses. These investigations are extended to some general theoretical interpretations of the role of the individual in history and of the role of history for the individual. They lead me to conclude that the development of the individual and the history of society do not merely consist in retrospective collections of past events nor in the recording of present achievements and changes, but, most importantly, in the activities of individuals and cohorts of individuals who through their efforts generate and thus change prospectively their own development and our own history.

CHAPTER 2

Development and History
in Social Science Theories

Since the publication of de Saussure's lecture notes (1916), linguistics has been cut into two: synchronic linguistics, the description of a particular "state" of a language at some "point" in time; and diachronic linguistics, the description of its historical development "through time." In deemphasizing the interdependence of these two approaches, linguistics has disregarded the human being as both the creator and the creation of language. This disregard is the result of the failure to understand individual and historical changes. The methodological, epistemological, and ideological implications of this issue may be clarified by the following examples.

TOWARD DEVELOPMENTAL–HISTORICAL ANALYSES

Linguistics Without the Human Being

Let us consider a synchronic study of the slang spoken in eastern American cities. Restricting, thus, the inquiry to a narrow domain, we eliminate the language spoken in other American and in British cities, in all rural areas, and in other English-speaking countries. Moreover, we lack precision because we failed to specify the sex of the speakers, their age, etc. Slang will vary in familiarity and type with the age of the speaker. At early age levels it may not be known at all, and at others, it may be the predominant mode of communication. With his concept of *parole,* de Saussure

9

made provisions for these variations. Although loosely defined, this notion, ultimately, forces us toward the viewpoint temporarily promoted by Kurt Lewin (1927; see also Riegel, 1958), who insisted that psychological laws ought to be based on "the description of one individual, at one time, at one location." The same should be concluded for synchronic linguistics.

If we were to extend our first investigation into a diachronic analysis, we would have to obtain records of the slang spoken in eastern American cities sometime ago in the historical past, let's say, around 1920. Since records of the spoken language are hardly available from that time period, such a comparison would pose some difficulties. In regard to written language, however, diachronic linguistics finds itself in a much more fortunate position than its counterpart in the behavioral sciences, i.e., developmental psychology, where achievement or production records, such as test data, may be available for the last few decades but not for periods prior to 1920. In linguistics, too, the farther one reaches back in history, the more one has to settle on a few records produced for selective purposes by selected people.

In the terminology of developmental research, a synchronic study represents a single *cross-sectional analysis*. A diachronic study represents a contrastive comparison of two (or more) of such slates that—commonly fixed upon a particular developmental level (e.g., teen-agers), a particular location (e.g., eastern U.S. cities), etc.—has been called time-lag analysis. These fixations are the main prerequisite by which linguists could have escaped the bewildering variability and ambiguities of concrete languages. But by aiming at descriptions of the language in general (*langue*), they rejected such idiographic limitations (as Lewin had proposed them for psychology) and reached for an abstract formalism. They failed to see that, thereby, they downgraded or rejected the most precious and central part of their exploration, the human being. Despite their liberal use of labels such as "generative," "productive," and "spontaneous," they forgot that language is not created by the elitist intuitions of linguists but by man who, at the same time, is created by language.

Psychology Without Human History

My criticism of contemporary linguistics should not be regarded as an endorsement of the personologism of Western psychologies, which in their uncritical commitment and frequent glorification of the individual not only removed cultural–sociological but frequently also biological–physical aspects from consideration. The limitations of this approach are most clearly apparent in developmental studies.

Developmental psychologists have thought to study changes by slicing one synchronic, cross-sectional slate into its age-specific substrata. By collecting data from a large group of people differing in age and, then, by subdividing this group accordingly, they tried to derive developmental descriptions. Without exception they failed to realize that people who differ in age also differ in their past histories and, therefore, in regard to the vast social changes that were brought about in education, welfare, health care, communication (newspaper, radio, television), transportation, etc. While these psychologists conceived of the individual as if he or she were growing up in a constant sociohistorical environment (if not in a sociohistorical vacuum), the diachronic linguists, studying precisely one aspect of these sociohistorical changes, i.e., language, acted as if these changes occurred without the participatory efforts of individuals and generations of individuals (cohorts).

Developmental psychologists have always excused their deficiencies by emphasizing that *longitudinal analysis* remains the ultimate goal of their efforts. In such an analysis, the performance of individuals is repeatedly evaluated over periods of time. Though recognizing many of the technical difficulties of carrying out such an investigation, the proponents of this strategy failed to realize that as the individual changes so society changes. Indeed, recent investigations in psychology and sociology have convincingly shown (Baltes *et al.,* 1970; Nesselroade and Baltes, 1974; Riegel and Riegel, 1972; Schaie and Strother, 1968a, 1968b) that in many instances changes in the physical and social environment are faster and more dramatic than those that individuals may undergo. Subsequently, the growing and aging individuals fall farther and farther behind; they become "outdated." If their cohorts succeed in retaining their power, a generation gap develops that places the new cohorts and ultimately the whole society under severe stress.

Developmental–Historical Research Designs

The conceptualization implied in longitudinal research designs makes the interdependence of individual and societal changes abundantly clear. Recent advances in developmental research designs by Schaie (1965) and Baltes (1968) have enabled us to unconfound these confounded changes. Table 1 (chap. 1) shows some of these possibilities. As indicated by the year of birth, each cell represents a corpus of data from one cohort. Under the conditions shown, we could make *two cross-sectional comparisons* between 20- and 70-year-old individuals. For this purpose, we would compare the two cells within each of the two rows. As evidenced by the different birth dates of the cohorts compared, a cross-sectional design (*CSD*) does not only reflect age differences (*AD*), for example, in the language spoken by 20- and 70-year-olds, but cohort differences (*CD*) as well, i.e., for the historical periods of 1850 and 1900 or 1900 and 1950, respectively. Assuming additivity, we obtain the following formula:

$$CSD = AD + CD$$

Also *two time-lag comparisons* are possible for our example. In this case we would analyze historical differences, for example, in the language spoken by 20-year-olds in 1920 and in 1970. The same comparison can be made for the 70-year-olds. Thus, we would compare the data of two cells lying vertical to one another in either of the two columns of Table 1. Time-lag designs (*TLD*) confound cohort differences (*CD*) with the time-of-testing differences (*TD*) both of which are historical in nature. Age differences are not considered or rather kept constant in each of the two possible comparisons. In a formula:

$$TLD = CD + TD$$

Finally, *one longitudinal design* (*LTD*) is embedded in the example shown in Table 1. We might analyze, for instance, the changes in language as spoken by a group of 10-year-olds in 1910 and by the same group at an age of 70 years in 1970. Any observed changes are reflecting both age and time-of-testing differences. In a formula:

$$LTD = AD + TD$$

According to these formulas, none of the three approaches provides us directly with "pure" estimates of either age, cohort, or time differences. However, by solving the three equations for any one of the three components, such estimates can be obtained:

$$AD = \tfrac{1}{2} (CSD - TLD + LTD)$$
$$CD = \tfrac{1}{2} (TLD - LTD + CSD)$$
$$TD = \tfrac{1}{2} (LTD - CSD + TLD)$$

While it is, thus, in principle possible to estimate the "pure" effects of age, cohort, or time differences, such attempts will always have to rely on the joint utilization of all three basic designs. This recognition represents a true breakthrough. Psychology may, now, justifiably describe individual developmental changes, sociology may describe cohort differences, and history may describe changes with chronological time. Our analyses make us also aware that none of these disciplines ought to remain in their isolation. An understanding of change can be achieved only if their contributions are recognized in their complementary dependence. Each alone produces fictitious results and interpretations. This conclusion has serious implications for psychology and linguistics.

Diachronic linguistics analyzes historical differences in form of time-lag designs. Thereby, the changing individual is disregarded. Developmental psychology analyzes either differences or changes in the form of cross-sectional or longitudinal designs. Thereby, the sociocultural differences or changes are disregarded. Diachronic linguistics and developmental psychology ought to supplement each other. Only both in conjunction can lead to a comprehensive understanding of language that, generated through the ceaseless efforts of man, in turn, transforms or regenerates man through each of the cohorts of growing individuals. Such a synthesis stands in diametrical conflict to the least imaginative approach of all, synchronic linguistics and synchronic or general psychology.

TOWARD DIALECTICAL INTERPRETATIONS
OF PSYCHOLINGUISTICS

Linguistics between "Chaos" and "Law and Order"

After the publication of his "Syntactic Structures" (1957), Chomsky became known to psychologists for his attack upon Skinner's operant behaviorism (1959). Although this article created the misperception that, thereby, he challenged psychology itself and not merely a deviant form of application, his critique appeared at a most appropriate time. It gave support to many psychologists who felt repressed by the mechanistic theories of behavior and learning that had dominated psychology in the United States for much too long a time.

With his emphasis upon change and with his disrespect for both inner and outer organization, Skinner deviates not only from Chomsky but also from such "hypothetical–deductive" attempts proposed by his colleague Hull (1943). While the emphasis upon modifiability makes Skinner's work refreshing, indeed, these changes occur without any respect for the socio-historical conditions. Therefore, they can hardly lead to any recognizable structure within the organism, an organization that, anyhow, Skinner is unwilling to search for. From moment to moment the organism is at the mercy of outer forces that must appear indeterminate and unstructured to him. Although the organism changes successfully and predictably through these encounters, Skinner makes no attempt to analyze systematically the organization of these outer forces; to provide, for example, a sociohistorical explanation of why a behavior modifier operates in one way when conditioning one organism and in a different way when conditioning another. Since there is no explanation of the past, there is no direction for the future. Unlike Pavlov's reflexology in the Soviet Union, Skinner's interpretations have not been supplemented by a theory of society and have not been integrated within a theory of history (see Rubinstein 1958, 1963).

In the modern Western world, Skinner, the "Agent of Chaos," is juxtaposed to Chomsky, the "Guardian of Law and Order" (see Wilden, 1972). Although Chomsky has placed the word "mind" into the title of some of his publications, his interpretations successfully strip linguistics of its psychological base. He aims toward abstract descriptions of the universal structure of language, of *language as it ought to be,* which, he maintains, makes the language of individuals possible at all. But when we ask how an individual acquires this language, he provides no answer except to regress toward a reductionism by arguing for "innate capacities" or "blueprints" of language. When asked how language was generated in society, he might either give a similar answer or retreat to pregeneticism and preformationism of Cartesian philosophy. For these spiritualistic extensions, language lies outside of the sensing and acting mind; it reflects the universal mind, HIS mind (Riegel, 1973a).

The Static Dualism of Linguistics

Ever since de Saussure, linguistics has suffered an identity crisis that de Saussure had tried to resolve by freeing linguistics from the dominance of psychology. With the growing emphasis upon the sensory-perceptual basis of sciences during the last decades of the 19th century, psychology had gained increasing significance. Even in the natural sciences such prominent scholars as Mach, Petzold, and Oswald, and mathematicians of no lesser renown than Dedekind and Frege promoted a psychological basis of knowledge at the expense of naturalistic, materialistic conceptions. In linguistics this influence became apparent in Wundt's writing although, I hasten to emphasize, he assigned to this discipline, as well as to sociology, anthropology, and history, much more independent roles than would be expected from a person whose name has been singularly connected with the growth of psychologism or psychological imperialism (Blumenthal, 1970).

But apparently these concessions by a prominent psychologist were not enough and thus de Saussure aimed toward a more radical separation.

The resulting break affiliated his antipsychologism with the biosociological dualism of Durkheim, which not only downgraded the significance of the individual but of development and change as well. I criticize both not so much for their antipsychologism and their implicit suspicion of psycholinguistics but for their a-developmental and a-historical interpretations. What we ought to adopt is an approach that gives attention to both the biological–physical and the cultural–sociological bases of language seen in their dynamic developmental interactions. Such a conception reintroduces the human being into linguistic interpretations, it promotes a human science of linguistics.

Linguistics between Intuitionism and Formalism

In Chomsky's case, the dualistic split took the form of relying, on the one hand, on the evasive, subjective notion of "linguistic intuitions" and escape into abstract formalism, on the other. The recognition of linguistic intuitions seems pleasing at first because it admits a nonrational and psychological basis of language and linguistic interpretations. But these intuitions represent the insights of a few selected persons only and not the concrete experience of common man. If, indeed, Chomsky were to accept intuition on such a common and concrete basis, he would be forced to reintroduce the whole psychologism from which linguists have been trying to escape so eagerly. Moreover, he would be forced to reintroduce the cultural–historical context through which such intuitions are determined (Halbwachs, 1925; Blondel, 1928).

For similar reasons it is also not surprising that modern linguistics has been unable to handle the problem of meaning. The biosociological dualism of Durkheim and de Saussure eliminated this possibility in a radical manner. This limitation afflicted also Bloomfield, whose affiliation with the psychology of his day provided only an apparent consolidation. The psychology that he promoted, behaviorism, followed a similar route to that of Durkheim and de Saussure, leading to the elimination of the experiencing human being and, thus, of meaning. The concrete and meaningful experience of the individual, nevertheless, has to form the basis for any interpretation of language. Linguists in their striving for independence have either delegated these experiences to the elitist few and/or have denied the participatory role of the common human being. Thereby, they escaped into formalism.

Undoubtedly formalism can serve the important function of increasing the precision of a description. It should not be an end in itself. But as the precision increases, so does the rigidity of the structure that it provides. Ultimately, the investigators may be captured within their own web and may be unable to see the limitations of their interpretations. This outcome resulted when modern linguistics was applied to the study of language development. As even the most conservative linguists must admit, real children learn to interact meaningfully within a sociolinguistic context; they learn to communicate. Transformational grammer describes an alienated formal system in the mind of the linguist that real children do not and should not acquire.

The Outer and Inner Dialectics of Development

Language acquisition does not merely consist in the externalization of internal structures through the organism's activities. It would also have to consider the cultural–historical structures as active forces participating in the developmental process, leading to the internalization of the external organization. Like Piaget, Chomsky has restricted the notion of activity and structure of the organism essentially to the biological organism. His theory restricts these interactions to process within the organism, in particular to those between deep structure and surface structure, competence and performance. Behaviorism, on the other hand, has disregarded both the notion of structure and of activity but has, nevertheless, dealt with interactions, limited to the mechanical interaction of external physical stimuli and response movements. The desired synthesis emphasizes the activities and structures of both the organism and of the environment that, in their dialectical interactions, produce the developmental and historical processes. Such a synthesis reintroduces the human being into linguistic interpretations (Riegel, 1973c, 1975c). It recognizes that we create ourselves through our own labor, by transforming nature to transform ourselves.

CONCLUSION

As seen from the Western perspective, the first part of my discussion was based on nothing more profane than the statistics of developmental research design; the second led to nothing more contemptuous than idealistic and materialistic dialecticism. It is the significance and beauty of true psycholinguistics that it would reconcile without effort these apparently incompatible tools of the human mind.

CHAPTER 3

Ecological Interpretations
of Development

Despite its impressive history, developmental psychology has not provided a clear answer to the question of why organisms grow and age. Some have tried to obviate the problem by declaring that time itself may serve explanatory functions. This means nothing else than to say, for instance, 4-year-olds have a certain height *because* they are 4 years old. Others have been satisfied by (commonly overappreciated) attempts to reduce psychological development to changes in nonpsychological conditions, particularly biological factors, and to substitute phenotypical by so-called genotypical descriptions. Such an interpretation is implied, for example, when we explain growth in size by changes in the endocrine system. For many purposes such explanations will be fruitful. But they merely delegate the problem to another area of study where the same question arises again and no satisfactory answer is provided as to why organisms grow and age.

A more abstract form of reductionism is implied when the time or age dimension itself is replaced by nontemporal factors. This possibility is inherent in all attempts to derive psychological or biological age scales independently from chronological age, for instance, by evaluating the potassium concentration, the calcification of certain organs, or merely the number of items solved on a mental-age scale. If the evaluation of psychological or biological age is theoretically well substantiated, powerful explanations of growth and aging can be derived. For clarification of this point, let

The original article was published under the title, "Development of language: Suggestions for a verbal fallout model," Human Development, *1966, 9, 97–120.*

us consider two biological theories of development (for a comprehensive discussion see Strehler, 1962; Curtis, 1963).

The first theory has been called the *waste theory*. Basic metabolic processes in cells lead to the production of waste products, such as lipofuscin, which cannot be completely removed and accumulate over the years until they reach a critical level and produce a slow or sudden decrease in functioning. This theory leads to the important notion that life itself implies growth and aging, namely, via the accumulation of metabolic waste. The waste theory may be called an intrinsic theory of development: The biological age is determined by the amount of waste accumulated by and within the organism.

The second theory has been called the *mutation theory* and is concerned with the instability of the chromosomes in somatic and gonadic cells. Mutations, which are generally deleterious for the organism, occur at random. The older a person is, the greater the number of mutations that have occurred and the more likely it is that structural and functional defects will result. Since the mutation rate depends on the amount of irradiation to which an organism has been subjected, some theorists regard the amount of radioactive fallout as a major determinant of changes during development and aging. This formulation is of importance not only because it suggests ways to manipulate developmental processes in the laboratory, but also because the determinant of age has become an extrinsic, nonbiological entity. Again, the amount of radioactive fallout to which an organism has been exposed may be used to redefine the time or age scale. Thus, we may rid ourselves of chronological time as a primary dimension and simultaneously develop a deterministic interpretation of growth and aging.

SUGGESTIONS FOR A DETERMINISTIC MODEL
OF LANGUAGE DEVELOPMENT

Contrary to what some experimentalists like to make us think, language does not consist of short responses in single situations, but as Anderson has put it, individuals are virtually "bathed in linguistic stimulation" (1949). A 5-year-old may speak 12,000 words per day and will receive even larger quantities of spoken language. In our search for a deterministic interpretation of language development, we first have to ask whether the amounts of verbal activity on one hand, and of "verbal fallout" on the other, are about constant throughout life.

Despite the practical importance of age differences in the amount of communication, few reliable studies are available. Link and Hopf (1946) reported some results of a sample survey on the amount of time spent daily in reading. Even though we might question whether the material listed (newspapers, magazines, books) represents adequately the total written input, let us for the sake of simplicity accept the results as they are presented; and, subsequently, let us conclude on the basis of these data that the amount of written input during a time period of specified length (e.g., day, week, month) is about constant for the adult years. Accordingly, the total number of messages received will increase linearly with age.

Messages differ in quality or information value and, on the average, the information value decreases with the length of messages. The precise relationship between these two variables has been investigated by researchers in literary statistics and a number of mathematical models have been suggested. Thus, Carroll (1938) analyzed the relationship between the number of different words (types) and the total number of words (tokens) in James Joyce's *Ulysses*. Plotting the first occurrences of all words in an accumulative manner against their locations in the text, he derived a negatively accelerated trend, which is shown in Figure 1. For our present purpose it is more appropriate to regard Figure 1 as representing the information *received* by a person *reading the book*. On the first few pages he will be faced with many different words (types). Then, after the more common words have occurred, the encounter of new words becomes less likely. Thus, the curve flattens out as the end of the book is approached.

In his study of the relationship between word variability and text length, Carroll has been followed by a number of other scientists. In an earlier publication (Riegel and Riegel, 1965), we have reviewed the pertinent literature and selected the best-fitting function for our own study. In the present chapter I will generalize these interpretations to the study of language development.

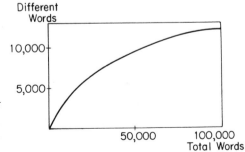

Figure 1. Predicted number of different words as a function of total number of words in James Joyce's *Ulysses* (Carroll 1938).

Generalizations and Empirical Support for the Model

If a word count were available on all the books and materials a person has read during his life span, we would expect a growth curve for his vocabulary quite similar to the one for the reader of James Joyce's *Ulysses*— only longer. Moreover, if we maintain our assumption on the constant amount of daily reading, we could substitute the total number of pages read by the age of the reader or vice versa.

Slicing off equal intervals along the ordinate of the curve, we may also use the enumeration of the different words as an indicator of a person's "reading age." During early years, reading age increases quickly in comparison to chronological age; later on, when the reader is far advanced in his "book of life," greater and greater amounts of reading are required to produce equal amounts of reading growth. But as long as a person continues to read, he will have a chance—even though a decreasing one—to encounter a word that has not occurred to him before. This word might be a new one, only recently introduced into the language, or it might be a rare word that requires an exceedingly large language sample for its occurrence.

Substantial evidence in support of my propositions has been obtained. During the first two years of life, scores on recognition vocabularies (McCarthy, 1954) show a positively accelerated increase. Thereafter, the trend becomes negatively accelerated, but even during the adult and later years of life a high stability or a slight increase in scores has been noted in most studies (Riegel, 1965b). Figure 2 includes a mathematical trend for a multiple choice vocabulary given to 500 persons (Riegel, 1968b).

The evidence reported above is for recognition vocabularies and does not represent the words actively used by individuals. Unfortunately, much less is known about age differences in the active vocabulary. The present author observed an increase in variability of responses in a word-association test over an age span from 17 to over 75 years (Riegel and Riegel, 1964), and similar results have been reported by Riegel and Birren (1966) in their study of syllable associations of young and old individuals. Since these and a few other investigations rely on cross-sectional comparisons, the increase in variability may express an increase in vocabulary specializations by the various persons, i.e., in interindividual variations rather than in intraindividual changes. Each individual, therefore, may become narrower rather than wider in his response variability.

The difficulty of deriving a separate estimate of intraindividual response variability is resolved in word counts of diaries and journals written by a woman at a median age of 35 years and of letters written by the same

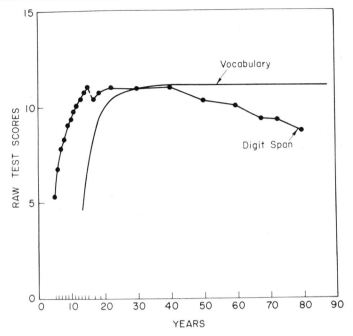

Figure 2. Mean scores on a vocabulary and digit span test for different age groups (Riegel, unpublished data; Wechsler 1949; Wechsler 1955).

person after the age of 68 years (see Figure 3). In the analysis of these records, Smith (1955, 1957) observed an increase in word variability up to an age of about 75 years. She attributed the decline thereafter to extraneous factors, particularly the declining health of the person.

The data of Figure 3 provide only indirect support for my interpretation. Ideally, complete counts of *all* the words heard or spoken, read or written during a person's life ought to be obtained. Of course, such a study would become an exceedingly expensive if not an impossible endeavor. Fortunately, simplifications of the procedures are possible: First, we may limit our study to time samples. Second, we may stratify our material and restrict our analysis to specific strata, for instance, to nouns or verbs or adjectives. Indeed, we may go so far as to study only words beginning with a certain syllable or letter of the alphabet. Undoubtedly the type of restriction will have its effects on the results, but by comparing different restrictions generalizations may be drawn.

If we restrict our study in the indicated manner, we approximate the method of testing verbal fluency as developed by Bousfield and Sedgewick (1944). In this procedure a person is asked to name as fast as possible all

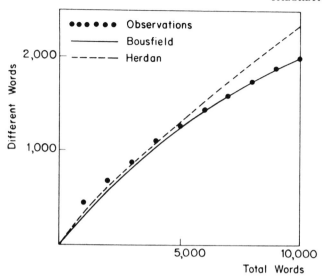

Figure 3. Accumulated record of different words written by a S after her 68th year of life plotted against text length. (After Smith, 1957.)

words of a particular type that come to his mind, for example all words beginning with S or Q. With this restriction on the individual's performance, we compress his output to such an extent that we may obtain our records during a single laboratory session.

Our comparison implies that individuals in the verbal fluency task are scanning through their repertoires in the same manner as readers would do when they go through the pages of a book in order to detect particular words, such as different S-words. To the person scanning a book for different S-words, the interspersed words are a nuisance and they become the more so the farther they have advanced in the text (because later in the text an increasingly greater number of words is likely to be interspersed between any new S-words). If the time intervals between the emission of adjacent words in the verbal fluency test are assumed to be proportional to the time intervals that elapse until a person scanning a book hits upon new words, and moreover, to the time intervals that elapse until a reader of the book encounters new words, we can derive a method of simulating developmental processes in the laboratory.

Simulation of Developmental Processes

Previously, I cited some evidence that old persons have larger active as well as passive vocabularies than young persons. Subsequently, their performance in verbal fluency tests ought to be superior. In order to test this hypothesis and, more generally, the idea of simulating aging processes with the verbal fluency test, I compared the accumulation of S- and Q-words in James Joyce's *Ulysses* with the production of such words by young and old individuals in 10-minute laboratory sessions.

In my study, 31 college students and 23 members of senior citizens' clubs were asked to write down as many words as they could think of beginning with the letter S or Q, respectively. They marked the end of each 2-minute period on their papers. The number of responses given during these consecutive 2-minute periods was used in the analysis.

According to the results of Figure 4, my prediction that the larger vocabulary of old individuals should lead to a superior performance in the verbal fluency test was not confirmed. The total number of different words emitted during the 10-minute periods was found to be much smaller for the old than for the young persons. Apparently factors other than vocabulary size affect verbal output and prevent the old from making full and efficient use of their large vocabularies. Subsequently, I have to examine possible sources of interference and, generally, to explain the failure of my prediction.

1. Thus far, I have dealt exclusively with the *physical environment* according to Lewin (1954) and *la langue* according to de Saussure (1916). I dealt only with the different words that occur in the surroundings of an individual but not with the question whether he does indeed register and per-

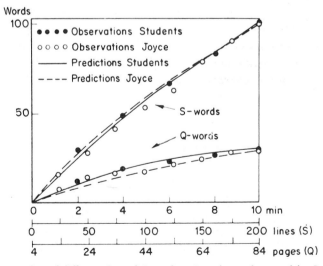

Figure 4A. Number of different Q- and S-words written by students and by James Joyce plotted against time or text length.

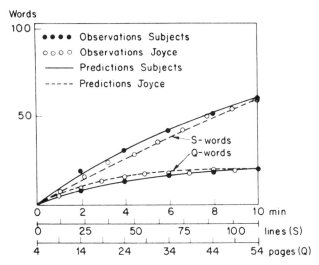

Figure 4B. Number of different Q- and S-words written by old Ss and by James Joyce plotted against time or text length.

ceive these words or not. I dealt with the words that he can possibly produce under optimal conditions but not with the limitations that a realistic situation imposes upon his performance. Quite different mechanisms representing inner biological changes rather than changes in outer physical or linguistic contingencies will be involved in perceiving (hearing or reading) or producing (saying or writing) words and sentences.

Figure 5 shows some characteristic data on age differences in the speed of silent reading and writing. Mature persons read about 10 times as fast as they write, but there is also a differential decline in writing speed beyond the age of about 50 years. The data of Figure 5 on silent reading speed have been collected for children between 7 and 14 years of age by Pressey and Pressey (undated) and for persons above 10 years of age by Hall and Robinson (1942). The data on writing speed have been obtained for children between 8 and 12 years of age by Wills (1938) and for subjects above 16 years of age by Birren and Botwinick (1951). Further information has been provided by Rader and O'Conner (1957, 1959). The decline in writing speed with age is one important factor that explains why old individuals produce markedly fewer words in the verbal fluency test than anticipated.

2. A writer of a book will avoid undue repetition of words, but he is not rigidly restricted in this regard. In the verbal fluency test, however, a person is prevented from using the same response twice, and thus he has to check carefully any response he is intending to give against all the others

previously emitted. This counterchecking of words causes interference and again differentially affects the performance of old persons (Riegel and Birren, 1966). Moreover, the checking of words requires a good short-term retention span, which, according to Figure 2, old persons lack. The data of Figure 2 represents the Digit Span Subtest of the Wechsler Intelligence Scales for Children and Adults (Wechsler, 1949, 1955). The differential susceptibility to interference and the decline in retention span are other factors that explain why old persons produce markedly fewer words in the verbal fluency test than anticipated.

3. The complexity of the sentences produced or comprehended is another important factor in the analysis of developmental differences in verbal behavior. Old persons may differ from young in the syntactic or semantic structure that they are using or able to comprehend at a certain reading rate. The problem of linguistic structures seems far remote from the present interpretation but since relations and classes are basic components of such structures, similarities become conceivable. After all, one major difficulty of the verbal fluency test consists in identifying members of a class and the

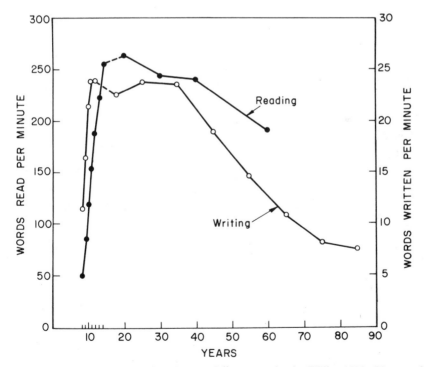

Figure 5. Speed of writing and reading at different age levels (Wills, 1938; Birren and Botwinick, 1951; Pressey and Pressey, undated; Hall and Robinson, 1942).

performance is greatly facilitated if categories, such as S-words or words denoting particular groups of objects, food items, pieces of furniture, animals, etc., are readily available to the individual.

In order to outline the role of linguistic structures for verbal performances, we have to analyze how classes are acquired, how class relations are recognized, and how transformations of these relations are performed. Although a detailed discussion of these problems is beyond the scope of the present chapter, I will briefly show that age differences do exist and are at variance with changes deduced from the model.

Figure 6 provides pertinent information on age differences in reading comprehension and sentence length. The data on the length of spoken sentences are taken from the review by McCarthy (1954, Table 5) and represent the average results of four studies. The data on the length of written sentences of children and adolescents are taken from the same source (1954, Table 6) and represent averages of two studies. The data for the adult subjects have been made available through the courtesy of Dr. Madorah Smith

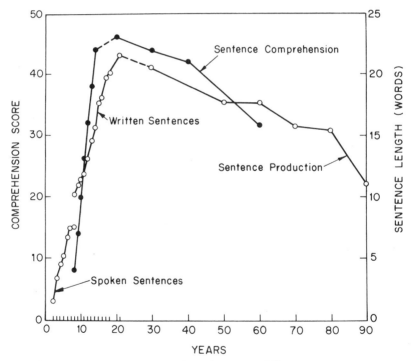

Figure 6. Sentence comprehension and production at different age levels (Pressey and Pressey, undated; Hall and Robinson, 1942; McCarthy, 1954).

(personal communication), and are based on large sets of letters written by three persons during spans of about 60 years of their lives. The results on sentence comprehension represent the scores on "paragraph meaning" of Pressey's Diagnostic Reading Test. The data on children's performances have been collected by Pressey and Pressey (undated) and those on adults by Hall and Robinson (1942).

Limitations and Further Explications of the Model

Since the results of the verbal fluency study seem to limit the statistical interpretation of language development, a reconsideration of the general purpose of the model seems appropriate. Primarily, the model will provide estimates of the upper limits of performance as a function of individuals' development. Because of inner biological and, subsequently, psychological constraints this upper limit will hardly ever be reached in real-life situations. In analyzing interfering factors, I proceeded to explain the observed differences between the data and the model.

Throughout my discussion, the individual has been regarded as an information-handling system that changes over time, i.e., with the amount of information handled. The total amount of information provided and, in particular, the total number of different words given increases with age. But because of intrinsic changes that are not primarily dependent upon environmental contingencies, a person's speed of intake (e.g., his reading speed or his ability to comprehend verbal messages) changes as well and thus the amount of perceived information is less than the amount of information provided to him. As suggested in Figure 7, individuals may be functioning most efficiently during early adulthood.

For most types of performances the perceived information has to be stored temporarily. Since there is a decline in immediate memory span, shown in Figure 2, further deficit will occur and the amount of information stored is less than the amount of information perceived. Some losses will also occur when individuals call upon the information stored. Because of slowness in expressing and because of difficulties in constructing complex sentences, the amount of information produced is smaller than the amount of information stored. The individual's failure to formulate complex sentences is, of course, also dependent on his immediate memory span and will lead him to the use of short and redundant formulations (Birren, 1955).

Because of these losses in the transmission of information, the overt performance does not match the total information provided. In order to evaluate this loss and the efficiency of the organism, we must obtain an es-

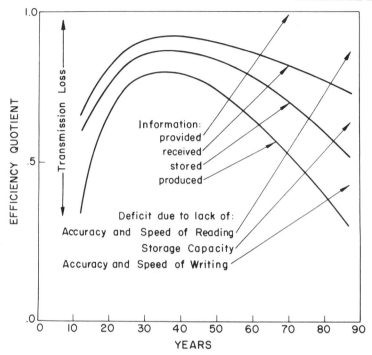

Figure 7. Hypothetical representation of transmission losses at different age levels.

timate of the information provided. It is here that the model will be useful and will allow us to derive specific hypotheses. What are, for instance, the effects of a poor versus rich linguistic environment upon the performance of individuals differing in age? How does the environment of a person interact with his verbal abilities? What are the interdependences of various abilities (perceptual, storage, retrieval) at different developmental levels? Does the efficiency change with age, etc.?

As an extension of our inquiry we may wish to study the determinants that bring about changes with age in perceptual, storage, and retrieval functions. Most likely, these determinants are not exclusively related to those long-term developmental changes that I have discussed, namely, the overall increase in information provided, but may rather be sought among the changing biological capacities of the organism, i.e., among the non-linguistic, intrinsic conditions of the organism.

Certainly, most of the questions raised are not new. Similar notions are implied in de Saussure's (1916) distinction between *langue* and *parole* and in Lewin's (1954) distinction between the *physical* and the *psychological environment*. Although Lewin has not given priority to the study of the physical environment, Barker and Wright (1949) as well as Brunswik (1949) have directed much attention to it. Barker and Wright regard the study of the contingencies in the physical environment rather than the study of particular psychological variables affecting the organism at any given instance as the most appropriate way of analyzing long-term changes in the growing organism. Similarily, linguistic contingencies have been analyzed, but are still waiting for treatment by psychological ecologists and developmental psychologists. It is here where the proposed model may prove to be useful.

Finally, the present analysis may allow us to redefine the age variable in terms of changes in the response variability. Accordingly, we regard equal intervals on the ordinates of Figures 1 to 4 as representing units of "verbal age." Because of the negatively accelerated shape of the curves, corresponding intervals on the abscissa increase toward the right end of the curves. In other words, verbal age progresses at a slower pace the larger the total amount of material already received or produced.

Scales of Developmental Progression

The possibility of deriving a developmental scale of verbal age brings out an important implication of our discussion: In contrast to most other interpretations in developmental psychology we have remained faithful to an absolute scale with interval properties instead of regressing to completely or partially ordered age scales. For example, Piaget's interpretations (see Flavell, 1963), with their periods of sensory–motor intelligence, preoperational intelligence, concrete and formal operations, constitute such an ordinal age scale. Only the sequence of the periods is unambiguously determined, not the distances within or between them. Since practical as well as theoretical difficulties arise when one attempts to map the boundaries of Piaget's periods or stages upon the chronological age scale, we need to explain how an interpretation of continuous changes would deal with these constructs.

1. Our previous interpretations were concerned with the continuous growth of the vocabulary as derived from the notion of an accumulating amount of information provided during the life span. However we also mentioned the contrasting trend of a continued decline in inner biological operations. Both interpretations point to theoretical limits rather than to concrete performances. If we were to test any individual in a real-life situation, various interactions will take place and the observable performances will be like those shown in Figures 5 or 6. Consider, for instance, age

changes in associative reaction time to verbal stimuli. Early in life the speed of reaction is high, but because their vocabulary is limited individuals are unable to discriminate and to respond quickly to different verbal stimuli. Later in life the verbal habits are developed but the speed of reaction is lowered. Thus, only during the middle period and because of the optimal interaction between two continuous functions is a maximum level of performance reached. Prior to that period speed in performance grows; afterward it declines.

2. The linguistic environments impinging upon the growing individual differ in quality and type. Undoubtedly the language spoken to a baby differs markedly from that used among playmates, in elementary school, high school, in church, at the job, among friends, etc. Thus, we may need to describe language development as a series of shifts between subsystems of the language. Most of these subsystems (*paroles* of de Saussure, 1916) are preselected for the growing individual in a more or less determined order and the confrontation with a new system is obligatory, as for instance, when a person enters one or another school, is drafted, retires, etc. Any new linguistic environment (even though it may share many properties with the preceding and the following ones) will shape the individual in a particular manner and will make behavior periods sufficiently distinct.

3. Most important, the continuous growth, such as of the vocabulary, consists itself of small discrete steps, any one of which may create a burst of knowledge and thus provoke qualitative leaps. Here, one is reminded of the implications that the acquisition of particularly mathematical and logical concepts, such as FUNCTION, INTEGRAL, or concepts such as PROPERTY, CONSTITUTIONAL RIGHT, etc. will have upon the behavior of an individual. This sudden increase in the available knowledge by the addition of single elements has been recently discussed by McLaughlin (1963).

McLaughlin attempts to explain differences in the "logics" of children at various developmental periods by differences in the immediate memory span. Even though the obtained developmental curves on the immediate memory span, such as those for digits shown in Figure 2, are smooth, a child in a concrete testing situation recalls either two or three or four, but never 3.6 items. The increase in the number of items retained implies a marked increase in the number of conceptual, logical operations that the child can perform. A person who can retain two items at a time is able to perform simple categorizations by recognizing the presence or absence of certain attributes or the membership or nonmembership of items in a class. If four items can be retained, they can be simultaneously categorized within two dimensions, and thus, the possibilities of analogical inferences, syllogisms and many other operations are open to the child.

McLaughlin's interpretation reduces the typology of a stage model to an interpretation of development as a continuous process. Developmental periods in the logical operations of children are reflections of their memory capacities, which attain only discrete values in concrete testing situations. Even though average values may be computed and will yield smooth developmental curves, because of the wealth of potential interpretations, it is more reasonable to separate discrete developmental levels corresponding to ages at which children are likely to retain one, two, four, or eight items, respectively.

McLaughlin's argument also holds for the acquisition of syntax. Syntax, and generative syntax in particular, allows the construction of an infinite set of linguistic expressions on the basis of a finite set of elements, classes, and class relations. In my discussion I have been primarily concerned with the acquisition of elements (words). As soon as classes and class relations are abstracted (Riegel and Riegel, 1963), a burst of generative possibilities occurs and the child will be able to produce many new expressions that, formerly, he could not generate without matching input information. Dependent on the number of classes and class relations which a child has abstracted, linguists may separate distinct periods in the acquisition of syntax. Again, the underlying learning process is a continuous one but the products to be utilized for syntactical performances, the classes and class relations, are qualitatively distinct and in turn create qualitatively distinct periods in language development.

CONCLUSIONS

I have emphasized the status of language as an objective and quantifiable system with which an individual is confronted throughout his life. The total amount of verbal input and output increases with the age of the individual and, subsequently, the total number of different words perceived or produced increases as well. The increase in the number of different words as a function of the total number of words has been empirically analyzed. The increase in vocabulary, for instance, is at first positively accelerated (1 or 2 years) and becomes negatively accelerated or zero during adulthood and later years of life. Also the active verbal repertoire, as tested in word counts of letters, journals, or responses to association tests, increases in this manner. Thus, older persons have available a larger passive as well as active vocabulary than young subjects.

The analysis of complete cumulative records is, of course, very laborious. Instead one might simply ask individuals to write or say all the different words that occur to them during a given period of time. Thus, by excluding all repetitions of words, one reduces extensive literary records to the tabulations of short laboratory sessions. The verbal fluency test represents such a method and the equation proposed by Bousfield and Sedgewick has been originally derived for the analysis of such data. It also predicts best the changes of both the active and the passive repertoires during the life span.

Throughout my discussion, the human organism has been regarded as a system that changes with the total amount of input it receives and/or the output it produces. Thus, my interpretations have been closely similar to the description of physical systems that change under the influence of external conditions. However, the analysis of my verbal fluency data has also revealed that a study of the physical, linguistic contingencies will provide an upper limit of performance only. Of greater importance for behavioral scientists will be the analysis of those factors that prevent the individual from making the most efficient use of the information provided. Deficiencies in perceptual, storage, and retrieval functions characterize such limiting factors. Explanations of the developmental changes of these functions need to be based on other than the physical and linguistic conditions in the environment of the individual. They need to be related to developmental changes in intrinsic, biological components. Any changes observed by the behavioral or social scientists represent the outcome of developmental interactions between changing inner and outer conditions.

CHAPTER 4

Nomothetic Interpretations of History

According to Windelband (1894), nomothetic sciences search for general laws and are trying to explain nature. Idiographic sciences aim for an understanding of social situations or individuals in their uniqueness and do not attempt to generalize these descriptions.

Dilthey (1894) and Spranger (1924) applied this distinction in their attacks upon the experimental and academic psychology. In arguing that research and theorizing by these psychologists touch only the surface of mental processes, they, essentially, denied with Kant the possibility of a science of psychology. According to Kant, psychology, in dealing with the mind, could not possibly apply systems of mental operations, i.e. mathematics, to itself. In particular, measurements and experimentation, which imply mathematical operations, could not be performed and therefore psychology could not become a science, at least, not a nomothetic science. Psychology had to be restricted to introspection and understanding.

Even though it was soon realized by Stern (1921) and Allport (1937) that from a methodological point of view Windelband's distinction is inappropriate, and that inferences and generalizations can be derived from data based on single individuals as well as from those based on groups, Windelband's distinction has remained of significance. Its survival is not so much due to its intrinsic validity but to the normative influence that it began to exert upon the following generation of scientists, provoking them to exclude one segment of science at the expense of the other.

A slightly more extended version of this article was published under the title, "History as a nomothetic science: Some generalizations, from theories and research in developmental psychology," Journal of Social Issues, *1969, 25, 99–127.*

This normative influence is most apparent among the historians who, in comparison to the psychologists, have not burdened themselves with such a split but have remained committed to an idiographic approach. Occasional attempts to provide quasi-nomothetic character to history by overemphasizing so-called factual knowledge have been futile, and interpretations have continued to be based on an understanding of individuals and historical periods. It is the main purpose of the present paper to show that a nomothetic science of history is possible and to discuss potential methodologies, research, and theories.

CLASSICAL AND MODERN SCIENCES

Idealized Events and Idealized Systems

A nomothetic analysis of historical changes will benefit from knowledge gained in scientific psychology. However, only a special area is of concern, namely, that of developmental rather than general (experimental) psychology. If we are to generalize this dichotomy to the study of social organizations, we would have to distinguish a general from a developmental social science. The latter represents the nomothetic description of history we are searching for. The distinction between general and developmental behavioral as well as social sciences that we are finally proposing is analogous to the distinction between classical and modern natural sciences.

The laws of classical natural sciences describe idealized events; those of modern natural sciences describe idealized systems. Perhaps one of the best examples of the classical approach is Galileo's law of gravity. By eliminating or abstracting all distorting factors, this law describes the ideal relationship between the spatial and temporal states of a falling body. Although most scientists would disagree with Lewin (1927) that such laws could be derived by observing a single event at an instant of time, they would accept laws derived from a few critical observations, provided extraneous factors are well controlled.

Unfortunately, extraneous factors cannot be sufficiently controlled in modern natural sciences, and the analysis of their covariation rather than their elimination provides the only possible solution. Subsequently, the derivations of laws are based on long series of observations and the laws represent statistical distributions rather than idealized, mathematical relations. Most important, instead of studying one-to-one connections, such as between forces and lengths of levers, modern natural scientists examine many-to-one relations between the underlying microcosmic processes, such as the movements of molecules, and the macrocosmic outcome, such as the temperature, pressure, or volume of an enclosed gas. Although changes in the state of the system are often imposed by macrocosmic manipulations, such as by moving a piston, they are mediated by changes in microcosmic conditions that cannot be studied as separate events; only their overall effect can be observed.

Since its beginning, general (experimental) psychology has been committed to the classical viewpoints. Wundt, for instance, attempted to detect psychological elements of sensations, images, and feelings, which in a one-to-one manner would be related to physiological events in the nervous system and to corresponding instances of physical stimulation. Variations in reactions between subjects were disregarded and variation within subjects were attributed to errors of judgment and measurement. Even when G. E. Muller proposed to consider thresholds as a statistical concept rather than as distinct psychological excitatory conditions, no major change of the model but only more complicated methods for data analysis were introduced.

Paired associate learning represents another example for the application of the classical viewpoints of natural science to psychology. Beginning with Ebbinghaus, the one-to-one relation of stimulus and response terms was studied as a function of list length, pro- and retroactive interference, serial position, and testing time. By inventing the nonsense syllable, by measuring its "meaningfulness," and imposing complex control conditions, extraordinary efforts were made to create the ideal learning situation uninfluenced by extraneous factors such as past experiences and selective response tendencies.

Even though most experimentalists have been applying lists of 10 or 20 items in order to obtain stable results, their approach remains diametrically different from that of a scientist interested, for instance, in the acquisition of the natural language during childhood. A developmental psycholinguist would not deny the usefulness of the laws described by his experimental colleagues, but the consideration of the hookup between a few verbal items is bound to be buried under the 20,000 to 50,000 words spoken in the linguistic environment of 4-year-old children during a single day (Brandenburg and Brandenburg, 1919).

In the past, "tough-minded" experimentalists have failed to recognize the theoretical power of developmental psychology. They can hardly be blamed for this failure, however, because until recently most developmental psychologists themselves have limited their efforts to the collection of descriptive data, rather than to the exploration of theories of development and to the search for explanations of growth. It is the specific purpose of the present chapter to discuss several models of development that may provide such explanations, and to apply them to the study of history.

The Concept of Causality
in Developmental Studies

The reorientation that characterizes modern natural sciences brought about a change in the notion of causality. While in classical natural sciences causal relations could be inferred from the one-to-one connection between the dependent and the independent variables, this inference was blurred by intervening microcosmic states in the modern analysis. In classical mechanics, for instance, the increase of the weight on a lever will be interpreted as causing a loss of balance. In modern physics as well, the scientist will state that increasing the pressure on an enclosed gas causes a rise in temperature, or that the release of two gases with different temperatures will cause their mixture and average out their temperatures. Thus, the actions studied are again implemented by gross, macrocosmic manipulations; the effects are produced, however, by the intervention of a multitude of untraceable microcosmic interactions and can be inferred only on a probabilistic basis.

Also in psychology, both the analysis of causative triggers and of causative forces have been considered. In the "classical" interpretation of the general psychologists, these factors were viewed as underlying drives, motivations, or volitions that moved an organism or changed the behavior from a distinct condition A, the stimulation, to the reaction, B. Thus, factor A is seen as the trigger for B. Drive or motivation provided the force for achieving such a change. Developmental psychologists, on the other hand, hardly realized the potential for causal interpretations but restricted themselves to mere descriptions of changes during the whole or parts of the life span. Since they also failed to discuss specific determinants that trigger a sequence of changes, they have been, appropriately, called tender-minded by the general psychologists.

In history the two modes of interpretation have been called personalistic and naturalistic. The former emphasizes distinct events and, in particular, persons who trigger historical developments; the latter considers the physical and social conditions of the people as the major causative forces in the course of history. Appropriately, the two interpretations have been characterized by such slogans as "men make history" versus "masses make history." The former maximizes the notion of causative triggers and the latter of causative forces. It is not surprising that both interpretations are not only confounded but remain confused by even such eminent historians of the behavioral sciences as Boring (1957).

While Boring, in general, emphasizes a Zeitgeist interpretation, i.e., considers the spirit of the age as a major determinant of historical developments, he nevertheless lists four triggers that "explain" the revival of learning in the Italian Renaissance: the invention of gunpowder, the invention of the printing press, the fall of Constantinople, and the discovery of America (1957, p. 7). Since all of these events occurred at a time when the Italian Renaissance was long on its way, they can be considered just as readily as effects rather than as causes for the revival of learning. Most appropriately, they ought to be regarded as symptoms of this important historical development. If historical causes are to be explicated they need to be found at a more basic level of sociopsychological processes. Neither the vague notion of Zeitgeist as an underlying force, nor specific incidents as triggers, can serve this purpose in a satisfactory manner. In my description of five models of historical growth, I will attempt to provide such explications.

SOCIOPSYCHOLOGICAL MODELS OF DEVELOPMENT

The first two models, the *branch structure* and the *root structure models*, are complements to one another. The first emphasizes the diffusion and divergence; the latter, the integration and convergence of ideas. Both interpretations are based on ordered relations. The third model, the *jigsaw puzzle model*, takes some of Kuhn's (1962) suggestions seriously and represents an interpretation of continuous, accumulative growth. The fourth model, the *fallout model*, extends the former as well as the theories of cellular growth mentioned before (see chap. 3). Most of our discussion of this model will be restricted to the individual's development. The fifth model represents a modified version of Piaget's theory of developmental stages. Like Kuhn's interpretations of scientific paradigms, it is of a mixed type in that it allows for transition between stages that, on the other hand, are treated as relatively distinct, noninteracting entities.

Branch Structure Model

History of Philosophy, an Example. The oldest known interpretations of growth and change can be attributed to Heraclitus. The few fragments of his teaching handed down to us refer to the notion of a basic contrarity and opposition that lead to a never-ending strife and produce a ceaseless flux.

If we take these ideas literally, we may conceive of a historical development such as the history of philosophy as the product of a continuous dialogue. At a certain moment in time and for reasons unknown to us, philosophical ideas were advanced. They found listeners, but because any student who was to make his mark in the history of ideas was bound to deviate from his teacher in one direction or another, some of them challenged and distorted these ideas. To be sure, there were many followers who did not dare or did not succeed in challenging their masters. They became the custodians, those who cultivated the memory and transmitted the teaching of their masters to future generations. However, by and large, the names of these students are lost. Only the names of the masters and those of their defiant colleagues and students survived in the history of ideas.

A traditional, idiographic analysis of the history of philosophy allows us to draw a fairly precise map of some contrarities and trends both for the Greek and modern European periods (see the more detailed analysis presented in chap. 10).

An upsurge in philosophical interpretations began with Thales. Already his student, Anaximander, and the student of his student, Anaximenes, initiated divergent intellectual trends that were to dominate the history of Greek thought. The first, Anaximander, sought for more abstract principles than his teacher who, relying on phenomenal analysis, had declared water to be the essential substance of the universe. Anaximenes, in turn, renewed and strengthened the reliance on the sensory basis of knowledge and with it the notion of change and flux.

After a few generations, the emerging trend of rationalism, accepting reasoning and introspection alone and denying the validity of perceptual knowledge, found its most outspoken representatives in the Eleatic School, whereas the opposing trend of sensualism led to the mechanistic–materialistic theories of Leucippus and Democritus. Even though carried still further into the subjective and relativistic interpretations of the Sophists, both trends seem to have reached their limits within the Greco-Roman world of ideas, and the major dualistic, synthesizing systems began to emerge.

The Model and Its Modifications. If we were to formalize our interpretations in the simplest possible manner, we would derive a tree diagram with binary branches whereby the number of different philosophical positions (y) attained in successive intellectual generations (x) can be expressed by the exponential function: $y = 2^x$. This function, characterized by a marked positive acceleration, is identical to that on the distributions in a lineage of descendants (see Figure 8). Dealing with only two descendants at each node, a present-day population of 3 billion persons would be reduced to a single ancestor living 31 generations ago or (assuming an average generation length of 25 years) at about A.D. 1200. This result, being clearly inadequate, leads to two possible modifications of the model.

The first modification proposes a certain limit in the capacity of a sociocultural group to process and incorporate information. The notion of such limitations has been implied already in discussions of the history of antique and modern philosophy. The Sophists in the former, and the philosophers of the Enlightenment in the latter period, set the limits that both historical developments were able to tolerate (with such notable exceptions as Socrates's persecution). Plato–Aristotle and Kant–Hegel, respectively, represent best the full range and breadth of these developments.

The second modification emphasizes the interactions and shared origins of ideas proposed by particular thinkers. For instance, Plato consolidates ideas of the rationalistic and sensualistic trends. While he gives somewhat greater attention to the rationalism of the Eleatic School, his student, Aristotle, shifts the emphasis to the naturalistic interpretations of Democritus. Similarly, Kant consolidates the rationalism of Leibniz with the sensualism of the British School, especially through Berkeley's influence. In these cases, as well as in numerous others, the interconnections reduce the divergence and redirect attention toward a common theme and synthesis.

Both modifications are essentially similar. The first is stated in general; the second, in more specific terms. If we accept them for more realistic descriptions of historical developments, we are converting the branch structure into a two-factor model whereby one factor provides for expansion and the other counteracts such an unlimited development. Compounded models of this type are not uncommon in the study of populations or economical trends. The growth of bacterial colonies, as well as of populations of various organisms, is often explained as the outcome of a reproduction factor and a limiting factor, such as food resources (Herdan, 1960).

If we assume that each philosopher represents an independent but comparable amount of knowledge, we have to conclude that a universally educated man, i.e., a person knowledgeable of all the contemporary ideas would have to carry an increasing amount of information as history advances from intellectual generation to generation. Early in history he could still direct his curiosity toward other, nonphilosophical endeavors. Later on he will be fully occupied by keeping up-to-date with the philosophy of his time. Finally, he will become eclectic, selecting ideas from different philosophers, or he will become a specialist, devoting his attention to one at the expense of others. Idiographic inquiries into intellectual history have indeed shown that universality (not restricted to philosophy, however) seems to have been difficult to achieve after the ages of Plato and Aristotle or Kant and Hegel, respectively.

The idea of an ever-increasing load upon the capacity of participants in a system is also implied in Parkinson's law of the rising pyramid (1957), which analyzes the growth of administrative structures. Also, some empirical data in the history of sciences are available that may be utilized to test such a model. Pledge (1947) has provided a master–pupil analysis of the natural sciences. Boring and Boring (1948) and more recently Wesley (1965) have surveyed contemporary psychologists about those teachers that were most influential for their careers. Since complete records of doctoral dissertations are available, at least for the past 100 years, it is conceivable to make a systematic analysis of the branch structure of modern sciences (see chap. 12).

Root Structure Model

Description of the Model. Directed toward synthesis rather than toward increasing diversification, the root structure model is the inverse of the branch structure model and is implied in Hegel's dialectical analysis of history. If two ideas are presented, for instance, in a scientific dialogue, development will result only if there is some form of consolidation. By incorporating two divergent ideas, such a synthesis necessarily will be more comprehensive than any of the previous ideas.

Hegel's dialectical scheme does not necessarily provide a developmental model that would be useful for our purposes. In maintaining that the thesis conceptually implies the antithesis in the same way as the concept of freedom implies the notion of captivity, one may elaborate a chain of merging pairs of ideas, but such a chain recasts and does not necessarily generate new knowledge. This interpretation raises the old platonic problem of whether the basic ideas remain essentially unchanged during the individual's as well as historical developments and are being merely translated into new languages characterized by increasingly greater formalism, methodological sophistication, and perhaps know-how for applications. However, by assuming an independent origin of the antithesis rather than stressing its conceptual implication in the thesis, this interpretation can be readily expanded to provide for a generative model of knowledge. In this way we describe a structure decreasing in diversity as we move forward in time.

Inasmuch as the branch structure model is congruent with the genealogical descendants of a person, the root structure model might represent the distributions of his ancestors. If we were to formulate the increase in the number of ancestors (y) by going backward from generation to generation (x) we arrive at the negative exponential function: $y = 2^{-x} = \frac{1}{2}^{x}$.

Again, serious limitations of this model become apparent if we determine the number of ancestors for a contemporary person. Assuming an average generation length of 25 years, we have to conclude that 31 generations ago or at around A.D. 1200 a total of about 3 billion ancestors must have existed. Since this figure exceeds by far the estimated size of the population at that time, a considerable amount of inbreeding between various lines must have occurred. We also realize once more that the root structure model provides a rather limited theory of growth. However, in conjunction with its inverse, the branch structure model, promising predictions may be made, as shown in the following applications.

Applications of the Model. The root structure model is closely akin to library search and retrieval systems. If a person had read, for instance, a scientific article and intended to trace the background of the ideas presented, he could look up some of the reference literature cited. Without exception these reference articles will be older than the original paper and, in turn, will suggest further references. In tracing back an idea in this manner, various trends will appear. However, many of these trends will merge somewhere in the past, indicating their common origin. In other instances, ideas will originate without further traces, thus representing original contributions. Disregarding such exceptional cases, particular books or articles will be repeatedly cited as sources for different publications. If this were not so, the total amount of literature would increase to an ever greater extent the farther we move backward in time. Library records, however, show the opposite trend, i.e., positive relation between the amount of literature and historical time.

Reference couplings and networks have been rarely used for retrieval purposes but are of great interest for the study of scientific communication and its change over time (Salton, 1966). Kessler (1963) developed and applied the method of biographic coupling to 10 case histories derived from more than 8,000 papers in the *Physical Review* appearing between 1950 and 1958. Tukey (1962) used a similar methodology in his study of literature in chemistry, as did Boll (1952), Osgood and Wilson (1961), and Xhignesse and Osgood (1967) in their analyses of networks of psychological journals. While these studies investigated the flow of information during restricted periods of history (see also the whole No. 11 of the *American Psy-*

chologist, 1966, Vol. 21). Price (1965) in physics and Cardno (1963) in psychology emphasized changes in reference networks over longer time intervals. However, the most extensive contributions to this topic have been made by Garfield. Garfield (1967) relied on an idiographic, historical account of the discovery of the genetic code by Asimov (1963), which he confirmed and elaborated further in his quantitative study (Garfield, Sher, and Torpie, 1964).

With the exception of sociometric studies, the analysis of relations and networks has not yet found a foothold in psychological research. In linguistic analysis (Lamb, 1966), as well as in psychological studies of language, especially when concerned with problems of meaning (Rapoport, Rapoport, Livant, and Boyd, 1966; Riegel 1970b), this method is becoming increasingly important as treatises on the mathematical theory (Harary, Norman, and Cartwright, 1965) become available to the behavioral and social scientists. In much the same way as a person's place in science can be operationally defined as a point of intersect in the network of scientific publications, so can the meaning of a term be defined by the set of relations diverging and converging upon it (Riegel, 1970b, 1970c).

Jigsaw Puzzle Model

The Concept of Scientific Paradigms. As suggested by Kuhn (1962) science progresses through successive paradigms, which do not merely represent ever more comprehensive and parsimonious systems but may be nonoverlapping and distinct in their emphasis. Within each paradigm—such as Ptolomaic astronomy, Copernican astronomy, corpuscular optics, wave optics, etc.—science proceeds as if a complex jigsaw puzzle needs to be solved.

As Kuhn admits, the concept of paradigms is not the most precise one. Paradigms might oversimplify the diversity of problems within an area, especially when associated with names of particular scientists. Although the orientations of outstanding scientists are usually much broader than the areas or principles for which they are known, each scientist could conceivably represent a paradigm of his own. On the other hand, the notion of paradigms could be considerably enlarged to embrace whole areas within a science, such as optics, acoustics, or thermodynamics. Ultimately, each science could be regarded as representing a general paradigm and so could periods of artistic or architectural styles or even the totality of a civilization or culture, as indeed proposed by Spengler, Toynbee, and others.

If the concept of paradigm is modified in the indicated manner, special problems arise concerning the interactions of (a) the scientist with a scientific paradigm, (b) the paradigm with the science of which it is a part, (c) one science with another, (d) all sciences with the civilization of which they are part, etc. While Kuhn touches upon most of these problems, he does not provide any definite suggestions for deriving a model of scientific and cultural growth.

Of still greater importance for deriving such a model are the sequential dependences of paradigms. Kuhn considers the paradigms as stages and the history of science as a progression in which bursts of activities alternate with periods of steady growth. This view resembles closely the stage models of individual growth as proposed by Freud, Buhler, Erikson, and especially Piaget. Unfortunately, Kuhn as well as most developmental psychologists are least precise in their treatment of the transitions between paradigms or stages. While I will return to this problem when discussing Piaget's theory, at this moment I can but take a one-sided view of Kuhn's contribution by giving exclusive attention to the growth within specific paradigms, or what he has called the growth of normal sciences.

Description of the Model. Kuhn compares the cumulative advances within paradigms with attempts to solve a jigsaw puzzle. Thus, a paradigm is comparable to a complex pattern, gestalt, or picture. At the onset only the general outlines or ideas but none of the details are recognized by the scientists. The development within a paradigm consists in the identification of specific problems and subtopics and of fitting them into the overall design. At the beginning it takes a considerable amount of ingenuity to fit particular items into the patterns. However, as more and more items are connected, performance will be accelerated and missing parts might be predicted with an increasing degree of accuracy. With the overall pattern recognizable and only a few random items missing, scientists will become attracted to new viewpoints or paradigms. Toward the end of the puzzle the performance becomes uninteresting.

On the basis of this reasoning I propose that the number of items (N) fitted together per time (t) is proportional to the number of items already assembled. This gives us the differential equation

$$dN/dt = mN$$
$$N = \frac{1}{m}(e^{mt} - 1)$$

In wishing to consider the decreasing number of items not yet assembled,

(D), we subtract the latter equation from 1 and obtain

$$D = 1 - \frac{1}{m}(e^{mt} - 1)$$

A search of the literature reveals no psychological research or published theory on the speed and changes in speed in solving jigsaw puzzles. The only exception is an unpublished study by Horvath (1963) in which a single subject solved a 500-item colored puzzle. In analyzing the time for assembling solitary pieces or clusters of pieces, the search and assembly process was found to be essentially random. The distribution of the number of moves made in each one-minute interval ranged from zero to nine, and could be adequately fitted by a Poisson distribution with a mean of 1.93 moves per minute.

Horvath also observed a slight acceleration toward the end of the 13 successive 20-minute intervals. While this deviation was not strong enough to warrant a modification of the random model, it is likely to become more significant as the puzzles decrease in size. In small puzzles the patterns of the anticipated pictures will be much more important determinants especially toward the end of the performance than in large puzzles where these patterns, composed of numerous subpatterns, remain less clear. These considerations suggest modifications of the formula, giving stronger weight to the dependence of the solution speed upon the size of the puzzle.

The jigsaw search process represents perhaps the less significant part of Kuhn's theory. As an idiographic historian, he pays greater attention to the delineation of the various paradigms, the conditions of their development, and the reasons for their substitution. He does not deny that paradigms merge into one another and that there are shared elements and interpretations that are to be reembedded into the newer system. Perhaps the interrelation is hierarchical and follows the general trend suggested in the root structure model, but Kuhn's outline does not allow for precise statements regarding these transitions and the overall growth of science from paradigm to paradigm.

Fallout Model

Description of the Model. The following model, originally proposed to account for the acquisition of language (see chap. 3 and Riegel, 1966, 1968a,) represents another case of accumulative, continuous growth. Like the jigsaw puzzle model, it relies on the notion of an extrinsic pool from which particular ideas are drawn. While this property makes it suited for explanations of developmental changes that are dependent on the interactions between the individual and a sociological (for instance, a linguistic) system, the growth of such a system itself can be explained only if we were to assume that the elements (for instance, the ideas and laws of a science) are expressions of nature itself and not man's creative interpretations and projections. Since this assumption limits its acceptability, the fallout model eventually needs to be supplemented by a model emphasizing generative aspects of historical growth.

The model is based on the assumption that the increase in the number of scientific events or ideas (D) with time (t) is proportional to the number of different events in a universe of events that have *not yet* been produced by the scientists. Thus, if L is the total number of different events in the universe and D is the number of different events that have occurred up to a certain point in historical time, the differential equation reads as follows:

$$dD/dt = M(L - D)$$

$$D = L - Le^{-mt}$$

The negatively accelerated growth curve thus derived contradicts our intuition and idiographic descriptions of the growth of sciences. What scientists seem to be experiencing is that scientific events occur at an increasingly faster pace the more recent a period in regard to the observer, i.e., scientific development seems to be positively accelerated.

The discrepancies between the individual's and the societal growth curves and the fact that the fallout model may account for the former but hardly for the latter is determined by the differences in the conditions under which these two systems operate. The individual has to grow into the social, linguistic environment that surrounds him. The social system remains relatively unchanged through his adaptations. For the growth of a social system, such as a science, the interactions of different scientists are of importance. Each scientist might contribute a small share of new knowledge, thus supplementing and supporting the others; each generates a few new ideas and does not passively receive them from the system. Thus, sciences grow actively and creatively as the scientists grow and interact. The creative and inventive use of the language (which undoubtedly represents an important aspect of the individual's growth process) remains insignificant for the society, however, in which an infinite number of other forms have already been used prior to the individual's encounter.

Interactions in the Growth of the Individual and the Society. Recently the interaction in the growth of the individual and the society has attracted considerable interest among psychological gerontologists, because it is in this area of long-term development that changes in the sociocultural conditions become most apparent and confound the psychological results. These considerations led to important explorations of research designs in developmental studies, including designs for historical comparisons, and extensive studies of the performance of outstanding individuals and its change with historical time.

The first problem has received detailed treatment by Schaie (1965) and Baltes (1968). These authors have shown that by embedding several of the three basic designs (cross-sectional, longitudinal, and time-lag designs) into complex developmental arrangements, it becomes possible to estimate the relative contributions of the individual's and of the society's changes to the overall trends observed (see chap. 5). While, thus, important steps have been taken toward the conceptualization of the interdependence between the growth of the individual and the society, this topic is much enriched if we look into the various areas in which such changes occur. This topic has been studied, almost single-handedly, by Lehman (1953, 1962).

Lehman assembled extensive production and performance records of famous artists, scientists, philosophers, politicians, and businessmen. While most of his attention has been directed toward comparisons in amount and peak productivity across disciplines and fields, he has also analyzed historical changes accompanying or modifying these differences. In regard to the mean age of attained political leadership, for instance, he observed a marked increase from the periods prior to the middle of the last century to the more recent times. He attributes this increase to growing political stability. In regard to historical shifts in scientific creativity, the great increase in the number of scientific publications and records has been considered as necessitating longer training periods and, subsequently, a delay in productivity. Contrary to this expectation, both quantitative and qualitative records show either no changes of this type at all or minor changes in the opposite direction. Lehman (1953) lists several reasons for this result: (1) Earlier scientists devoted long periods to the development of tools and techniques. (2) Earlier scientists served as trailblazers and started in areas different from the ones for which they are known. (3) Modern scientists are stimulated by greater rewards, competition, and pressure to publish early during their careers. (4) Earlier scientists withheld publications to safeguard their rights.

These interpretations become still more confounded when the known increase in longevity during historical times is taken into account and, especially, when it is noted (Riegel, Riegel, and Meyer 1967) that early death affects selectively persons with lesser intellectual capacities and interests. Again, Lehman has analyzed these questions at considerable length by partitioning creative workers from different fields on the basis of their ages at time of death. His findings suggest "that increasing the average length of man's life will result in greater average output on the part of our most creative thinkers, but that the most fruitful years for creative work will still be those between 30 and 39" (1953, p. 309).

Models of Developmental Stages

It has always been one of the most cherished intellectual activities of developmental scientists and historians to divide the course of events into distinct phases or periods. But even though many efforts have been directed toward such delineations, the outcome has remained ambiguous and arbitrary. Psychologists, in particular, have fluctuated between interpretations that attribute different periods to normative social contingencies and even to legislative decisions, e.g., on school age, voting age, retirement age, etc.; and those that emphasize maturational, psychobiological processes, e.g., periods of self-assertion, dependency, stability, etc. While their discussion has remained unsatisfactory for a long period of time, Piaget has recently approached these problems in a more rigorous manner and delineated psychological stages rather than attempted to reduce them either to sociological or to biological events.

Piaget has described four systems of logical operations representing successive stages of cognitive development and has assembled a large body of evidence demonstrating that children at varying ages operate at the levels described in his theory. Since Piaget considered himself a genetic epistemologist (1950), he devoted much attention to developing the idea that the same concepts and operations that emerge sequentially in the growing individual also characterize the intellectual growth of society. Since Piaget's model does not represent a system simple enough for our present purpose, I will direct our attention to a much simplified version proposed by McLaughlin (1963).

McLaughlin's (1963) brief outline seems even more ambitious than Piaget's because he equates the four successive stages of cognitive growth with increases in immediate memory span. However, his interpretations are also simpler because he reduces the intellectual performance to logical operations with classes. If concepts are distinguished by a number of attributes (N), then each distinct concept is derived by one of 2^N possible combinations of the presence or absence of these attributes. Each value of N specifies a unique logic that McLaughlin equates with successive levels in children's cognitive development (see chap. 5).

In emphasizing the serial embedding of the stages of logical operations, Piaget's and McLaughlin's theories represent transitions between models of relations (branch and root structures) and those of stages. The transitional nature is most clearly expressed in McLaughlin's attempt to equate these stages with successive systems of class operations. Indeed, his formal expression, $y = 2^N$, is identical with that derived for the branch structure model and, thus, can be represented by the diagrams of Figure 8.

Taking this equivalence seriously leads us to the interpretation that successive generations of philosophers represent stages comparable to the cognitive operations in the child. At level 0 (Thales/Anaximander/Anaximenes), the number of distinctive attributes is zero, $2^0 = 1$ (see Figure 13, p. 164); the philosophical theme is identified. As appropriately as for childhood, and emphasizing the phenomenal–operational method of approach, this stage might be called the sensory–motor period of Greek philosophy. At level 1 (Pythagoras/Heraclitus), one attribute characterizes the conceptual split between rationalism and sensualism. Appropriately, this stage might be called the preoperational approach to philosophy. Both rationalism and sensualism are derived by experiential generalizations and have not yet received the explicit formulations that they are to obtain through the schools of Elea and Democritus. At level 2 (Elea/Socrates/Anaxogora/Democritus), two distinctive attributes characterize the conceptual splits leading to four schools of thought. The first attribute explicates the former distinction between the rationalistic and sensualistic approaches and separates the Eleatic school and Socrates on the one hand from Democritus and Anaxagoras on the other. Even though not fully explicated until the next generation of thinkers, the second attribute separates the monists (School of Elea, Democritus) from the dualists (Socrates, Anaxgoras). In analogy to the cognitive development of the child, we may speak of the level of concrete operations that is characterized by "processes of restructur-

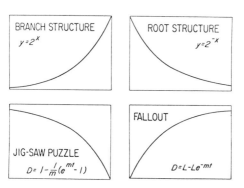

Figure 8. Four models of development.

ing concepts, that can be illustrated by grouping tangible objects" (McLaughlin, 1963, p. 65). This type of conceptualization is represented by the paradoxes of the Eleatic School (Achilles' inability to pass the turtle; the flying arrow is at rest; etc.), or the concrete partitioning process in Democritus's demonstrations of the atom.

It is questionable whether Greek philosophy ever advanced far beyond the level of concrete operational intelligence. At least our system of hypotheses does not cover the full range of eight conceptual possibilities at the fourth intellectual generation. Of course, this proposition is not likely to be accepted without further argument based upon a detailed analysis of Greek philosophy, and even my own further exploration as described in chapter 10 may not be sufficient to settle these issues. But whatever the outcome of such a discussion, level 3 ought to be characterized by three distinct attributes, two of which represent explications of those already presented at the earlier levels. Performance of such complexity is neither attained by all children nor are eight conceptual distinctions applied by all adults in all situations. Both the ability to perform triple-classifications as well as retention span of eight independent items represent upper bounds rather than estimates of performances in average situations or by average persons. Of course, such considerations are not necessarily relevant for a discussion of the history of sciences or philosophy because these developments, in comparison to individual growth processes, will be carried and sustained by the exceptional rather than the common persons.

Discrete and Continuous Growth Models. My generalization of developmental logic to the study of history has been possible only under the exceptional conditions where there exists a well-delineated system of propositions, such as for the history of philosophy. In most other cases, stages in historical development, such as the scientific paradigms discussed by Kuhn, have to be described in terms of their specific content. Even though students of history thus seem to face an exceedingly difficult task, it should not be forgotten that the situation in developmental psychology is not much better. Interpretations, such as those by Piaget and McLaughlin, have been possible only after painstaking inquiries and still remain the exception rather than the rule in psychological research.

Aside from the difficulties in delineating specific stages, Piaget's and McLaughlin's discussions provide some general insights concerning the transition between stages and the relationship of stage sequences to chronological or historical time scales. According to McLaughlin, preceding logics are successively embedded into the following ones. Thus, while at each level "qualitatively" different operations become available, there is nevertheless an ordered transition between the stages, and the information attained at earlier periods is not lost.

Piaget has assigned chronological age boundaries to the successive stages. Thus, by superimposing an absolute time scale upon the ordinal scale of stages without providing a rationale other than empirical evidence, he has gone beyond the theoretical possibilities of his model. Of course, Piaget (and, to a lesser extent, the majority of developmental psychologists) is not taking too seriously these chronological boundaries but, primarily, attempts to satisfy the practitioner's needs and curiosity.

If we generalize these interpretations to the study of the history of sciences, we find ourselves much in agreement with several suggestions by Kuhn. Undoubtedly, the time boundaries for most scientific paradigms are quite arbitrary. Different paradigms co-exist over fairly long periods of time. Subsequent paradigms are, generally, more comprehensive, even though perfectly ordered sequences represent exceptions rather than the rule. Most important, scientists work either within one paradigm or another at one time, but rarely within several simultaneously.

In extension to Kuhn, and relying on McLaughlin, the reduction of the growth in logical operations to increases in immediate memory span may find its counterpart in the historical growth of material and intellectual communication within civilizations. The change in the means of communication characterizes not only the most recent centuries but also the later periods of the Greco-Roman or Egyptian civilizations and can be traced from the trader and foot messenger to the electronics, rockets, and laser beams of modern technology. As suggested by Rashevsky (1968), the change in communication might explain and not merely describe the acceleration in intellectual productivity during recent periods.

CONCLUSIONS

The last-mentioned model is based on successively embedded categorization systems, each representing a different stage in the individual's development and a different paradigm in the history of science. In psychology, it emphasizes distinct operations that emerge from within but require experience for their realization. In history, it emphasizes distinct forms of communication styles or theoretical viewpoints of organization. Even though most powerful for psychological elaborations, this model does not answer the question as to why organisms grow.

In comparison to this interpretation, both the branch and the root structure models emphasize sociopsychological interactions rather than distinct psychological operations. Growth is seen as the outcome of a continuous dialogue leading to increasing conceptual differentiation and integration. Inasmuch as social interactions can be regarded as intrinsic tendencies for any human being, these models are deterministic and explain growth. Like the first interpretations they do not elaborate, however, the triggering conditions leading to sudden bursts in productivity. When applied to historical analyses, they elaborate specific relations between persons and incorporate these relations into a general order. Only secondarily do they lead to classifications of particular events or persons.

The third type of interpretation, the jigsaw puzzle and fallout models, directs still greater attention to external social rather than to internal psychological conditions. The fallout model has been successfully applied under conditions where there exists an extrinsic body of information, such as the language, which has to be adopted by the growing individual. Its usefulness for the study of historical changes is limited because it is difficult to imagine a comparable set of information existing outside or beyond the society in which the historical processes are taking place. The growth of a science has to be considered as an interaction process that generates, rather than incorporates, information. Both the jigsaw puzzle and the fallout models analyze the most general trends rather than particular groupings and traces. Single contributions lose their identity in the analysis of the growth process. For the same reason these models provide, if successfully applied, the most deterministic explanations of growth.

Thus, when progressing from the categorical via the relational to the continuous growth models, we turn our attention from intrinsic psychological to social psychological and, finally, to extrinsic sociological and physical conditions. As our explanations become more deterministic and the models more powerful, we face growing difficulties in justifying the necessary assumptions. Even though the third model has been considered in theory, explorations of individual developments have concentrated on the first approach. The relational model has not been applied in studies of psychological developments, but the major interest of the historians has been directed toward this approach.

CHAPTER 5

Models of Growth and Change

Cross-sectional and longitudinal investigations of development have resulted in an accumulation of large masses of data in which differences or
changes of particular variables have been plotted against chronological age,
revealing the various growth trends reported in texts and handbooks such as
those edited by Mussen (1970) on child psychology or by Birren (1959) on
aging. Despite the wealth of data collected, the records are insufficient for
at least three reasons: (1) Almost none of the reports have been addressed to
the question of *why* organisms grow and change, but have remained descriptive and prescientific. (2) The uncritical application of physical time
scales has been harmful for the development of theoretical interpretations of
growth. (3) Without exception, individual and cultural changes have been
confounded.

In the following section I will analyze these three issues by discussing
qualitative and quantitative growth models as well as the interaction between individual and cultural development. Throughout, the focus will be
on changes—i.e., on systematic modifications of behavior—rather than on
time, which represents an abstraction from experienced changes. The following presentation modifies the innovative proposals made by Van den
Daele (1969).

---

*An extended version of this article was published under the title, "Time and change in the development of the indi-
vidual and society," in H. W. Reese (Ed.), Advances in child development and behavior, Vol. 7, New
York: Academic Press, 1973, pp. 81–113. Some of the parts omitted from this chapter have been included in
chapter 14.*

QUALITATIVE AND QUANTITATIVE GROWTH MODELS

Properties of Qualitative Growth Models

Most models of qualitative developmental changes assume an invariant order of some sets of behavior. A model, stated in such a general form, fails to account for individual differences in the development of these sets as well as for variations within individuals, e.g., between different modes of behavior. It also disregards the question of how much of an early form of behavior is transferred, retained, or incorporated into the later and succeeding forms. Despite these limitations, the property of an invariant order is a necessary prerequisite for all of the more complex models.

If we define an ordered collection, D, which contains the sets U, V, and W, the *single sequence model* (Van den Daele, 1969) implies that the features or structures studied emerge in the fixed order for all members of D:

$$U \rightarrow V \rightarrow W \tag{1}$$

This model does not consider any inter- or intraindividual variations except in a rate of progression, which, however, would imply comparisons between these ordered sets and metric time scales upon which an evaluation of the rate of progression would have to be based. Logically, such a match between different types of scales is inappropriate.

If we want to allow for inter- or intraindividual variations in developmental progression, we need to specify that D may contain single or several subsets, i.e., $U \supset u_1, \ldots ; V \supset v_1, v_2, \ldots ; W \supset w_1, w_2, w_3, w_4, \ldots$. If these subsets are mutually exclusive, i.e., $w_1 \neq w_2, \ldots$, we may generate three types of multiple progressions, a *divergent branch structure*, a *convergent root structure*, and *parallel seriation*. Most likely, the three types of combinations will be confounded into partially convergent and partially divergent progressions. Below, the digraph for a divergent progression, for the *multiple sequence model*, is given:

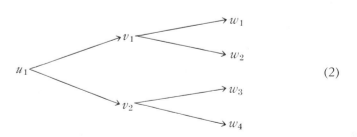

$$\tag{2}$$

If, as above, there is more than one subset for some set of D and if some subsets are mutually exclusive and others are not, i.e., are intersecting or correlated, we are accounting for differences between traits within persons or within behavior and trait compounds. For instance, trait compounds might represent linguistic skills (including phonetic, semantic, and syntactic components), mathematical skills (including analytic and synthetic modes of thinking), but also, in a more general sense, perceptual, storage, and motor aspects of behavior. If we allow that a skill of an individual may represent a composition of traits different from that of another individual but with an equal overall effectiveness characterizing the particular, developmental stage attained by both, we would have to delineate these differences by specifying the elements $a, b, c, \ldots$ of the u_i, v_i, w_i.

If intersections occur also in the transition between stages, i.e., through an accumulation of behavior or trait components over time, we posit within persons alternatives, namely, that more than one stage might characterize the behavior or traits of a person at a given time. Subsequently, a person on one occasion might regress and respond in a more primitive manner; on another occasion he might progress and respond in a more mature manner. Similarly, a complex performance might be predominantly related at one point in time to one trait, such as linguistic skills, at another point in time to another trait, such as mathematical skills. The fluctuations within as well as between stages are depicted in the *complex sequence model* of digraph (3):

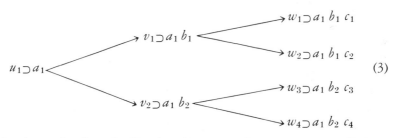

$$(3)$$

As shown in digraph (3), the element a_1 intersects across all three stages; the elements b_1 and b_2 intersect across the last two stages only. There are many ways of such sequential intersection or accumulation; the intersection can be partial or can extend over the whole range of stages. Also, some within-stage intersections are depicted in digraph (3). Element a_1 connects all the different branches at the last two stages; elements b_1 and b_2 connect two branches each at the third stage only. A pure, sequential intersection or accumulation across stages is possible for parallel seriations only. In most other cases, as in digraph (3), both *sequential* (between stages) and *parallel* (within stages) intersections co-occur.

Applications of Qualitative Growth Models

The single sequence model of digraph (1) represents Piaget's theory of cognitive growth as well as many other interpretations emphasizing developmental stages, such as the popular distinction of infancy, childhood, adolescence, maturity, and old age. It excludes alternative progressions and alternative organizations. Piaget (1963) has extensively discussed the issues of transition, successive embedding, and structural transformation across stages, however; therefore, this assignment greatly oversimplifies his contribution.

If, in the study of history, we rely on such distinctions as Pre-Socratic, Socratic, and Post-Socratic periods, or if we compare the Greek-Roman with modern Western philosophy without specifying the transitional influences, we are applying the single sequence model. Kuhn (1962) has emphasized such an interpretation in his discussion of the history of sciences. As he suggests, with sufficient precaution, science progresses through successive paradigms, which do not merely represent ever more comprehensive and parsimonious systems but to some extent, are nonoverlapping and distinct in their emphasis. Within these paradigms—such as "Ptolomaic astronomy," "Copernican astronomy," "corpuscular optics," "wave optics," etc., science proceeds as if complex jigsaw puzzles were to be solved and, thus, a supplementary model for the progressions within stages is suggested.

The multiple sequence model represented by digraph (2) implies alternative developmental progressions originating from each node. The developmental branches may represent different persons as well as different traits or behavior within a general trait or behavior compound. Both possibilities might be confounded. Thus, Erikson (1968) allows at each stage for mutually exclusive binary choices, such as between trust versus mistrust, identity versus identity confusion, integrity versus despair, etc. The progression results in increasing individual as well as developmental differentiations.

The application of the multiple sequence model to the history of sciences has been elaborated previously (see chap. 4). The description of divergent lines of thinking, the branch structure model, or Heraclitean model, represents but one possible system of multiple progression that needs to be supplemented by the converging root structure model, or

Hegelian model, as well as by noninteracting seriations through which ideas are preserved in an unmodified manner. Most reasonably, history (as well as an individual's development) represents a complex compound of all three of these basic paradigms.

The preceding two models did not consider interactions between persons or between traits of a trait compound either within or between different developmental stages. The complex sequence model of digraph (3) takes account of such variations. In order to provide a convincing application of this model to psychology, we will describe a modified version of Piaget's theory of cognitive development as proposed by McLaughlin (1963) (see chap. 4).

McLaughlin's brief outline, on one hand, is even more ambitious than Piaget's theory because he equates successive stages of cognitive growth with increases in immediate memory span. On the other hand, his interpretations are simpler because he reduces the intellectual operations of children to logical operations of classes. If classes are distinguished by a number of attributes or dimensions (N), then each class is characterized by the binary choice of the presence or absence of these attributes. Each value of N specifies a unique logic (2^N) that McLaughlin equates with successive levels in cognitive development.

At level 0, the child is able to operate $2^0 = 1$ concept at a time. This period corresponds to Piaget's stage of *sensorimotor intelligence*. During this time the child learns to attend to objects and to develop a notion of object constancy, but is unable to operate logically with concepts since he lacks a basis for comparisons. The selection of a particular object is not based on a specific attribute or dimension, but the child seems to focus his attention upon items that happen to be within his reach and available for manipulations.

At level 1, the child is able to retain $2^1 = 2$ concepts simultaneously and thus, to classify objects according to the presence or absence of the attribute. This period corresponds to Piaget's stage of *preoperational intelligence*. At this level the child cannot yet perform seriations since this would involve the simultaneous retention of at least three concepts. For instance, a child may start to sort items into two classes by their color; when other items are added, he may shift to the attribute of form even though size is a transitive criterion but, now, would require the simultaneous comparison of the three sets of objects, i.e., large, medium, and small.

At level 2, the child is able to process $2^2 = 4$ concepts simultaneously. This period corresponds to Piaget's stage of *concrete operational intelligence*.

Now a child is able to consider simultaneously not only the attribute of the classes A and A', but also to form a third concept, that of their sum, B. By accommodating a fourth concept, the complement to B, called B', he is able to perform class additions. Such a performance is evident when the child combines items into superordinate classes, as well as when he orders items into extended series on the basis of a transitive criterion.

At level 3, the child is able to process $2^3 = 8$ concepts simultaneously. This period corresponds to Piaget's stage of *formal operational intelligence.* An individual retaining up to eight concepts and distinguishing up to three attributes at one time can perform logical operations in conformity with the intellectual demands of everyday situations. Conceivably, at level 4 a person would be able to categorize items on the basis of four attributes. This would require the simultaneous consideration of 16 concepts. For all practical purposes such operations are not only beyond daily and even scientific needs, but can be reduced to successive performances of more limited operations or can be transcribed into a formal language that will greatly facilitate their solution.

McLaughlin's interpretation of cognitive development represents the complex sequence model. Each stage develops its logic by embedding those preceding it. At level 0, the child merely focuses upon single objects; at level 1, he distinguishes items along one dimension; at level 2, he superimposes a second dimension; at level 3, a third, and so on. Since each categorization system is conceptually implied in the following system, with one new dimension added at each stage, there is transitivity between the stages, i.e., digraph (3) is applicable.

The complex sequence model is also implied in some empirical studies of the history of sciences. For instance, Garfield, Sher, and Torpie (1964) relied on such a model in their cross-reference analysis of the history of the discovery of the genetic code. The present author compared eight books on the history of psychology and eight books on the history of philosophy (see chap. 14) by applying the same model of qualitative changes. In this way it became possible to provide systematic interpretations for the observation that historical writers allot a disproportionally larger number of pages to early figures in the history of science, i.e., to persons who have no or only a few competitors. As the number of scientists increases with historical time, the number of pages allotted to them decreases inversely. Therefore, the number of pages assigned to different time periods by historical writers remains about constant; during the early periods few persons received much attention, during the late periods many persons received little attention.

Relation between Qualitative and Quantitative Growth Models

Piaget has assigned chronological age boundaries to the successive stages. Thus, by superimposing an absolute time scale upon the ordinal scale of stages without providing a rationale other than empirical evidence, he has gone beyond the theoretical possibilities of his model. Of course, Piaget (and, to a lesser extent, the majority of developmental psychologists) does not take these chronological boundary markings too seriously. Primarily, he attempts to satisfy the practitioner's needs and curiosity. McLaughlin's interpretations have the advantage of allowing for a more succinct analysis of the relationship between qualitative models of stages and quantitative models of chronological age changes.

McLaughlin reduces, as we have seen, the progression across stages to increases in immediate memory span. When averaged over several subjects or when averaged over repeated measurements, such tests show a continuous and smooth increase with age in the number of items retained. The ages at which, on the average, 0, 2, 4, or 8 items are retained correspond reasonably well with the suggested age boundaries for the successive levels of logical operations, i.e., 2, 7, and 11 years (see Wechsler, 1958). But while an individual's performance will fluctuate around a fractional average (which is characteristic for his capacity at a particular chronological age) in any given testing situation, he reports only a whole number of items. His concrete performance is always of an all-or-none or digital type; he either reports 3, 4, 5, or 6 items but never 4.58. Correspondingly, his mode of logical operations will shift back and forth from more or less advanced levels. His assignment to a developmental stage represents a best estimate of his performance during a certain period of time but always remains artificial.

Stated more generally, qualitative growth models imply temporal order but not temporal distances; quantitative models imply both. Since the choice of the measurement unit is arbitrary (although often dependent on technological refinements), the differences between the two approaches are often less marked than they appear to be at first glance. Even within a system of continuous changes, measurements will always be taken in discrete steps, for instance, in hours, minutes, seconds, or milliseconds, respectively, dependent on the precision requested and/or the instruments available. Let us consider, for instance, the set of relations shown in the matrix of Table 3. Each row and each column represents one discrete measurement. Theoretically, there can be as many rows and columns as desired.

Table 3. Matrix Representation of Digraph (3)

	a_1	b_1	b_2	c_1	c_2	c_3	c_4
a_1	1	1	1	1	1	1	1
b_1	1	1	0	1	1	0	0
b_2	1	0	1	0	0	1	1

Table 3 represents digraph (3) of the complex sequence model, which has been rewritten into a matrix form in order to make apparent the relationship between qualitative and quantitative growth models. Each row represents one discrete element in u_i, v_i, or w_i; the same is true for the columns. Dependent upon the number of branches (or roots) most qualitative growth models have several cell entries for single rows (or columns). For example, element a_1, shown in the first row, is connected with all other elements of the matrix. This is indicated by entries of 1. Elements b_1 and b_2, on the other hand, are not connected with all of the other elements. In comparison, continuous growth models have, in general, only one entry per row and one corresponding, i.e., functionally related, entry per column. Moreover, the entries in the rows, with few exceptions, represent a different type of variable than those in the columns. The columns always represent the time variable (mostly chronological age); the rows represent the dependent variable (mostly some psychological measure). Since the entries in continuous growth models, usually, represent the set of all real numbers, their magnitude can be decreased or increased indefinitely.

Without providing a formal description of the properties of continuous growth models, a system of relations (qualitative model) is functional (quantitative model) if each member of the domain of one variable is paired with one and only one member of the range of the other variable. Although this statement can be accepted for most practical purposes, important exceptions exist in the form of multiple value functions for which each member of the domain is paired with several members of the range. This possibility is implied when we consider intraindividual differences, e.g., task differences, and interindividual differences, e.g., group differences, in developmental trends, as well as the important problem of the spread of growth functions along the time continuum, i.e., the problem of the interaction between changes in the individual and the society. In some of the following sections we will discuss these implications. Before we do so, we return to a concrete example of a quantitative growth model introduced in chapter 3.

Applications of Quantitative Growth Models

In the past, several successful attempts have been made to depict changes in word variability with length of a text and/or age. A model discussed by Carroll (1938), Chotlos (1944), and Herdan (1960) assumes a frequency distribution of the items incorporated, represented by Zipf's (1949) standard curve of the English language. In a large universe of items, such as words, some occur at very high frequencies, e.g., articles, auxiliaries, prepositions, conjunctions, etc., whereas others occur less often. When such a model is applied to the analysis of language acquisition, the individual is assumed to draw successive samples at a constant rate and to incorporate any new items into his repertoire that have not occurred to him before. Subsequently, common items are likely to be acquired early in the development. Late in life, only rare items will not have occurred and, therefore, the accumulation will proceed at a slower pace.

The negatively accelerated growth curve thus derived provides estimates of language acquisition time or "language age" that are at variance with the traditional measures of chronological age. If for the purpose of obtaining such estimates we were to assume that the occurrence of an equal number of new items represents equal time units, we would have to conclude that language age progresses faster during the early than during the later periods of development. As shown in Figure 9, this inference can be well supported by research data on the growth of the synonym vocabulary and other psycholinguistic skills (Riegel, 1970b).

For all practical purposes, the language universe from which vocabulary items are sampled is infinitely large and the acquisition of any one item represents an exceedingly small step in the acquisition process, which,

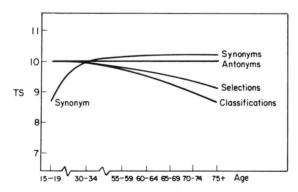

Figure 9. Differential trends for four verbal tests.

thus, might be described by a continuous function. The growth of the vocabulary, representing only one example out of a set of psychological performances, is frequently contrasted with the acquisition of sensory-motor skills that follow different developmental trends. A comparison of various growth curves, all sharing the same origin, represents an example of multiple value functions. For any individual at any particular age, there exists a set of different values characterizing different psychological skills. In such an analysis of *differential changes,* the vocabulary, generally, shows a fairly slow rate of growth and a zero or very small rate of decline. Skills dependent upon sensory-motor capacities and their coordinations show a fast rate of growth and a fast rate of decline coupled with short-lasting periods of peak performances. As shown in Figure 9, even within the narrow range of verbal skills, differential changes have been observed.

The continuous differential changes of verbal skills, depicted as a case of multiple value functions, are analogous to the qualitative differentiations described by the multiple sequence model of digraph (2). Another example of this model relates to differential changes of particular skills as a function of interindividual differences. As shown in Figure 10, superior subjects do not only exhibit higher average performance along the whole age continuum but a faster growth rate during the early years and a slower rate of decline during the later years of life. Inferior subjects show a slow rate of growth and a fast rate of decline. Observations like these have been reported for nonverbal intelligence tests and a vocabulary test (see Raven, 1948) but have not been accepted unequivocally (see Baltes and Nesselroade, 1973; Riegel and Riegel, 1972; Schaie, 1972). They depict the *dependence of changes upon the original level of performance.*

The examples of Figures 9 and 10 describe intraindividual differentiations (differences between skills within subjects) and interindividual differentiations (differences between subjects in one skill). As recent evidence has shown (Riegel and Riegel, 1972), both components interact during development, e.g., superior subjects retain their lead only on tests requiring complex cognitive organizations but not on recognition vocabulary tests. Thus, the complex sequence model of digraphs (3), which also takes into account interdependences between skills or persons or both, represents the more appropriate analogy for the continuous differential changes presently discussed.

I will not pursue this issue in detail. We have to take notice that all the examples of qualitative and quantitative changes describe cases in which the developmental trends share the same origin or zero point. Important further modifications of the interpretations involve cases in which the

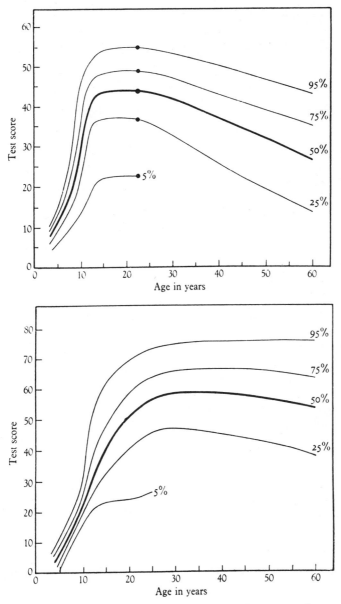

Figure 10. Top: Changes in the Matrices Test percentile points as age advances. Bottom: Changes in the Vocabulary Test percentile points as age advances (from Raven, 1948).

points of origin are scattered along the time or age axis. Strictly speaking, all developmental observations are of this type, i.e., no two subjects are precisely of the same age, but for reasons of simplicity we pool our subjects into groups "equal" or, rather, similar in chronological or school age.

While such an adjustment or averaging seems all but reasonable, serious problems arise if these points of origin are spread out widely over historical time, i.e., if we compare subjects belonging to different cohorts or generations. Figure 11 shows an hypothetical example of the results that we might expect. Since an increase in intelligence with historical time has been documented in the literature (e.g., Tuddenham, 1948), each of the last two curves shown will be elevated in comparison to the two earlier ones. Because of the considerable improvements in the quality and availability of education, the rate of growth during the early years might also be assumed to have increased with historical time, i.e., intellectual growth might have been accelerated. Finally, improvements in communication, adult education, and health care might have prevented a fast deterioration of the performance during later years of life; i.e., the rate of decline might have decreased with historical time.

Without exception, developmental psychologists have disregarded the results as well as the problems shown in Figure 11 and have pretended that a child born in 1900 would have to reveal the same developmental changes as a child born in 1970. Contradictory evidence, such as reported by Tuddenham (1948) on the differences in intelligence between draftees in the First and the Second World Wars, have been noticed with bewilderment but have not led to any reformulations of the developmental analyses. Extensive further evidence and interpretations by Ryder (1965) have been disregarded. Only when Schaie (1965) proposed a theoretical extension of

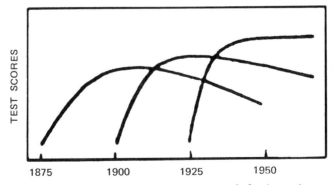

Figure 11. Hypothetical developmental trends for three cohorts.

developmental research designs did at least some psychological gerontologists become seriously concerned about this problem.

None of the qualitative developmental models discussed takes account of the problem that the growth of different persons originates at different points in historical time and that this growth, therefore, is subjected to sociocultural influences that change as well and, perhaps, at a faster rate than the individual. Changes in the individual and in the society have been kept confounded by developmental scientists. The research designs proposed by Schaie (1965) allow for an unconfounding of these changes. Since the models described are equally applicable to the study of changes in the individual as they are to the study of changes in the society, it is all but reasonable to conclude my presentation with a brief review of the problem of unconfounding confounded changes.

INTERACTION BETWEEN CHANGES IN THE INDIVIDUAL AND SOCIETY

As shown in an insightful manner by Baltes (1968), certain variables—for instance, the amount of physical mobility and intellectual communication—may yield developmental gradients increasing in magnitude from generation to generation. If these increases are linearly related to age and if, furthermore, we were to assess age differences by the traditional cross-sectional method, i.e., by testing, at one time, samples from different age groups (thus, representing different generations or cohorts), the results, indicated by the heavy line in Figure 12 might be obtained. Curves like this one are all too familiar to the developmental psychologists but represent nothing but artifacts because neither the generation (cohort) nor the time of testing effects (history) have been eliminated as contributing factors.

As we have seen in chapter 2, it is in principle possible to obtain estimates of the "pure" effects of age, cohort, or historical time differences. But such attempts will always have to rely on the joint utilization of all three basic designs, i.e., cross-sectional, longitudinal, and time-lag designs. The remaining problem, therefore, is to derive complex arrangements that incorporate the three basic designs in different manners, optimizing thereby the precision with which estimates of either age, cohort, or historical time differences can be obtained. Consequently, Schaie (1965) has proposed three strategies that he has called cohort-sequential, time-sequential, and cross-sequential methods.

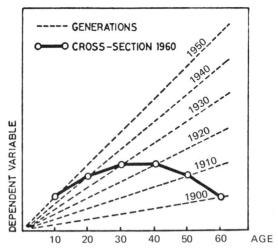

Figure 12. A hypothetical example for the effects of generation differences on the results of a cross-sectional study. Broken line, generations; solid line, cross-section 1960. (From Baltes, 1968, Figure 1, p. 12.)

CONCLUSIONS

As our knowledge of developmental processes advances and as the field of developmental studies matures, we need to become more fully aware that this area, as well as any other area or discipline, does not emerge within a vacuum, but is intimately dependent upon general sociocultural conditions. Studying history as a developmental sociology (by drawing generalizations from reseach and theories in developmental psychology) and studying developmental psychology as a systematic inquiry into individuals' histories (by retrospectively analyzing their pasts) might help to accelerate such an awareness.

Subsequently, developmental psychologists ought to give up their antiquated views of time and change. They ought to divorce themselves from separated studies of cross-sections of the population, e.g., of infancy, childhood, adolescence, adulthood, or old age. Only functional changes over time ought to be of concern to them. If this were not the case, they would be concerned with static conditions rather than with dynamic modifications during individual and historical time.

With these claims I neither propose an uncritical progression to longitidinal studies nor do I abandon qualitative growth models for the sake of quantitative models. I do not recommend the adaptation of a simple longitudinal strategy because such a methodology would fail to unconfound the changes in the individual and in society. Only the more advanced and complex developmental designs enable us to solve this problem. At the same time these designs direct our attention once more to the dialectical interactions between the individual and society. They make us recognize that the human being (like any living organism) is a changing organism in a changing world, which he creates and by which, at the same time, he is created. To separate out static conditions would be as useless for the study of development as would be the abstraction of universal, unchanging dimensions of time, space, substance, causality, etc.

The differences between *qualitative* and *quantitative growth models* are related to the type of measurements obtained. If time measurements represent sets of ordered relations, a qualitative model is all that can emerge. If time measurements represent real numbers, we develop models of continuous changes. In practice, however, we cannot obtain time measures of infinitesimal magnitude but always chunk the continuum in technically manageable units. The outcome is a time scale of concrete steps that, as the example of McLaughlin's theory of cognitive development has shown, is also psychologically reasonable.

The differences between qualitative and quantitative models of change are conceptually clear but they do not reflect "real" differences of a nature independent of the scientific observer. As convincingly argued by Reese and Overton (1970), they reflect viewpoints projected by the observer upon nature; they represent his way of constructing "reality." Therefore, he should aim at developing psychological interpretations that, at the same time, determine the type of measurements taken. Only when interpretations and observations are seen in their dialectical interactions can incisive knowledge be gained.

PART II

Case Studies

CHAPTER 6

Developmental Psychology and Society

Inquiries into the distant past of our society are similar to attempts by psychoanalysts to discover points of choice and/or catastrophe in the life of an individual (Wyatt, 1963). The psychoanalyst restricts his efforts to the discovery of these points; it is left to the patient to reconstruct his life in a new and "healthier" manner. Similarly, our historical inquiries aim at uncovering points in time at which crucial choices were made. We can trace the history back to these points, but any distinct groups, such as minority groups, would have to construct on their own a new interpretation of life, a new philosophy of man and his development. They alone can find their identity and aim at its conceptual description.

A great many philosophers and psychologists have expressed similar viewpoints. In his theory of human development Erikson (1968) distinguishes various binary choice points that lead to either trust or distrust, autonomy or doubt, initiative or guilt, industry or inferiority, identity or identity confusion, intimacy or isolation, generativity or stagnation, integrity or despair. Erikson extended his interpretations to cultural developments, for instance, by relating the identity choice to the historical period of the Reformation and by demonstrating this interpretation by means of an analysis of *Young Man Luther* (1958). Minority groups face similar identity problems. Thus, like an individual, they need to go back to such choice points in history in order to find their identity and to construct their own philosophy of man and his development.

The original article was published under the title, "Developmental psychology and society: Some historical and ethical considerations," in J. R. Nesselroade and H. W. Resse (Eds.), Life-span developmental psychology: Methodological issues, *New York: Academic Press, 1973, pp. 1–23.*

In contrast to Erikson, Jung's work (Jacobi, 1962) has focused more strongly upon universal features of civilization. By looking at art, symbolism, customs, and social conventions across developmental and historical stages, he searched for those forms and expressions common to all men. Jung (unlike his teacher, Freud) emphasized the constructive, active aspects in the therapeutic process. It is not enough, he maintains, to rediscover and identify the choice points of the past, but it is necessary to construct new perspectives, a new philosophy of life. This ought not to be left to the patient; the therapist should be of active assistance.

In his *Comparative Psychology of Mental Development,* Werner (1926) draws parallels between the development of children and that of so-called primitive societies. Thus, he revived the recapitulation hypothesis of evolutionary theory and extended it to psychological and social conditions, claiming that children undergo developmental sequences similar to those that characterize historical progression. Psychopathological conditions are regarded as regressions to or fixations upon early developmental levels. With much support from the extensive collections by cultural anthropologists (Frazer, 1890; Lazarus and Steinthal, 1859–1920), Werner focused his interpretations upon noncognitive behavior. In comparison, Piaget in his studies of genetic epistemology (1950) claims that in the development of intellectual and logical operations as well, children follow the steps through which societies had to pass in order to attain the knowledge of modern civilization.

HISTORICAL NODE POINTS OF THE PAST

I do not intend to draw upon the above interpretations in order to specify in detail different conceptualizations of man and his development. However, historical studies make us aware of critical node points at which alternative modes of interpretation were still existent but afterward were repressed for the sake and success of the dominant civilization. By reconstructing the choices made, we gain a fuller understanding of our past and a greater consciousness of our present conditions.

Pre-Grecian Civilizations

In a recent presentation, Noel Smith (1970) delineated modes of conceptualization that characterize the civilizations preceding the Greek-Roman period. While the latter has been described as an ontological dualism between being and becoming, and modern Western civilization as the epistemological dualism between mind and body, the ancient civilizations of Sumer, Babylon, Assyria, Persia, Egypt, etc., emphasized distinctly different dimensions and dichotomies (Moscati, 1957). The corresponding philosophies of the universe, life, and man need not concern us in detail, but it is of interest to analyze briefly how these conceptions were overcome or repressed through the emergence of the Greek-Roman civilization.

During the early periods in the Greek-Roman civilization, i.e., during the pre-Homeric and Homeric period (1000 B.C. to 600 B.C.), we find an array of different world views with which the Greeks became acquainted. This confrontation has been emphasized by several scholars. Nestle (1940), in particular, considers the entire development of Greek civilization as a struggle between *mythos* and *logos,* between the forces of darkness and light and, as elaborated by Nietzsche (1872) and Ruth Benedict (1934), between the Dionysian and Apollonian ideals. During the history of the Greek civilization the latter, and thus rational thought, attained dominance and the "alien" ecstatic forces of emotionality were successfully controlled and repressed.

Early in Greek history, the term "barbarians" denoted nothing else than "the others," i.e., persons of non-Greek origin. Soon, however, this term became connotatively loaded, indicating uncivilized, alien, inferior persons. This change characterizes the efforts among ancient Greeks to facilitate their own cultural identity by downgrading persons and groups with different languages, habits, customs, and conceptions of man. Since many of these so-called barbarians had attained a much higher level of civilization than the Greeks of the Homeric period, their attempts appear highly artificial. Indeed, at that period the Greeks were the barbarians.

For similar reasons, romantic and idealized interpretations of Greek civilization have dominated modern historical views since the Renaissance and, especially, since the Classicism of Winkelmann, Herder, and Goethe. Consequently, the Greek civilization appears as an elevated historical period initiated by a distinct historical break. Only recent research and interpretations have revealed the heritage from pre-Greek civilizations, especially from Persia, Mycenae, and Egypt. It has been documented, for instance, that even such distinct and typically Greek innovations as the mathematics of Thales, Pythagoras, and Euclid had their origin in earlier civilizations. Pythagoras gained his insights while working as a surveyor in Egypt and it is likely that the theorem named after him was already known in his host country.

It is not my intent to downgrade the astounding intellectual achievements of the Greeks. What I would rather like to note are the strenuous efforts within this civilization and on the part of sympathetic historians to maximize its distinctiveness and to neglect the transitions. These activities indicate the relentless efforts to achieve a unique cultural identity by neglecting alternative conceptualizations. At the beginning, alternatives were readily available; as the civilization advanced, these choices were successfully suppressed. If we look for alternate models of man and his development, we might have to go back to these early periods of a civilization at which different views co-existed. The pre-Greek period represents the first node point to be considered if we were to develop a non-Western developmental psychology.

Scholastic Period

At about A.D. 400 the Greek-Roman civilization had collapsed and the Middle Ages had begun. Judean-Christian ideology penetrated the areas around the Mediterranean and those north of it, i.e., the areas that were to become the basis of modern Western civilization. The intellectual life during this period aimed toward a consolidation of religious ideas and an absorption of the sociopolitical remains of the Roman Empire. These developments led to the foundation of dogmatic theology and to the establishment of the administrative organization of the Christian Church. At the same time a slow revival of commerce and trade occurred, spreading from the northern shore of the Mediterranean toward the central parts of Europe. Here, between 700 and 800, a political consolidation took place that led to the formation of the Carolingian Empire (Duckett, 1962; Hay, 1964).

Preceding these developments by about 150 years, an upsurge occurred in the southern section of the area dominated by the Semitic civilizations, i.e., in the Arabian peninsula. The emerging civilization conquered both politically and intellectually the whole Near East and swept within less than a century through northern Africa and the Iberian peninsula deep into France. The rapid advance of Islam brought about important intellectual conflicts representing a second historical node point in the modern conception of man.

At the time of the Islamic conquest, and especially during the reign of Charlemagne, the spread of Semitic civilization was by no means regarded as a threat. On the contrary, and as persuasively documented by Pirenne (1939), deep admiration existed for the more advanced civilization represented by the Arabs. Material and intellectual exchanges were sought and diplomatic relations were maintained. This beneficial competition was soon destroyed, however, through the continuing theological and philosophical attempts toward an identification of a Christian-Western civilization. Intolerance and degradation began to take the place of intellectual exchanges. The Moslem civilization was increasingly seen as alien, inferior, and in the derived and connotative sense, as "barbaric" or, as it was now to be called, "heretic."

The scholastic theology and philosophy represents the culmination of this development. Scholasticism, in attempting to consolidate Greek philosophy with Christian religion, led to the elaborate systems of Thomas of Aquinas and other theologians. Although the knowledge of Greek philosophy was transmitted through the Arabs, increasingly this assistance was downgraded and the competing Semitic civilization, represented by Islam, was sharply rejected.

Scholasticism provided the "blueprint" for modern Western civilization, in which the major philosophical and scientific trends were already implicitly represented. Comparable to the present-day actions within the Communist party of the Soviet Union, it marked off the acceptable boundaries within the Christian world. From this time onward, philosophy, sciences, and the arts had to operate within the confines of these conceptualizations or, if not, were prosecuted as heretical.

The dogmatic constraints imposed by Scholasticism, which maintained and elaborated a continuity with the Greek-Roman civilization but rejected the Semitic civilizations represented by Islam, faced a serious challenge during the liberating movements of the Renaissance. Even though stimulated by the rediscovery of Greek-Roman civilization, Renaissance philosophers such as Giordano Bruno and Thomas Campanella, as well as Francis Bacon, rejected the tradition of Greek philosophy, which, by that time, had been thoroughly distorted and rigidified. Renaissance philosophers, therefore, regarded the rejuvenation of man's thinking and the throwing-off of ancient philosophical constraints as their main task. That they succeeded in abandoning the scholastic dogmatizations of classical philosophy is well documented by the sudden burst of intellectual advances during the following historical periods, but ultimately the Greek-Roman tradition in its purified form was not only retained but gained greater influence than ever before.

Conclusions

The first node point in the history of the conception of man occurred prior to the Greek-Roman civilization. We know least about these developments but from the little that we know, we comprehend the attempts by the ancient Greeks to downgrade outside influences originating within the older civilizations of the Near East. These rejections served to establish the identity of the Greek-Roman civilization, a tradition that laid the foundation of our modern conception of man. In order to gain a fuller understanding of man and his development, however, we might have to return to these earlier, alternative interpretations.

An historical node point of greater impact for modern Western conceptions terminates the pre-Scholastic period of the late Middle Ages. Originally the influence of the outside civilization, represented by Islam, was seen as highly beneficial. In the search for an identity within the Western civilization, these connections were soon denounced as heretical, however, by the secular and spiritual leaders of the Christian Church. Among these leaders, the Scholastics represent the most important intellectual group explicating what might be called the blueprint of modern Western civilization.

A more dramatic challenge yet is being provided by the philosophy and dogmatism that has emerged in the Soviet Union. While we shall return to this issue on a later occasion, we now draw attention to the post-Scholastic developments in Western civilization that, again, led to the differentiation of competing conceptions of man and his development.

OPEN AND CLOSED DEVELOPMENTAL SYSTEMS IN WESTERN SCIENCES

Qualitative growth models (see chap. 5) imply a progression in leaps and are sensitive to multigenerational and multicultural differences. They were developed and flourished in continental Europe, with its mercantilistic economic systems (Riegel, 1972). Quantitative growth models imply a continuous progression toward an abstract achievement ideal. They were developed in the capitalistic countries, especially England and the United States, with their emphasis on free trade, competition, and entrepreneurism. In chapter 7, I will outline these models and show the dependence of their development upon social, political, and economic conditions.

Related to, though not identical to our comparison of quantitative and qualitative growth models, is the distinction between open and closed developmental systems.

In the past, developmental psychology, dominated by the notion of continuous growth, has shown a preference for what we shall call open developmental systems. According to such an interpretation, growth consists in the acquisition of bits and pieces of information, habits or experiences that are being accumulated in the subject's repertoire, making him or her increasingly more able. If, at a given time, problems cannot be resolved, the *individual will have to acquire more information so that he finally may succeed.* In contrast to the notion of unlimited expansion, a closed developmental system is characterized by the principle that *everything that grows, grows at the expense of something else.* Such a model assumes limits in basic capacities. Development consists in an increasingly finer organization and, perhaps, in systematic restructuring of information, habits, and experiences, but not in a ceaseless addition of new materials.

1. Our distinction of open and closed developmental systems has a wide range of applications. Some of the most dramatic comparisons are those of political, economic, and administrative operations. Here, the concept of open systems has become singularly associated with the development of the modern industrialized world. The West and the East, Democrats and Republicans alike subscribe wholeheartedly and completely to the social and economic philosophy of ceaseless expansions. Whenever problems arise, such as a business slump, a high rate of unemployment, a trade deficit, an instability of international exchange rates, etc., the single, overall solution proposed consists of accelerating production and increasing spending. Undoubtedly, there are variations between different camps. The Democrats willingly suscribe to Keynes and deficit spending, the Republicans are more reluctant and aim for a balanced budget; the farmers care less about the unemployed, the urbanites favor increases in welfare subsidies. But despite any specific and often forceful disagreements, the belief in the open system is not questioned. Closed systems, in contrast, are seen as backward and unable to produce solutions, and generally, as representing the antithesis of growth. As Looft (1971) has put it so ably, our thinking is dominated by the "psychology of more."

Underdeveloped rural societies are frequently cited as counterexamples of open social and economic systems. Typically, members of such communities have been engaged in the same activities for countless generations. Changes in these activities are often viewed by the participants with suspicion and, if possible, prevented. It would be inappropriate, however, to limit the description of closed systems to underdeveloped societies. There are numerous other communities that, though stable in the size of their population or in the area occupied, have shown considerable growth through internal reorganization, better utilization of their resources, and more efficient planning. Most of the former city states in central Europe as well as in the eastern Mediterranean are cases in point. In modern times the smaller European countries such as Sweden, Netherlands, and Switzerland serve as outstanding examples, having increased their productivity and the quality of their products, education, and welfare to a degree much higher than that of the most advanced expansionist nations.

The differences between open and closed social systems are also revealed by administrative policies. For example, the uncritical support ot continuous land annexation in communal development has been challenged by the policy of zero growth aiming toward improvements of internal organization, such as traffic, transportation, schooling, housing, and recreational facilities. Similarly, in the evaluations of our large professional and scientific organizations we have become cognizant of the strains caused by our commitment to an open system. For example, we have realized that the disarray of such organizations as the American Psychological Association can result in nothing but its replacement by smaller, structurally more efficient (and aesthetically more pleasing) organizations. The same fate might befall large universities and colleges that, by committing themselves to ceaseless expansion, have sacrificed organizational efficiency and the quality of higher education. On the basis of these experiences, it is reasonable to reconsider the underlying administrative philosophy of such organizations and formulate alternate ways of conceptualization and operation.

2. In regard to psychological functioning, open systems consider development as a ceaseless expansion, produced by the addition of bits and pieces of information, habits or experiences. The more material an individual has accumulated, the brighter, more knowledgeable, and more successful he is thought to be.

A good example of a closed developmental system, in comparison, is the interpretation of Piaget's developmental theory by McLaughlin (1963) (see chap. 5). This author described the four major developmental periods of Piaget as successive enlargements of the child's ability to operate with classes. During the sensory-motor period the child attends to one concept only and does not discriminate along any dimension or attribute. During the period of preoperational intelligence, the child handles two concepts along one dimension, such as red versus nonred. During the period of concrete operational intelligence the child succeeds in double classifications of four concepts along two dimensions, and during the period of formal operational intelligence he performs triple classifications of eight concepts. Thus, the child apprehends and operates with the same material in successively more differentiated and structurally more complex ways. At the beginning he lacks discrimination; at the end he makes succinct differentiations and performs complex operations and judgments.

While McLaughlin's interpretation might be accommodated within a closed developmental system, Piaget's own theory requires modifications of such a system. To Piaget, the intellectual operations of a child during successive periods of development are characterized by distinctly different logics that are only partially embedded in one another. Development does not merely consist in the discrimination along a series of dimensions, but in the appearance of new types of operations. Thus, the child, at each period, acquires a unique logic that he continues to improve until, suddenly, he shifts toward a more complex form of behavior and a more advanced logic. Piaget's theory, therefore, represents an open system that, during long-term development, incorporates different closed systems, i.e., a system that accumulates information but also changes its internal organization.

3. Piaget's theory of cognitive development resembles the theory of scientific growth proposed by Kuhn (1962). Kuhn distinguishes between paradigmatic and normal sciences. The former provide new perspectives and interpretations of data either already available or collected in view of the proposed paradigm. Different scientific paradigms may co-exist, such as the wave theory and the particle theory of light. They shift the attention to scientific aspects that were disregarded in the past or they put them into a new context. Like Piaget's theory of cognitive development, Kuhn's interpretation proposes an accumulation of information within paradigms, a process that he compares with the solving of a jigsaw puzzle. Major progression in sciences is brought about, however, by shifts from paradigm to paradigm.

Kuhn's interpretation of the history of sciences, like Piaget's theory of cognitive development, suggests a synthesis between closed and open developmental systems. "Pure" cases of the latter have traditionally dominated interpretations of the history of sciences. Progress was seen as a ceaseless accumulation of information, leading to more and more "factual" knowledge, thereby stripping "nature" of its secrets. Such an interpretation is quite compatible with utopian views of political and cultural history as expressed both in democratic and socialistic theories. A "pure" interpretation of political and cultural history in terms of a closed system has been proposed by Spengler (1918–22). According to his view, a civilization starts with a basic theme that, through artistic, philosophical, and scientific advances, is explicated in successive steps until, toward the end, it deteriorates through overdifferentiation. Even though such an interpretation, when adopted for the description of the history of philosophy or sciences, is one-sided, it provides a challenging alternative to the traditional view of history in which events follow events and persons follow persons without any explicit origins and goals.

DIALECTIC INTERACTIONISM IN
SOVIET PSYCHOLOGY

In the first section I described historical node points in human conception. In the second section I compared two major models of development predominant in modern Western behavioral and social sciences. The present section represents a further historical extension that should be of interest for several reasons. First, it attempts to synthesize the two developmental models previously described. Second, it represents a node point in our conception and development that we are experiencing in its very own emergence. Third, and in contrast to past historical conditions, it represents a choice pointing toward future actions rather than an enumeration of decisions and biases of the past.

The two models of growth that I have described conceive of development as either an accumulation of environmental information by an essentially passive organism, or as the spontaneous emergence of new modes of operation for which the environment merely provides information as necessary material in order to enable the organism to make his or her own selections. Soviet psychology incorporates both these viewpoints and, thus, overcomes the dualism outlined by Reese and Overton (1970). In this synthesis, new operations represent the internalization of external structures, such as language, but these modes of operations also represent the outcome of internal structural processes. Both the material basis within and the material basis outside of the organism represent origins of interaction processes through which activity and consciousness emerge.

The trends in Soviet philosophy and sciences are comparable to those that led to the consolidation of Greek philosophy with Christian thoughts and beliefs. Much as the Scholastics incorporated Aristotelian philosophy but warded off the influences of the Skeptics, Epicureans, and Stoics, so does Soviet ideology incorporate the dialectical philosophy of Hegel but rejects his idealism and "Machian" positivism. Whereas the Church and the Scholastics repressed the Islamic influences (although Arab scholars were the main transmitter of knowledge from the Greek-Roman period to the late medieval world), Soviet philosophers and scientists seem to remain free of such an external, intellectual "threat" and, therefore, are directing additional defenses against Western philosophy, whose traditions they nevertheless cultivate and transcend.

The Beginning of Soviet Psychology

Among the few surveys of Soviet psychology, the treatise by Payne (1968) on S. L. Rubinstein seems by far most sensitive to the intrinsic dynamics of Soviet sciences. According to Payne, the postrevolutionary history of Russian psychology can be subdivided into the Mechanistic Period (1917–1930), the Dialectical Period (1930–1950), and the Period of Synthesis (after 1950).

1. The period immediately after the Russian Revolution saw the elimination of the existing teaching and research traditions that were following Western, especially German, introspective psychology and philosophical idealism. This development was terminated at the time of the First All-Russian Psychological Congress in 1923 and through the appointment of Kornilov as Director of the Moscow Psychological Institute in 1924. At the same time Pavlov, and especially Bekterev, established themselves firmly. By considering behavior as a biosocial phenomenon they denied any distinct place to psychology. This view was opposed by Kornilov as mechanistic and reductionistic and as failing to consider the dialectical roots of communism, according to which the objective and subjective have to be brought into an organic synthesis.

During the ensuing controversy between the mechanistic materialists (who considered all changes as quantitative and reducible to biological contingencies) and the dialectical materialists (who insisted on Hegel's notion of "dialectical leaps" through which qualitative transformations were achieved), the latter received strong support through the posthumous publication of Lenin's *Philosophical Notebook* (1929b) and through the efforts of Deborin. Although the latter gained a clear victory over the mechanistic materialists, after two years he was criticized for adopting Hegel's idealistic dialectics without sufficient consideration for the materialistic reformulation by Marx and Engels. Nevertheless, dialectics, stripped of its idealistic features, continued to win out over mechanistics, as confirmed at the First All-Union Conference for Human Behavior in 1930.

2. The period from 1930 to 1950 was characterized by intensive criticisms and reevaluations. Of greatest consequence was the purge of the educational movement known as Pedology.

According to a decree by the Central Committee of the Communist party in 1936, this movement (especially connected with the work of Blonskij) had undermined the responsibility of the teacher and developed a laissez-faire if not a negative attitude toward so-called backward children. The use of psychological tests had been accepted for the categorization of these children who, then, were kept in their backward states by assigning them to "special" schools in which "bad habits" became even harder to correct. Individual differences were either related to inherited biological factors or to the social environment. The proponents of the former view, the "biologists," came under sharp attack for preserving the aims of the bourgeois classes instead of emphasizing the duty of the educators toward active modification of the child's development. Instead of accepting the child's development as predetermined, the participatory role of the teacher as a representative of the historical–cultural conditions of the society became the dominant theme not only for education, but also for behavioral and social sciences in general.

Although criticized for his support of the bifurcation into heredity and environment, Vygotsky, the most prominent "sociologist," was credited with directing full attention to the normative effects of the sociocultural factors. This interpretation was consonant with the dialectical materialism of Marx, Engels, and Lenin, especially since Vygotsky emphasized the historical impact of these factors (1929). Consciousness, according to this interpretation, emerges through the process of historical and social evolutions, which, in turn, originate from a material basis through human labor.

The victory of dialectics was greatly enhanced by Vygotsky. After his early death, his arguments were carried forward by his associates and students, especially Leontjev and Lurija. The late thirties and, due in part to the disruptions of the war, the forties were not marked by any major confrontations, and it did not become apparent until the late fifties how thoroughly Vygotsky's interpretations had introduced the dialectical materialism of the "Classics" into psychology. When consolidated with Pavlov's interpretations of the "first and second signal systems," a theory could emerge in full conformity with the goals of the communistic ideology.

3. The third major period in the history of Soviet psychology was initiated by the Pavlov Conference in 1950. This meeting was dominated by physiologists and medical researchers although the psychologists were but a small minority that remained on the defensive throughout the proceedings. The conference had the declared purpose of firmly establishing Pavlov's legacy and, primarily, consisted in proclamations of allegiance coupled with self-criticisms by those who had failed to appreciate his contributions

in the past. Stated more positively, the conference by rejecting the psycho-physical parallelism of Western thinking, adopted dialectical interac-tionism. Such an interactionism had been made possible through the devel-opment of Pavlov's theory of the "second signal system" and, thus, the conference accepted and promoted this change in interpretation with its far-reaching consequences.

According to Pavlov, "conditioned and unconditioned reflexes realize the connection of the organism with its environment and are directed towards the maintenance of a state of equilibrium between the systems of the organism and external conditions" (Payne, 1968, p. 14). The activity involved in the formation of this connection is called higher nervous activ-ity in distinction from lower nervous activity, which serves to integrate the different parts of the organism. The stimuli from the environment, sig-nalizing the objects necessary for the organism's survival, represent the "first signaling system," which is common to human beings and to ani-mals. Throughout our culture and history, we have developed, however, a second signaling system that "does not directly signalize reality but rather the data of the first signaling system" (Payne, 1968, p. 14). The second signaling system allows for a much higher degree of abstraction and for an expansion of activities resulting in the cultural–historical achievements of society.

Pavlov's extension of his early theory of conditioning thus paved the way for a consolidation of the dialectical materialism of Marx, Engels, and Lenin with the mechanistic materialism that characterizes his earlier work. This possibility was realized and accepted by the participants of the Pavlov Conference. One of the most penetrating proponents of this development was S. L. Rubinstein.

The Psychology of S. L. Rubinstein

Rubinstein's synthesis tries to overcome the mind–body dualism that has remained unbridgeable in Western thought and has led to development of several different "psychologies." On the one hand, the introspectionists focused exclusively upon consciousness. Because of its absolute, subjective character, consciousness has remained unattainable for scientific descrip-tions, however. The methodologically powerful countermove by beha-viorism (being intrinsically weak in its epistemological basis) represents, according to Rubinstein, nothing but vulgar mechanism and the denial or inverse of introspectionism and thus is not of much greater worth.

1. Rubinstein's synthesis emphasizes the unity of consciousness and

behavior. These terms do not denote separate systems, nor is the former all internal and the latter external, but both interpenetrate each other. Consciousness is not a passive contemplative state but an activity; behavior is not merely a movement, but is directed by internal organization. On the one hand, activity objectifies the inner subjective world; on the other hand, the objective world is reflected in and by the subject. This distinction is very similar to Piaget's comparison of accommodation (of the subject to the object) and assimilation (of the object to the subject). Both processes are interdependent, leading to adaptation of the subject. Rubinstein refers to Marx: "By acting on the external world and changing it, he [the subject], at the same time, changes his own nature" (Marx, 1954, p. 177).

For Rubinstein, the study of the ontogenesis of consciousness is not conceivable without the study of phylogenesis. Piaget, likewise, emphasizes both, genetic individual and historic–cultural epistemology. Development in neither case consists in the continuous accumulation of information but progresses in qualitative leaps. For Rubinstein, modifications are brought about by changes in the structure of the organism. But as these structures change the functions change also, because structure and functions develop as a unit. At the beginning, development of organisms is determined by the laws of biological evolution. At higher levels of phylogenesis, however, development becomes increasingly co-determined by the laws of sociohistorical evolution. In particular, people, through their activities and labor, transform their environment and create new conditions for individual development. As stated by Payne, the human being "creates himself by his own labor—by transforming nature to transform himself" (1968, p. 90).

When focusing upon the ontogenetic evolution, the individual's development consists in the acquisition of human culture through his own activities. In rejecting Pedology, Rubinstein insists that this process has to be supplemented by the activity of the society. In other words, it is insufficient merely to point out the sociohistorical conditions of the culture; society has the duty as well of imposing, if necessary, these conditions upon the growing organism. The activities have to permeate in both directions: from the individual to the culture and from the culture to the individual. Knowledge is acquired through the individual's activities, but the activities of the society are of equal importance. Knowledge is social in nature.

2. In the preceding paragraph, I emphasized the dialectical interactions between individual and cultural conditions. The individual is co-determined by a second system of interactions, i.e., those between psychic states and higher nervous activities. Rubinstein does not elaborate this interaction at length but refers to the work of Pavlov and his followers. With

this renewed emphasis on the biological, material basis Rubinstein completes his synthesis. In the words of Payne:

> The relation of the psychic to the material world is fundamentally twofold: to the inner matter of the brain (this relation constitutes the psychic in the quality of higher nervous activity) and to the outer matter of the external world in which relationship the psychic takes on the quality of ideal and subjective. The first quality Rubinstein calls the *ontological* aspect of the psychic; the second he calls *gnoseological* or theory-of-knowledge aspect. (Payne, 1968, p. 98)

The seriousness with which the notion of dialectical interactions penetrates all of Rubinstein's interpretations is most clearly revealed by the concept of "constitutive relationism" that he adopts from Hegel and Lenin. Lenin emphasized, "Every concrete thing, every concrete something, stands in multifarious and often contradictory relations to everything else: ergo it is itself and some other" (1929b, p. 124). In Payne's formulation, ". . . every phenomenon or thing is determined and constituted by its relation to all the other phenomena of reality" (1968, p. 99). Consequently, psychic states have a plurality of structures. There are several intrinsic structures relating higher nervous activities to the brain, and several extrinsic structures relating these psychic activities to the external reality. Thus, relations are both logically and genetically prior to the elements that they connect; our experiences are always contextual, and meaning, for instance, is prior to words (Riegel, 1970c).

Rubinstein's interpretations imply nothing else than a reformulation of the old mind–body problem. Traditionally, the solution of this problem has been sought by determining the nature of both, the mind and the body and then by contemplating their interdependence. For Rubinstein the solution has to proceed in the reverse order. The relationship determines how we conceive of mind and how we conceive of body. In particular, the psychic is determined by the dual relationship to outer and inner matter. But matter also appears in this dual relationship. For instance, a crystal is determined by its inner atomic structure as well as by its relationships to the external, material conditions. Thus, the boundaries between mind and matter become fluid. Similar to Leibniz, "The material world has traits which are, in some faint way, similar to consciousness and which provide the premises for its natural evolution. The psychic is therefore one link in the chain of properties of the material world" (Payne, 1968, p. 106).

The two anchoring conditions of the internal and external material reality characterize a new dualism of Soviet philosophy. Since both represent processes rather than synchronic entities such as the body and mind, they relate to the contrast between ontogenetic and phylogenetic changes. Psychic activities emerge through the interactions with both. Thus, mind and body collapse upon the intersect of these two interaction processes. At the same time psychic activities are delegated to a secondary position. Their study has to be founded upon that of internal biochemical processes as well as upon that of external sociocultural processes. Psychology without these foundations would be fictitious.

Conclusions

Rubinstein's synthesis tries to reformulate on a relational basis, and thereby tries to overcome, the old mind–body dualism of Descartes. With the exception of the latter himself, who formulated on a somewhat superficial level an interactionistic interpretation (by placing the locus of interaction in the pineal gland), Western philosophy and psychology either adopted parallelism or materialistic and idealistic monisms. These Western approaches placed all their efforts into the separate descriptions of these two entities; they studied their relative contributions in terms, for instance, of the hereditary and environmental influences upon development, but by splitting them apart at the beginning, they precluded the possibility of bringing them together again.

This split also characterizes the two major Western branches of developmental psychology that I have called its capitalistic and mercantilistic modes (see chap. 7). Only recently have attempts been made, notably by Piaget and by Chomsky, to emphasize interaction processes rather than parallel descriptions. Both these scholars have restricted their discussions to mental states. Thus, they have created a neo-mentalism and have failed to emphasize the interaction of the growing organism with the sociohistorical contingencies. Rubinstein, by reviving the early interpretations of Vygotsky but, most important, by taking the "Classics" seriously (i.e., Marx, Engels, and Lenin), has provided a synthesis that leads to new perspectives in social and psychological philosophy. As for Piaget and Chomsky, the individual is no longer seen as a passive recipient of external information, but unlike Piaget and Chomsky, the notion of activity is not restricted to the individual alone.

PHENOMENAL, LOGICAL, AND EXISTENTIAL BASES
OF SCIENCES AND KNOWLEDGE

Psychological operations have been categorized into those that focus upon motor-productive, sensory-perceptual, or symbolic-structural processes. Recently, this distinction has been emphasized in Bruner's (1964) description of *enactive, iconic,* and *symbolic* modes of representation. By enactive representation Bruner means:

> a mode of representing past events through appropriate motor response. We cannot, for example, give an adequate description of familiar sidewalks or floors over which we habitually walk, nor do we have much of an image of what they are like. Yet we get about them without tripping or even looking much . . . Iconic representation summarizes events by the selective organization of percepts and of images, by the spatial, temporal, and qualitative structures of the perceptual field and their transformed images . . . Finally, a symbol system represents things by design features that include remoteness and arbitrariness. A word neither points directly to its referent here and now, nor does it resemble it as a picture . . . The other property of language that is crucial is its productiveness in combination, far beyond what can be done with images or acts. (1964, p. 2)

In the present section, I will use this distinction in a quite different sense than Bruner, namely to characterize and evaluate the state of knowledge and science. Generally, in Western thinking the criterion for knowledge and science has been predominantly a sensory-perceptual one or, as I shall call it, *iconic;* the "truth" of a scientific statement is evaluated by the degree to which it corresponds to sensory data, regardless of whether these are of a common-sense type or attainable only under complex observational conditions. Since even the simplest statement implies a structure of logic and grammar, the iconic criterion blends into that on the *symbolic* level. Here, in conjunction with sensory-perceptual information, an isomorphism is sought between the structure of the observed phenomena and that of their common-sense or formal description. While Western sciences and philosophy have emphasized the second criterion through the elaboration of mathematical formalism and the first through empirical research, they have hardly ever considered *enactive* representation as a criterion for knowledge and science; i.e., they have disregarded the effects of particular scientific contributions upon science as well as upon society.

Iconic Evaluations

Western philosophy step-by-step abandoned naive realism, which assumes nothing less than the existence of a physical world with its substances and movements. Locke first rejected the notion that our impressions of hardness, color, warmth, etc., are directly representative of the physical world; rather, they represent the interpretations of the observer. Nevertheless, Locke did not question the existence of the physical world, which in his opinion causes our sensations and impressions.

The subjective contributions of the observer were more strongly emphasized by Hume and the positivists of the late 19th century, especially by Mach. Consequently, it became necessary to explain how different observers, on the basis of their subjective experiences, could nevertheless agree on the quality of these experiences, e.g., could agree to denote some experiences as red, warm, or hard, etc. The positivists, especially Poincaré, proposed that such agreements are the result of conventions and, thus, emphasized the importance of sociocultural contingencies. Unlike the materialists, these contingencies were regraded as arbitrary inventions. By declaring sensations, perceptions, and cognitions as the only information available to us and statements about the existence of a real physical world as metaphysical speculations, the positivists found themselves, surprisingly, in the company of the phenomenologists (who did not share their elementaristic zeal, however), as well as rationalists such as Descartes who, after all, maintained that all our knowledge comes from the mind and is in our mind (downgrading, of course, reliance on sensory data).

All of the schools and philosophers mentioned share a commitment to cognitive judgments. The criteria for truth lie exclusively in rational decisions, regardless of whether knowledge is gained from a sensory basis or through thinking alone. For Locke the truth criterion is external and either lies in the primary qualities of the real world or is based upon the linguistic agreements of the community. For Hume and Mach these conventions remain the sole criterion. For Descartes the truth criterion is internal and, ultimately, consists in rational self-observations. However, like Locke, he does not take this idea to its radical conclusion but, relying on the mediation of God, reintroduces sensory data from the real, mechanistic world.

The positivists of the late 19th century, especially Poincaré and Avenarius, realized that it would be insufficient to reach agreements on labels for subjective experiences, but that knowledge and sciences also depend upon agreements on the logical, syntactic organization of the labeled impressions and interpretations. Earlier, these structures were thought of as intrinsically given and, subsequently, as universally true and immediately apparent to the observer. Kant, for instance, insisted on the universality of Euclidean space and, therefore, on the indisputable status of traditional geometry and algebra. The positivists, on the other hand, regarded the choice of logical and syntactic structures as arbitrary and dependent upon social conventions as well as upon their utility in providing economic though comprehensive descriptions for a particular field of investigation. With this shift they supported an increased flexibility in the development and application of formal systems to empirical research. In physics, for instance, they justified the shift from Euclidean geometry to those of Lobachevski or Riemann. In the behavioral and social sciences they promoted the utilization of a great variety of mathematical and logical models.

Enactive Evaluations

Marx was one of the first to deny the arbitrary character of social and linguistic conditions and thus emphasized the noncognitive basis of knowledge and sciences. The material conditions force people to activity; through their labor they produce a world that, in turn, imposes changes upon them. The internal and external material conditions are realized only through the actions that, thus, become part of the criterion for truth and knowledge. Instead of asking how I can gain distinct and firm knowledge the question now becomes, how do my actions change the world (and knowledge) and how does the changed world affect the individual?

The shift from iconic to enactive truth criteria is not only characteristic for the Marxists of the 19th century but also for existentialism as initiated by Schopenhauer, Kierkegaard, Nietzsche, and others. In contrast to the material, deterministic foundation of Marx's philosophy, this movement aims toward nonscientific or antiscientific interpretations and, for this reason, is of lesser interest in the present context. The emphasis of an action-criterion for knowledge has gained momentum in the Western world through the realization of political injustice and social irrelevance of some of our scientific efforts. Among several contemporary proponents ranging from Heisenberg (1952) to Merleau-Ponty (1963), Amedeo Giorgi (1969) has written a thoughtful analysis of the socioepistemological problems from a phenomenological–existentialistic point of view; and Klaus Holzkamp (1970) has provided action-related interpretations of knowledge and sciences in his critical review of the more conservative theories.

The behavioral sciences, in their attempt to reach the standards of the natural sciences, have made extraordinary efforts to improve their methodological bases and the formalism of their theories. This has led to a disregard of the relevance of psychological investigations. As long as a study was based on a firm methodological foundation, it was argued, any type of investigation would add at least some small bits of information to the growing repertoire of psychological knowledge and thus, ultimately, would contribute to the advancement of science and society. This attitude has produced the enormous and rapidly increasing number of research reports by which the progress and status of a science have been evaluated. Little or no attention was given to the question of the usefulness of the material.

The criterion of social relevance remained overshadowed by the request for methodological rigor and abstract formalism.

To the philosophical realist, the goal of sciences was to detect the "laws of nature." Any social or political considerations would only sidetrack the scientist in this task and thus were not only inappropriate but positively harmful to his efforts. Even more so to the rationalists, the social relevance of science was of little concern; truth was found through contemplative introspections and, ultimately, was guaranteed through the intervention of God. With the advent of the positivists, social factors gained importance as a basis for scientific knowledge. Subsequently, societies with different languages and social conventions might not only produce different types of sciences but also arrive at different scientific "laws." Thus, these philosophers emphasized the social determination of the sciences but still paid little or no attention to the problem of how scientific activities would, in turn, influence the conditions of the society. Scientific efforts were seen as passive reflections of external and, in the latter case, of culturally dependent conditions. The active character and the normative effects of scientific efforts were not yet emphasized.

Much as Piaget and Vygotsky provided us with new interpretations of children's development, so do we need new perspectives on the growth and the direction of knowledge and science. In contrast to the behaviorists, Piaget maintained that intellectual development does not merely consist in the passive accumulation of data from the environment but that the individual participates actively in a search and exploration process. For Piaget, the environment still represents little else than a source for material from which the individual selects according to his or her wishes and level of intellectual competence. Vygotsky and Rubinstein, on the other hand, also emphasize the active role of the environment in developmental processes.

For Piaget, a scientist actively imposes modes of interpretations upon environmental data. For Rubinstein, these modes not only represent possible ways of interrelating scientific phenomena but also signify the wider social context into which they are embedded. Thus, the scientist needs to ascend a hierarchy of interpretations, each successive level representing a wider context and emphasizing more strongly the social significance of observations and interpretations. At the same time, the scientist has to determine what effect, in turn, any of these interpretations will have upon the society of which his or her science is a part. It is not only the scientist's task to provide interpretations of scientific observations and to consider their relevance for society, but also to determine how society and the changes in the society brought about by such scientific activities will influence the future activities and well-being of other individuals as well as his or her own.

Scientific activities consist of much more than the recording of so-called facts. They involve a weighting for social significance. These evaluations are not left to the reviewer and the critic but each scientist is, from the beginning, expected to consider his activities in regard to the modifications that they produce (Lynd, 1968). Universal criteria for scientific activities are, of course, hard to provide. These criteria will vary from society to society. Thus, a socialistic society will develop criteria different from those of a capitalistic society. What we can attempt, however, is to compare different conceptualizations of man and his development on a cultural–historical basis. In this way we may clarify some of the issues in the determination of criteria for social relevance in scientific activities.

CONCLUSIONS

In summary, I contrast four major viewpoints of man and his development. The first regards both the environment and the organism as essentially passive. Such theorizing is based upon the sensationalism, associationisms, and mechanism of such British philosophy as, for example, initiated by Locke. Combinations of events in the environment that happen to occur in the presence of a subject are imprinted into his mind. On the basis of the contiguity of these stimuli, their frequency, recency, etc., the mind of the individual—originally an empty box or *tabula rasa*—is being built up. Modern proponents of such interpretations can be found among the behaviorists and students of verbal learning.

The educational philosophy implied in the first model has hardly ever been rigorously applied. Even the most rigid trainer, sticking firmly to drill, memorization, and rehearsal, chooses his material and reinforcements selectively and, thus, determines actively the direction of the learning process. In a more general sense, however, this model represents the status quo behind which the teachers and administrators of our public educational systems try to hide. All too often, their main concern seems to be to stay out of conflicting situations, be it a simple quarrel among two or three first-graders or racial and political strifes that tear apart the whole nation. By maintaining that these conflicts have to be worked out between the individuals themselves or within the groups, these teachers fail to see that their evasion nevertheless implies a decisive choice, which generally lends the upper hand to the physically rather than intellectually more forceful individual and to the dominant power group.

The second type of theory retains the notion of a passive environment but introduces the individual as an active agent. Such viewpoints were very common among the Greeks and were reintroduced into philosophy through Leibniz's monadology. Monads change their internal state from passivity and trance to activity and consciousness but do not compound in order to form complex percepts. The theory of cognitive development by Piaget and of language and mind by Chomsky are the most outstanding examples of the modern revival of such an activity model. Both regard the environmental stimulation as a necessary prerequisite for development; neither of them spells out and emphasizes, however, its influence in detail. Environmental stimulation might be compared to surrounding material contingencies from which the organism makes spontaneous selections. If there were no such contingencies he or she could not make such selections; development is, however, internally initiated and directed.

In recent years, there has been a growing and understandable interest in applying Piaget to education (Aebli, 1951; Bruner, 1966; Furth, 1970). By putting "activity" back to where it belongs, namely into the organism, Piaget has profoundly changed our concept of humanity and its development. As pointedly emphasized by Hans Aebli, the application of his ideas to education has, however, serious limitations. For example, in intellectual progression, as long as a child attends to one form of thought, e.g., at the preoperational level, there is no point of training him for more advanced, i.e., concrete, operations: he would not yet be able to comprehend and apply them. Once a child has attained the level of concrete operations, there is no need to provide such training either; he is, now, competent to perform these operations anyhow.

Undoubtedly, such a *laissez-faire* attitude is more characteristic for the Summerhill school program (Neill, 1960) than for Piaget and my statements overemphasize the limitations of his theory. They also indicate the similarity between these educational viewpoints and the hermeneutical theory of Socrates and Plato in which the influence of the educator is compared with the skills of a midwife. Knowledge is implicit in the child; the educator merely assists the individual to explicate and to become conscious of these ideas. Since the educator will use skills selectively—for instance, by choosing certain tasks or toys for a particular child at a particular time—he or she participates actively in this explication process. After all, the educator, as much as the child, is an active organism. Piaget, and especially Chomsky, have disregarded the educator's participatory role in transforming the historical-cultural conditions for the developmental benefit of the child.

If we were to make our comparisons complete, we would have to search, thirdly, for an interpretation of a passive organism in an active environment. Perhaps Skinner's educational models, as represented in *Walden Two* (1948) and by the technology of the teaching machines, may serve as cases in point. The manipulations by the conditioner must appear as arbitrary and willful to the conditioned subject. Stronger yet, even the conditioner appears to operate without any overall directions; there is no theory of culture and history, nor of social ethics, that guides his or her interventions. In comparison with the fourth theory to be mentioned, little emphasis is given to the structure of the educational input.

The notion of a passive organism in an active environment is also implied in some sociological theories. Ryder (1965), for example, provides a developmental interpretation in which changes are brought about by generational (cohort) substitutions rather than by psychological growth. Individuals successively lose their places without modifications in their own behavior. Also, the early interpretations by Vygotsky can be considered as examples for such a theory emphasizing, in contrast to Skinner, the structure of the environmental conditions. Since in complete dialectical theories the penetration is always in both directions, however, i.e., from the environment to the individual and from the individual to the environment, an active role of both is implied. Thus, dialectical interpretations lead us to the fourth and most important theory in which both the organism and the environment are active participants in two-way interaction processes.

It is to the merit of S. L. Rubinstein to have proposed a psychological, developmental theory in which both the organism and the environment fulfill active roles and in which, thus, both the conceptual issues and those of social ethics are fully realized. Rubinstein distinguishes between external contingencies and what might appropriately be called the organism's internal, material environment. Through two interaction processes, connected with these contingencies, psychic activities emerge into consciousness and attain their organization. Thus, Rubinstein, on the basis of the material and historical dialecticism of Marx, Engel, and Lenin, incorporates into a theory of the human being and his or her development all three criteria of science and knowledge, namely, the enactive–existential, the iconic–phenomenal, and the symbolic–structural. The enactive–existential criterion is realized through the emphasis upon the social relevance of scientific efforts and by viewing consciousness as the result of the organism's activities. The iconic–phenomenal criterion is expressed by viewing sciences and consciousness as reflections of the sociocultural contingencies. The symbolic–structural criterion is realized in the organization of interactions between the internal and external material conditions on the one hand and the psychic activities of the individual on the other. Needless to say, both behavioral science and education are far remote from realizing the practical and theoretical potential of such a viewpoint.

CHAPTER 7

The Ideological Bases of
Developmental Psychology

The recent unrest in our society has made us once more aware of the intimate connections between economic and political ideologies and the development of sciences. This statement does not imply that I intend to address myself to the well-documented preferences of most governments for defense-related rather than socially significant spending, or to the political frustrations and problematic decisions that modern scientists have to face. Rather, I will deal with the general economic and cultural conditions of societies that provide a necessary basis for the growth of sciences. This dependence can be persuasively documented for developmental psychology, which exploits two traditions that are identifiable by certain philosophical, educational, economical, social, and political orientations. For the sake of convenience, these are labeled the "capitalistic" and "mercantilistic" traditions. The first has been dominant in the Anglo-American world, while the second has prevailed in continental Europe. I will discuss these traditions in the first two parts of this chapter, and in the third, attempt to synthesize these two trends in what might be called a relational or dialectical interpretation of developmental processes as well as suggest "what we must do" *
in developmental psychology.

* This expression is borrowed from the title of the challenging article by John Platt (1969),
   which in turn seems to have been taken from Lenin's pamphlet (1929a), which in its English
   translation reads "What is to be done."

The original article was published under the title, "Influence of economic and political ideologies on the development of developmental psychology," Psychological Bulletin, 1972, 78, 129–141.

THE CAPITALISTIC ORIENTATION

Most textbooks on the history of psychology, if they are treating the topic of individual differences and development at all, pay much, if not exclusive, tribute to Darwin's (1859) theory of the origin of species. Darwin (1809–1882) revived, on the basis of rich naturalistic observations, some ideas that were familiar to the British philosophical tradition and that were expressed most distinctly in Hobbes's (1588–1679) analysis of the development of social organizations. At the beginning, Hobbes (1669) argued in his *Elementa philosophica de cive* that each individual is engaged in a struggle against everyone else. Only sufficient damage makes us, motivated as we are by egoism, realize that our security and future are guaranteed only if some cooperation and social contract is achieved. Such arrangements ultimately lead to the establishment of reasonable social orders, especially through the development of property rights.

   1. Darwin, with his notions of the "struggle for survival" and the "survival of the fittest," proposed an open-ended developmental interpretation quite similar to the social philosophy of Hobbes. For Darwin, development is a process of continuous competition and selection, whose direction and goals are represented by the "successful survivors" here and now. When translated into the matrix of behavioral and social sciences, the "successful survivor" becomes the white, middle-class adult most likely engaged in manufacturing or business enterprises.* His success was not so much seen as due to his generative capacities but rather to the fit between his activities and the demands of the society that he represented.

   From this point of view, deviant persons or nonstandard groups attain negative attributes only: Children are regarded as incomplete adults; old persons as deficient; criminals, mental defectives, colonial subjects, and nonwhites as far below the rank of white middle-class adults. It cannot be denied that many of the privileged, especially in Britain, vigorously engaged in humanitarian efforts to better the "deplorable" lot of these "inferior" persons, but in all these activities they never abandoned their basic ideological and evaluative schema. Instead, they reinforced it through these efforts in much the same way as the role of the beggar is reinforced by giving him alms. Occasionally, they pitied the fate of their own making as the "white man's burden."

---

* This translation was promoted by Spencer (1897) (1820–1903) and Pearson (1904) (1857–1936) in Britain, but especially by Sumner (1963) (1840–1910) in the United States.

Darwin's theory of evolution was most readily accepted in England. France was most resistant, and Germany took an intermediate position (Norderskiöld, 1928). These national differences can be explained on the basis of economic and cultural conditions. The Englishmen with their cherished tradition for hunting and breeding—but especially the Englishmen as entrepreneurs, traders, and manufacturers—should be more than superficially susceptible to interpretations in which success emerges through restless competition. Of course, the idea of an apelike ancestry shocked the more conservative circles, but such considerations were easily outweighed by the relevance and similarity of these interpretations with the politico–economic ideals of a free, competitive trade system.

While the strong emphasis upon competition placed the young, the old, the deviant, and, generally, the "different" persons into inferior positions, the positive identification of the successful adult was, nevertheless, far from a simple matter. By posing an open-ended ideal, such a prototype became more a topic of wishful thinking than an observable phenomenon. Dependent upon personal preferences and values, the ideal may represent the imaginative manufacturer, the aggressive businessman, the clever politician, or the ruthless general; dependent upon stereotypes and illusions, it represents adventurers, movie stars, princes, and charlatans. In emphasizing prototypes rather than real people, it mattered little that the private affairs and mental states of such ideal persons (consensual heroes) might be pitiful or even more deplorable than those of the average and presumably less successful and happy individuals. The goal for every member of the society held fast: to strive toward these abstract ideals; and if the result was unsuccessful, to expect to be regarded with less respect.

2. One of the earliest proponents of the theory of evolution and of its translation into the behavioral and social sciences was Francis Galton (1822–1911). Under the strong influence of his older sister, and endowed with sufficient wealth, Galton developed into a brilliant superman scientist with a feminine sensitivity, as described in Nietzsche's writings and also as demonstrated by Nietzsche's own life. Aside from extensive travels and explorations, Galton conducted numerous innovative studies on crossbreeding, inheritance of traits, and individual differences. He invented and applied many methods, such as the free-word-association and psychomotor tests, as well as procedures for their analysis, including the regression technique. Most important for our present purpose are Galton's *Hereditary Genius* (1869) and *Inquiries into Human Faculty and Its Development* (1883).

Emphasizing a biogenetic basis, Galton, in the first book, traced the lineage of famous persons in order to show the hereditary nature of superior abilities. In his conclusion he did not hesitate to argue for selective in-breeding of gifted persons in order to improve the human race. This perspective led him to establish the field of eugenics, which he justified as follows:

> It may seem monstrous that the weak should be crowded out by the strong, but it is still more monstrous that the races best fitted to play their part on the stage of life should be crowded out by the incompetent, the ailing, and the desponding. (1869, p. 343)

Supported by the like-minded Count Gobineau (1816–1882, reference dated 1884) and generalized to cultural–historical comparisons by Houston Stewart Chamberlain (1855–1927, reference dated 1909), the uncle of the late British prime minister Neville Chamberlain and son-in-law of Richard Wagner, these ideas, when merged with continental European ideologies and applied with political fanaticism and military expediency, led directly to the holocaust of Belsen, Buchenwald, and Theresienstadt.

In his second book, *Inquiries into Human Faculty and Its Development,* Galton (1883) introduced impressive biological, psychological, and anthropologic records among which his psychometric measures—reaction time, strength of grip, coordination speed, etc.—across the full life span still are some of the most accurate and extensive data available (see Koga and Morant, 1923; Ruger and Stoessiger, 1927; Elderton, Moul, and Page, 1928). Other reports were more dramatic but less serious. Thus, during his numerous journeys in England, he counted the number of beautiful women seen per unit time and in his "beauty maps" reported that London had the most and Aberdeen the fewest. Nevertheless, his extensive recordings became the prototype of a developmental research strategy that, at least on the North American continent, was to dominate this field for many decades to come. Theoretically more sophisticated approaches, as well as experimental methodologies, have only recently begun to play a significant role in this branch of behavioral science.

Galton's thinking was dominated by the interpretations of his famous cousin. These interpretations were based on descriptive evidence and, from our present point of view, resemble scientific speculations rather than scientific theories. Even though progress was soon to be made, for instance, through the rediscovery and extension of Mendel's laws of crossbreeding by Correns, de Vries, and Tschermak, it took several decades until an experimental basis for genetic studies and appropriate methodologies for their analysis were developed. Undoubtedly, Galton was one of the early contributors to this development.

3. Similar though less credit has to be given to the American followers of Darwin's theory, especially G. Stanley Hall (1846–1924). While his continental European colleagues, including such outspoken promoters of the theory of evolution as Ernst Haeckel (1834–1919), engaged in experimental genetics and comparative anatomy and physiology, Hall tended to emphasize far-reaching generalizations rather than tedious research details. He strongly supported the theory of pangenesis with its notion that "ontogeny recapitulates phylogeny." In these interpretations Hall deviated from Galton by placing greater emphasis on environmental factors. While Galton, for instance, supported the notion of gemmules as carriers of hereditary information, Hall made some concessions toward Lamarck's (1744–1829) notions of the inheritance of acquired traits and of changes actively accomplished by organisms. In this regard, surprisingly, he found himself in agreement with Darwin himself, who also took a rather liberal view when dealing with questions of human development. Galton was indeed the extremist, arguing for the inheritance of mental traits, whereas Hall's interpretation represented a compromise between hereditarian and environmentalistic views. Recently, these differences have been cogently discussed by McCullers (1969) and Charles (1970).

Up to adolescence, Hall argued, development is biologically determined; thus, one has to allow "the fundamental traits of savagery their fling till twelve (Hall, 1904, p. X)." During adolescence and early maturity, however, genetic changes could be effected; thus, society has a heavy burden. Moreover, as expressed by Hyatt (1838–1902), an American naturalist:

> . . . all modifications and variations in progressive series tend to appear first in the adolescent or adult stages of growth, and then to be inherited in successive descendents at earlier and earlier stages according to the law of acceleration, until they either become embryonic, or are crowded out of the organizations, and replaced in the development of characteristics of later origin. (1890, p. IX)

Hall's compromise in the United States and Pearson's psychometric zeal in England initiated the long-lasting struggle between supporters of hereditary interpretations and the environmentalists. This controversy still burdens heavily our conceptualization of development as the recent excitement about Jensen's (1969) review and the reply by the Society for the Psychological Study of Social Issues (1969) has revealed. As will be discussed in the next section, the continental European, developmental psychology is freed of such an extrapsychological issue by dealing with psychological development in a nonreductionistic manner; that is, by trying to explain psychological development on a psychological rather than on a biogenetic or sociocultural basis.

Hall's compromise began to shift the emphasis from the competition between genetically determined to that between socially determined factors. This shift, much more than Galton's biogenetic interpretations and his notion of an applied field of eugenics, was to influence the developmental views in the major capitalistic country of today. Hall's students, especially Terman (1887–1956) and Gesell (1880–1961), continued within the empiricistic orientation of Galton, however, and in the following decades there was a burst of descriptive information on child development in the United States. All these studies contributed to establishing trends and standards with which the performance of the young and old, the abnormal and the deprived, could be compared. As long as the middle-class, white adult remained the sole standard–ideal, the outcome of all these evaluations was bound to remain negative.

THE MERCANTILISTIC ORIENTATION

Since the economic and social structure of a nation is strongly determined by geographical factors, it is not surprising that England emerged as a power on the seas and as a nation of entrepreneurs and merchants successfully trading their manufactured goods across the continents. Even though a monarchy, the government was not suppressive and the taxation was not severe enough to hamper seriously the industrial and financial developments. Colonial exploitations served to foster even further economic growth, which reached its culmination during the late nineteenth century (Beard, 1962). These conditions led to the emergence of a specific developmental science, representing the capitalistic mode of thinking.

In comparison to England, quite different economic and social conditions prevailed on the European continent, especially in France and in major parts of Germany and Italy. These conditions brought about a distinctly different type of developmental science that might be called its mercantilistic form.

1. All three countries, but especially France and Germany, remained land powers and were dominated by warrior aristocracies that controlled large land holdings. While, in general, the industrial and economic progress was delayed and slower than in England, the maintenance of large armies and courts made the development of manufacturing necessary. These developments were usually initiated and supervised by the state, with the

occasional exception of military production during times of increased demands. They were either manipulated by the rulers themselves, such as in Prussia, or by powerful advisers such as Jacques Coeur (1395–1456), Maximilien Sully (1560–1641), Baptiste Colbert (1619–1683), and Jacques Necker (1732–1804) in France. Whenever exceptionally successful, these entrepreneurs were ultimately suppressed, however, either as individuals or as a group. The French Huguenots, for example (especially after the cancellation of the Edict of Nantes in 1685), were forced to flee in large numbers to neighboring countries, where they contributed much to the development of trade and industry, in England, in the city ports of the North Sea, and as far away as in Russia.

The increased amount of manufactured goods and the increased trade within the continental European countries led, nevertheless, to the rapid expansion of a third, middle class of citizens which, though better off than the laborers, servants, and farm workers, was less privileged than the ruling aristocrats. Eventually, the incongruency between their social significance and their social privileges led to the French Revolution.

From the perspective of modern Western ideology, the prevalence of distinct classes with graded duties and countergraded privileges seems less than desirable. On the positive side, however, these conditions helped to strengthen an awareness and sensitivity toward group and age differences. In philosophy it produced the conservative attempts to justify the existing social orders, for instance, as implied in Leibniz's (1646–1716) *Théodicé*. By disregarding ceaseless competition between (but not within) classes, the continental European conditions generated a social and educational philosophy appreciative of multicultural and multigenerational differences. The home base for this movement lies at Geneva, the locus of intersection of the three major nations involved.

2. Influenced by Leibniz and supported by German representatives of philosophical Enlightenment, such as Mendelsohn (1729–1786), Lessing (1729–1781), and Herder (1744–1803), the first key figure in this development is Rousseau (1712–1778). In Rousseau's treatise on the future of science (1750), but especially in his book *Émile* (1762), he outlined an educational philosophy in which the child is set apart from the adult world of comparison and is educated and evaluated in view of the standards of his peer group alone. In support of a romantic ideal of a "noble savage," and in sharp contrast to Hobbes, people—and in particular primitive peoples and children—are considered as basically good. The adult world and civilization resemble a restrictive cloak that covers and spoils the natural beauty of the mind and body. We are all basically equal. Civilization creates individual

and group differences that make some rich and powerful and others poor and feeble. Rousseau's educational philosophy aimed toward preserving as long as possible the natural state of the child and tried to reaffirm the equality of men.

In a short period of time, Rousseau's educational and social philosophy began to influence the emerging educational institutions on the European continent. Although public education had become obligatory during the 18th century, these attempts mainly served the purpose of advancing the production potential of these states. Little thought was given to educational strategy, and since the teaching was often in the hands of retired army sergeants, drill and punishment were the predominant means of training. With the rapid spread of the new educational philosophy, especially through Pestalozzi (1746–1827), attention was given to educational approaches appropriate for the child, and the profession of specially trained teachers began to emerge in the more advanced European countries.

While this movement, initiated by Rousseau, can be considered as a revolution in support of the child, other upheavals originated from within the youth groups themselves. The early student organizations in the German states represent the first case in point. Originally conceived as paramilitary training groups against Napoleonic suppression, these organizations began to carve out distinct roles and privileges for students and teachers that were to influence the academic community for generations to come; only recently have they been challenged by radical student movements in the European universities.

After the educational breakthroughs for the pupils of elementary schools and by the students at the universities, the next movement was in support of preschool education and is especially connected with the names of Fröbel (1782–1852) and Montessori (1870–1952). The former, in close affinity to Pestalozzi, introduced the child-centered approach in "kindergarten," a term coined by him. Maria Montessori, giving stronger emphasis to an achievement orientation, emphasized nevertheless a child-initiated and self-paced type of educational strategy. Both charted a special role for and educational approaches to the preschool child, the former most liberal and laissez-faire, the latter more rationalistic and goal-directed.

The next major movement was again youth-initiated and influenced several better-known educators and developmental psychologists who, during their early years, actively participated in it. This movement, called the youth movement, was concerned with the liberation of adolescents from the establishments of the Victorian adult culture. It sought a "return to nature," and expressed itself in a preference for scouting, hiking, and camping. Unlike its counterpart in the capitalist countries (which persisted much longer), it was dominated by the thought that youth should be led by youth, and therefore the leaders were exclusively chosen from within the groups themselves.

As a participant in his youth, Spranger (1882–1963) became a developmental psychologist who formulated his educational experiences within a phenomenological psychology of understanding and empathy. In Spranger's (1924) influential book on adolescence he claimed that the thoughts and culture of this group, as well as of their deviant (i.e., their so-called delinquent) members, should be appreciated on the basis of sympathetic understanding and should not be evaluated in terms of the adult culture within which they exist uniquely.

3. Spranger's interpretations might stand for those of a good many other continental European psychologists who formed a group quite distinctly apart from their American and British contemporaries. The continental European movement originated, flourished, perpetuated, and spread from Geneva to reach its latest peak in the work of Piaget. This movement is characterized throughout by the notion of a stepwise, rather than continuous, progression in development. Each stage has to be evaluated in the framework of its own standards and, strictly speaking, is incompatible with any other level of behavior. While competition within stages is conceivable, it is not of great importance and is rejected as a driving force across stages.

Piaget has been criticized for his disregard of environmental, especially linguistic, factors and their impact upon cognitive development. Piaget's view is understandable within the developmental interpretations preferred among most continental European scientists (see Aebli, 1951). Language as a universal matrix for shaping the thoughts of the growing child is disregarded in favor of the conception of language as a succession of specialized sublanguages characteristic of different developmental stages. This distinction has been expressed by the Geneva school of linguistics, especially by de Saussure's (1916) *la langue* and *les paroles*.

The early controversy raised in Piaget's (1923) discussion of egocentric and socialized speech of children suggests a secondary conceptual distinction within the European tradition. Piaget, agreeing with Hobbes rather than Rousseau, regarded the young child as self-centered and egoistic. Development changes the individual into a social being. This interpretation was radically challenged by Vygotsky (1962), who, relying on equally dramatic observations, argued that children are basically social. Experience induces a self-concern and awareness of the overt social, for example, linguistic, actions. This experience, ultimately, leads to thought as an internalized form of speech. At the midway point, that is, around 6 or 7 years of age, the child produces self-centered speech that is not yet completely internalized and also lacks social and communicative features.

DIALECTICAL INTERPRETATION OF
DEVELOPMENTAL PROCESSES

The influence of continental European conceptualization is rapidly growing among American scholars as well as within the American society. Such a reorientation seems most appropriate. It not only assigns appreciable places to individuals at various stages of development, and more humane roles to the aged and deviant, but also allows us to deal fairly with various subgroups and subcultures striving to find their own identity. While the Anglo-American tradition has come to measure all individuals and groups along the same yardstick, the continental European educational and social philosophy promotes a diversity of standards and, thus, is sensitive to multigenerational and multicultural aspects.

Undoubtedly, the continental European social philosophy has serious shortcomings. In its extreme version it promotes the establishment of classes and castes. However, such implications might represent the lesser evil under conditions where the communication between generations and between incompletely realized subcultures is either lacking altogether or has been weakened to such an extent that no means other than revolution might induce the established groups to change their perspectives in order to make communication and mutual appreciation possible again.

But despite other conclusions that might have been drawn from these statements, I do not promote the adoption of either of the two views, because science and knowledge, as well as the society in general, can advance only if the divergent viewpoints are integrated at higher and more abstract levels. Behavioral scientists and developmental psychologists in particular have not succeeded in synthesizing the two viewpoints presented. This failure has to be explained by a lack of educational, social, and political awareness on the part of the individual scientist, by his preference for mechanistic rather than dialectical considerations, and by his naive "fact-finding" orientation.* Recently these issues have been brought into the

* Such a naive "fact-finding" orientation is clearly revealed by a quotation from Jensen in a recent report in *Life:* "I don't see why people should be disturbed by unequal representation of different groups in different occupations—or educationally, if it should be found that there are real differences" (Neary, 1970).

open in theoretical discussions (see Holzkamp, 1970), and by the promotion of interaction models.

1. Undoubtedly, the idea of writing a psychology in interaction terms is not an original one. Such attempts have been suggested by several continental European as well as Anglo-American scholars. For instance, von Uexküll's (1909) interaction paradigm is gaining much delayed though increasing attention from ecologists studying organisms in their natural environment. While von Uexküll (1864–1944) avoided any abstract formalism in his interpretations, Lewin (1890–1947), with due recognition of von Uexküll, tried to provide such an analysis (Lewin, 1936). Also, Anglo-American psychologists have proposed interaction models, most notably Kantor (1959) in his interbehavioral psychology, without receiving appropriate recognition.

For several decades a similar fate seemed to have befallen Piaget until his contributions were rediscovered through the efforts of Berlyne (1957), Hunt (1961), and especially Flavell (1963). Piaget (1968) based his theorizing on the paradigm of a dialectical interdependence between the process of accommodation (of the subject to the object) and assimilation (of the object to the subject) leading to continuous adaptations and readaptations. While Piaget is a strong case in point, the most explicit theory of interactions has been provided in Chomsky's transformational grammar.

Originally, Chomsky (1957) regarded linguistic transformations as devices that would make the production of utterances more efficient by deriving them from a limited set of kernel sentences rather than by deriving each sentence independently and anew. In his recent writings (1965), he has given a more central role to the concept of interaction, however, by proposing a distinction between a universal base structure and the surface structures of the utterances produced. By carrying this idea still further, one might disregard the surface structures as superficial and idiosyncratic, and the abstract base structure as intangible. What remains and what represents the essential features of language is the system of transformations.*

Such an interpretation of Chomsky's theory may seem one-sided. But, if nothing else, it makes us apprehend the insufficiencies of the traditional approaches to the problem of interaction. Looking at language again, we can see that these insufficiencies have been created by an undue emphasis on linguistic particles at the expense of contextual interpretations. Prior to Chomsky, language acquisition was seen as consisting, first, in the learning of elements, such as phonemes or words; and second, in the learning of

---

* Strong support for such an interpretation is given by Piaget (1970) who stated, "Transformations may be disengaged from the objects subject to such transformation and the group solely defined in terms of the set of transformations" [Piaget, 1970, pp. 23–24].

sequential dependences that, ultimately, were expected to explain the production of meaningful and complex utterances. But such interpretations reflect merely the bias of the analytical scientist because we cannot seriously doubt that all linguistic as well as perceptual–cognitive experience is relational. We receive elements always in contexts, never in isolation. Words, for instance, are always related to other words or to the objects, events, or qualities that they denote. Only in the ivory towers of the psychological laboratories, with their focus upon nonsense syllables, are elements viewed in isolation. These exceptional conditions aside, relations are given immediately; elements as well as classes are derived or abstracted from relational information, and in this way interactions are intimately embedded in our experiences.

In modern philosophy, the idea of a relational interpretation originated with Hegel's dialectical idealism and reappeared, especially, in Lenin's writing. Rubinstein, a Russian psychologist, has given it renewed expression in what he called *"constitutive relationism* according to which every phenomenon or thing is determined and constituted by its relation to all the other phenomena of reality" (Payne, 1968, p. 99). Rubinstein (see chap. 6) emphasized the material basis from which relations originate and through which they generate double interaction systems, namely, between psychic and external sociocultural conditions (representing the historical dialectics of Soviet psychology) and between psychic and internal biological conditions (representing the material dialects). Similarly, Rubinstein regarded the material world as having both an internal structure, for example, the molecular structure of a crystal, and an external structure that relates the crystal to other objects as well as to subjects. The observable results of this external interaction can be defined by the crystal's tangible qualities; for example, the crystal will appear hard and pointed to a particular observer. Finally, both interactions represent processes within individual and historical developments, which they both influence and by which they are both influenced.

2. According to Rubinstein, psychological processes are constituted by two interactions, those with external sociocultural contingencies and those with internal biochemical conditions. As an outcome of these interactions, the organism changes; as the organism changes, the interactions change. This intimate connection between psychological changes in the individual and the changes in intrinsic and extrinsic contingencies has only recently received appropriate emphasis in developmental studies. The present section draws attention to models of developmental analyses that seek to explicate the dynamic character of the interaction processes described.

In his analysis of the extensive testing records of military draftees during World War I and II, Tuddenham (1948) noted that the mean intelligence of the recruits of 1941 coincided with the 82nd percentile of those of 1917. Therefore, a considerable improvement in intelligence was observed that (if both samples could be regarded as representative of the same population) could be due to improved economic conditions, education, health care, etc., of the younger generation (i.e., to changes in the external, sociocultural contingencies). If the subjects of 1917 were retested in 1941 (by which time they would have been over 40 years old), deficiencies of their retest performance in comparison to that of the 17-year-old draftees of 1941 could not necessarily be attributed to aging, that is, to changes in the intrinsic, biological contingencies. Since the 40-year-old subjects of 1941 did not attain, when they were young, the level of the 17-year-old draftees of 1941, the results indicate equally well the enormous sociocultural changes, that is, differences between cohorts (Riegel and Riegel, 1972; Ryder, 1965).

While the traditional method of developmental psychology (the cross-sectional comparison), is insufficient for unconfounding the interaction of individual and historical differences or changes, the same conclusion has to be drawn for the longitudinal research methodology, which in the judgments of most developmental psychologists ranks so much higher than cross-sectional comparisons. If, in 1941, we compared the retest results of the draftees of 1917 with their original performance, such a longitudinal comparison would have been accomplished. But we would have equally failed in determining whether any observed differences were due to the individual's intrinsic changes or to those in the extrinsic sociocultural conditions affecting the individual (in this case, those occurring between the first and second testing rather than those influencing selectively the two different cohorts). Most likely, both components will be effective in a confounded manner.

Schaie's (1965) and Baltes's (1968) research designs for developmental studies make possible the unconfounding of the interaction between the changes in psychological and sociocultural conditions. Their success is due to the recognition of the third basic design embedded in such a set of data in addition to the cross-sectional and longitudinal arrangements. This design (called time-lag design) compares the performances of one age group, tested at different historical times; for instance, it compares (as did Tuddenham) the performances of 17-year-old draftees in 1917 and 1941. Since age is held constant, only sociocultural differences and changes can become effective. In conjunction with the other two basic developmental designs it becomes possible, therefore, to estimate the relative contributions of these extrinsic differences and changes to psychological growth.

According to Schaie, similar explications are possible for the interaction between psychological growth and intrinsic biological changes. Such analyses would require a basic design analogous to the time-lag design except that sociocultural rather than the biological changes of individuals need to be held constant. Although it might be difficult to conceive of changes in individuals that occur in such a sociocultural vacuum, attempts to raise children in complete isolation have been reported in the literature (see Brown, 1958), the first of which was attributed to Pharaoh Psammetichos I, who reigned almost 2,600 years ago (see Herodotus, 1931). Naturally, these quasi-scientific experiments did not resolve the problem satisfactorily, since the children remained affected by changes in the physical conditions such as the weather, diurnal and seasonal cycles, etc., which are part of the extrinsic contingencies. On the other hand, these attempts are not as exceptional as they might appear because many of our children remain to be raised under conditions of severe sociocultural stagnation. Thus, we do not need to generate such "experimental" conditions in which the influence of sociocultural factors is kept to a minimum or is held constant. They continue to exist in our society despite our advances in science, technology, and economy.

CONCLUSIONS

Hopefully, the fate of these children also makes us aware that science and knowledge, as much as our children, do not develop in a sociocultural vacuum. Science and knowledge are also functions of the actions taken and of the actions that they demand. These actions are determined by the economic and political ideologies of the societies in which we live. It has been the major purpose of this chapter to make us cognizant of these dependences so that we might better appreciate the alternative viewpoints of development and synthesize them at higher theoretical levels.

CHAPTER 8

Structure and Transformation in Modern Intellectual History

This chapter introduces structuralism from several different angles. In the first section, the concept of *structure* (and in extension those of schema, pattern, gestalt, etc.) will be contrasted with that of *function* (and in extension those of activity, interaction, transformation, etc.). Such a comparison will not merely reconfirm the old dichotomy as introduced into psychology by James and Titchener, but will emphasize the mutual dependence of structure and functions. In this attempt I rely on Piaget's interpretations and, thus, emphasize genetic aspects. Reference will also be given to recent trends in linguistics, especially to Chomsky's transformational grammar.

In the second section, I trace the origin of these ideas to some reformulations in mathematics proposed during the second half of the 19th century by Dedekind, Frege, Russell, and others. The new emphasis stressed the analysis of relational orders and classes and thus contributed to the foundation for structural interpretations.

Further steps in this direction were taken in Carnap's early work, which is represented in the third section. Carnap provides explicit descriptions of structural interpretations by relying on some positivists of the late 19th century, especially Mach, Poincaré, and Avenarius, whose contributions—unfortunately—have frequently been viewed in clear antithesis to structural descriptions. Carnap's interpretations come closest to those held by Avenarius; Mach relates to the psychologism of Wundt, and Poincaré to

The original article was published under the same title in K. F. Riegel, and G. C. Rosenwald (Eds.), Structure and transformation: Developmental and historical aspects, *New York: Wiley, 1975.*

the early positivism of Comte. Poincaré, in turn, influences the school of French sociology, with Durkheim, Mauss, Blondel, Halbwachs, and Lévy-Bruhl, which finally leads to the structural anthropology of Lévi-Strauss and to the genetic structuralism of Piaget.

In the fourth section I question, in alliance with modern sociologists and anthropologists, the role of the psychic self as a primary base of knowledge and of psychology as an independent science. Piaget has been criticized for viewing development as emerging, essentially, from within the individual and for failing to give equally strong emphasis to the interactive changes of the sociohistorical conditions. Rubinstein's theory, with which I conclude my presentation, proposed such a dialectical interpretation of a changing organism in a changing world.

PSYCHOLOGY AND LINGUISTICS

Early Structuralism

The distinction between structure and function gained its directive influence upon psychology through Titchener. Although previously discussed by James (1890; see also Ruckmick, 1911), Titchener (1898) elaborated this distinction in detail and thereby, paradoxically, helped his adversaries in founding functionalism in America (Boring, 1957, p. 555). Titchener, by drawing an analogy from biology, proposed a threefold distinction:

> We may enquire into the structure of an organism, without regard to function—by analysis determining its component parts, and by synthesis exhibiting the mode of its formation from the parts. Or we may enquire into the function of the various structures which our analysis has revealed, and into the manner of their interrelation as functional organs. Or, again, we may enquire into the changes of form and function that accompany the persistence of the organism in time, the phenomena of growth and of decay. Biology, the science of living things, comprises the three mutually interdependent sciences of morphology, physiology, and ontogeny. (1898, p. 449)

Titchener delineates this distinction not only in regard to the individual organism but also in regard to the species, the "collective life." He continues:

> Corresponding to morphology, we have taxonomy or systematic zoology, the science of classification. The whole world of living things is here; the organism, and species and sub-species and races are its parts. Corresponding to physiology, we have that department of biology—it has been termed "oecology"—which deals with questions of geographical distribution, of the function of species in the general economy of nature. Corresponding to ontogeny we

have the science of phylogeny: the biology of evolution, with its problems of descent and of transmission. (1898, p. 449)

Titchener's contrastive description of structuralism and functionalism (under exclusion of the third major possibility for scientific psychology, geneticism) has had a formative influence upon the development of American psychology or, at least, upon its historical description (especially through Boring's work, 1957). Nevertheless his view of structure, being atomistic and mechanistic, was an exceptionally unfortunate choice. More appropriately, his approach ought to be called the psychology of content, a denotation commonly reserved for Wundt in distinction to the psychology of act by Brentano. Titchener's structuralism emphasizes the analytic identification of psychic constituents (sensations, ideas, and emotions). Organizational aspects enter into the discussion only secondarily.

Gestalt Psychology

Structural considerations were firmly introduced into psychology by the Gestalt movement of Wertheimer, Köhler, and Koffka. Here, organized patterns became the foundation of scientific inquiries as well as of the phenomenal experience of subjects. The identification of constituent elements attains negligible importance if any importance at all. As for Titchener, genetic aspects remain neglected. Gestalt psychologists analyze psychic conditions from an "a-historical" point of view. They are concerned, however, with functional aspects that, as introduced by the forerunner of Gestalt psychology, von Ehrenfels (1890), are implied in the so-called second law of Gestalt.

As commonly expressed, the first law states that a gestalt is more than the sum of its parts; i.e., organizational, structural properties are implied. The second law concerns transpositions or transformations through which all parts may lose their absolute positions, though the structural properties are retained, i.e., are kept invariant. Convincing cases of the second law are the transpositions of a melody into different keys, or in a more general sense (i.e., keeping fewer properties invariant), the variations on a musical theme. In regard to spatiovisual conditions, the perception of a simple object, e.g., a suspended triangle, is subject to ceaseless transformations. Not only do the location, illumination, and color of the object change relative to the observer, but also the sensory organs of the observer undergo ceaseless transformations produced by their gross and fine movements. Thus, the scientific exploration of perceived pattern is as much an abstraction from the ongoing physical and psychic activities as was the abstraction of constituent elements from these patterns by the pre-Gestalt psychologists. What underlies both these abstractions, and therefore ought to be of main interest to the psychologist, are ceaseless sequences of transformations.

Gestalt psychologists recognized this issue, especially through their investigation of the phi-phenomenon. The phi-phenomenon is produced by switching two light sources on and off. Dependent upon the rate of switching, the lights are either perceived as alternating discrete stimuli, as two continuously lighted stimuli, or as a connecting lighted line. These investigations have primarily been used in refutation of earlier atomistic viewpoints in that they question the identifiability of discrete sensory elements. They could be used equally well to criticize the preponderance of fixed stimulus patterns. The investigations of the phi-phenomenon clearly support a transformational or transactional interpretation, i.e., an interpretation that characterizes psychic operations, such as perception, by sets of invariant transformations both within and outside the organism rather than on the basis of fixed inner and outer properties. The opposite dominated, however, through Köhler's (1920) analysis of the isomorphism between external physical and internal neurophysiological patterns with its implied priority of the former in the tradition of philosophical realism. A convincing argument for transposition as the key principle has been published by Witte (1960). More recently, Henle (1972) has thoroughly reviewed Wolfgang Köhler's contributions to this discussion.

Cognitive Developmental Psychology

Among present-day psychologists, only Piaget (1970) has drawn a conclusion similar to the transformationists, and has, thereby, reversed the order of the laws of Gestalt psychology. The "law of transposition," now, gains priority over the "law of the Gestalt." As an organism engages physiologically and psychologically in ceaseless transformations, he attains patterns during his internal transitions and attends to patterns as transitional external conditions. These patterns represent momentarily objectified states of equilibrium, but the organism moves forward through a stream of transformations. In his considerations, Piaget is willing to conclude that "transformations may be disengaged from the objects subject to such transformation and the group defined solely in terms of the set of transformations" (Piaget, 1970, pp. 23–24).

Piaget is, of course, best known for his "stage theory" in which he proposes a fixed sequence of synchronic structures for the characterization of developmental progression. If we take the above quotation seriously, however, development should be characterized by groups of permissible transformations rather than by fixed forms or schemata. The notion of the "group" implies that the freedom of transformation is never unlimited. In regard to mathematical systems, e.g., measurement scales, it implies that basic properties have to be kept "invariant," e.g., in metric systems the relative distances between points. In Piaget's theory of cognitive development, conditions of invariance are represented as temporary states of equilibrium from which the individual will constantly divert, but to which he will always return.

With his recent emphasis on transformational processes, Piaget (1970) inverts the meaning of structure and function as originally conceived by Titchener. Now structures emerge through continuous transformational activities; they are determined by functions. Moreover, structures emerge from within, whereas for Gestalt psychologists they originate from without. In further contrast to these and to most other structuralists, Piaget relates both the concepts of structure and function to genetic interpretations. Structures not only emerge through quick transformations but are subjected to slow, continuous changes. The individual's development is characterized by shifts in structures brought about by transformational activities. Thus, Piaget relates all three aspects of Titchener's outline to one another; his theory is structural, functional, and genetic. Development is not characterized any longer as a sequence of synchronic schemata, but by developmental transformations.

Linguistics

Piaget's emphasis on the connection between structures and transformations directs our attention to some recent developments in linguistics. Two major schools in linguistics have been called structuralists and transformationists, respectively. The former adopted the methodology of the behaviorists in order to determine the major linguistic forms and their arrangements in the natural language. With their emphasis on methodological rigor, they share with the behaviorists a disrespect for any notions about underlying organizations, forces, or meanings. They initiate their inquiries from the surface of the linguistic corpus. Quite paradoxically, of course, the denotation of these linguists as structuralists cannot be transferred to their allies, the behaviorists, who, from Titchener's point of view, were regarded as functionalists. Titchener reserved the label of "structuralism" for his own school of introspective elementalism.

Structuralism, as proposed by Bloomfield (1933), dominated Ameri-

can linguistics for many decades. Although objections were expressed repeatedly—for instance, Jesperson (1937) claimed that the purpose of a
linguistic analysis is "to denote all the most important interrelations of
words and parts of words in connected speech. . . . Forms as such have no
place in the system" (1937, pp. 13 and 104)—a major revision was not
undertaken until the appearance of Chomsky's transformational grammar.

As for Piaget, Chomsky's (1957, 1959) publications reveal some
major changes in his own thinking. He started with describing alternative
models of syntactic structures (1957) and by polemizing against behavioris-
tic interpretations (1959). Then he elaborated his syntactic theory
(Chomsky, 1965, 1968), which is of primary interest for our present discussion. His most recent interpretations, nevertheless, are not as radical as
those by Piaget (1970). In contrast to Piaget's transformationism, Chomsky
argues at two distinct levels: for grammars of the surface structures of the
natural languages and for that of an underlying universal deep structure.
Most of his efforts are directed toward the delineation of the latter. As such
a description is achieved, attention can shift toward the specification of
transformation rules by which the former are derived from the latter.
Transformations are thus performed upon given structures and do not attain
the priority that Piaget is willing to assign to them. Instead of considering
these transformations as the universal basis, they merely operate upon the
deep structure to which such a priority is assigned. Not surprisingly,
therefore, some of his followers (Lenneberg, 1967; McNeill, 1968, 1970)
have identified these universal forms of the deep structure with innate
schemata of the organisms, and thus have revitalized the nativism of 19th-
century psychology. What needs to be done is to relate the transformations
to intrinsic activities of the organism but not to their forms.

The concept of transformation, as used by modern linguists, creates as
many difficulties as the concept of structure used by Titchener. Transformations have their well-defined place in the logic and mathematics of numerical systems. As first elaborated by Hölder (1901) and discussed in many
different treatises in the behavioral and social sciences (see Stevens, 1951;
Coombs, 1964), measurements can be based upon numerical systems of
varying complexity, i.e., upon cardinal, ordinal, rational systems, etc. As
their complexity increases (and with it the number of operative prerequisites that have to be fulfilled), the complexity of the transformations that
can be imposed upon these systems decreases. Thus, cardinal numbers can
be subjected to a wide range of transformations, rational numbers only to a
few. In other words, with increasing complexity larger sets of properties

have to be kept invariant unless the structure of the whole system is to be invalidated.

Whereas the structure of these numerical systems and their sets of permissible transformations can be specified with precision, the use of the latter term in linguistics is rather ambiguous. Linguistic transformations do not only change the order of times within strings but also basic features of expressions; for example, they change declarative statements into negatives, questions, passives, and vice versa. Since the dimensions of linguistic expressions are difficult to determine and vary from investigation to investigation, linguistic transformations also lack descriptive rigor. In particular, the invariant properties are not spelled out. Indeed, mathematicians seem to emphasize the invariances, while linguists point to the modifications brought about by transformations.

MATHEMATICS

Theories of Numbers

In discussing some reformulations in mathematical thinking that contributed to the development of modern structuralism, I direct our attention to the work of Cassirer (1910). As implied in the German title of his book, *The Concepts of Substance and Function,* early philosophizing relied heavily on the concept of smallest, substantive elements. With the objective basis of these particles taken for granted, the task for philosophy and sciences consisted of analyzing the systematic connections between them. In opposition to such conceptualizations, Cassirer argues for the priority of functional relations or operations, a switch in thinking that characterizes structural interpretations. This shift in conceptualization also occurred in mathematics.

During the early historical periods, at least up to Descartes, mathematics was seen as a reflection of or an ideal abstraction from the real world with its substantial particle properties. A major reformulation was brought about by Leibniz, for whom the basis of knowledge did not lie in the reflection and abstraction of ideas themselves but in the relationship between ideas. As a general example of this change in thinking, consider the notion of geometrical points and lines. Traditionally, points were taken for granted, and thereafter notions about their shortest connections, i.e., by straight lines, were derived. Thus, the solution was achieved through operations performed on these points. Similarly, in algebra, the natural numbers, as experienced by counting real objects, were taken for granted.

Whenever problems arose, e.g., when a larger number was to be subtracted from a smaller one, extensions of the system were introduced, in this case, an extension into the domain of negative numbers. In many other cases, new numbers were interspersed between the natural numbers, such as fractional, irrational, and imaginary numbers. Thereby, the notions of the infinity in extension and in partition of the domain of numbers emerged. But at the same time it became even more apparent that the prerequisites, which made these developments possible, lie in our full use of operative capabilities rather than in better and better approximations of the range of real objects. In other words, gradually, mathematics was becoming a system of operations rather than a reflection of substantive givens. Since the full range of these operations has hardly been explored, many new forms of mathematics could emerge. Developments since the second half of the 19th century have confirmed this possibility, leading to non-Euclidean geometries and to some of the number systems mentioned above, e.g., irrational and imaginary numbers.

Related to these developments are changes in the concepts of time and space (Riegel, 1976b). Traditionally, *time* had been regarded as finite and discrete; thus, the concept of time was similar to the concept of substance. As the natural number system was extended and as the slots between numbers were filled to a greater and greater extent, the notion of infinity was introduced through induction. Now, instead of emphasizing the periodicity of time, its beginning and its end, an abstract continuum was derived. To Cassirer, however, the question of whether time is discrete or continuous, finite or infinite, relative or absolute depends solely upon the operations selected by the observer and not upon external, nonintellectual criteria.

Cassirer relates our concept of time to the theories of numbers and algebra. Geometry, on the other hand, he relates to the simultaneity and co-existence of several such number systems. Subsequently, our concept of *space* can also be continuous or discrete, absolute or relative, Euclidean or non-Euclidean. Originally, according to Cassirer, the concept of space was discrete and bound by the three-dimensionality of our experience. Through inductive generalizations the notion of a continuous space was derived and attempts were made to shift from the three dimensions of the experienced space to non-Euclidean interpretations. Although this has been intellectually achieved, Cassirer insists that our concept of space ought not to be regarded as a generalization from objective, substantive conditions of the real world, but rather as a fuller elaboration of our intellectual operations that enable us to generate these notions as well as many others not yet proposed.

Dedekind, Frege, and Russell

Cassirer's views, which occasionally have been called logical idealism, are shared by the mathematician Dedekind (1893), who argues that our concept of numbers, being a representation of pure laws of thinking, is independent from our concept of space and time. Quite to the contrary, only through the logical derivation of a theory of numbers and the attainment of a monotone domain of numbers have we become able to explicate our concept of space and time. If, in the pursuit of these explorations, we try "to determine what we are doing when counting a class or a number of things, we are bound to recognize the capability of the mind to relate things to things, to compare one thing with another, or to map one thing upon another; without this capability thought would not be possible at all" (Dedekind, 1893, pp. III–IV, author's translation).

According to Dedekind, our basic concept of numbers is relational. Through implicit mental comparisons we derive ordinal numbers. By explication we become able to categorize numbers or items. For example, we might, within a given range, group all those items into a class that are below a certain value a. Items above that value are assigned to a different class. Following this procedure (the well-known Dedekind "cut"), the criterion itself, a, cannot belong to either of the two classes that it defines. Therefore, we need to elaborate other operations that will lead to a new numerical system and include the criterion a, i.e., the system of irrational numbers. By applying these deductive procedures step-by-step and thereby extending the domain of numbers encompassed, Dedekind and the following generation of mathematicians succeeded in deriving the whole field of mathematics from such a deductive basis.

Dedekind's procedure is based on ordinal judgments. For the derivation of cardinal numbers and categorizations in general, as has been argued by Frege (1903) and Russell (1903), judgments of equivalence are more fundamental. Contrary to the traditional view, according to which numbers are considered as given and subsequently judged as equivalent or not, it is the goal of their approach to determine an operation of equivalence first, and then to derive sets of equivalent and nonequivalent numbers on the basis of such an operation. As stated by Frege, "It is our intention to form the content of an operation which can be expressed in an equation in such a way that there is a number on each side of it. . . . Thus, by means of the familiar concept of equivalence we are to obtain what we have to consider as equal" (1903, p. 27).

In comparing the approach by Dedekind and Cassirer with that by Frege and Russell, their similarities and dialectical interdependence need to be emphasized. First, both camps rely on relations, the former on asymmetric relations of different kinds, the latter on the symmetric relation of equivalence. Second, both emphasize operative, constructive aspects through which complex structures are derived. They neither regard these structures nor the equivalences and relations as given in the external world but as founded in the operations of the organism. Thus, their interpretations are closely in line and anticipate Piaget's cognitive developmental theory. They are at variance, however, with sociocultural theories that assign these operative, constructive, or transformational activities to society, which, in turn, will determine the activities of the individual. Before we discuss these trends, a brief overview will be given of some philosophical developments that parallel those in mathematical theory. In particular, we will refer to Carnap's (1928) early work.

PHILOSOPHY

Positivism and Conventionalism

The philosophical roots of modern structuralism lie in rather unusual grounds that, at first sight, we might not connect at all with such an interpretation. This is due to some common misconceptions about these schools, especially those of French and German positivism and, to a lesser extent, phenomenology.

The German positivism of the late 19th century became instrumental and supportive for a scientific psychology of which Titchener was one of the late representatives. Contrary to frequent statements, especially those expressed by American writers, positivism of this type was not at all supporting a blind search for "facts" but would argue against the notion of "facts" as a form of evidence independent of the observer and solely determined by external conditions of "nature." To Mach (1886), for example, there were only sensory impressions; all knowledge had to be derived from them and, thus, was in the mind. He supported the "psychologism" of the late 19th century, which epistemologically subordinated all other sciences to psychology, and emphasized, though timidly, the constructive aspects of scientific efforts in maintaining that "facts" are merely theories to which we have become sufficiently accustomed.

Quite similar in orientation, though with much stronger emphasis on the sociocultural basis of knowledge, Poincaré's conventionalism leads us back in the history of philosophy, at least to Locke's critical realism. The notion of sociolinguistic conventions was introduced in order to account for the agreement between different observers in regard to secondary qualities, i.e., those qualities that do not directly reflect properties of nature (primary qualities) but depend upon the observers' interpretations, such as their impressions of warmth, redness, brightness, etc. Poincaré carries this interpretation to its conclusion by considering all our impressions (not only those representing secondary qualities) as dependent upon socioliguistic conventions. Each individual has his subjective experiences; in order to make general knowledge possible, certain agreements have to be reached on how to talk about these impressions. Subsequently, knowledge is not only dependent upon the sensory impressions and observations but upon the constructive efforts on part of the observers to state their experience in communicable terms.

The last issue received focused attention in the work of Avenarius (1894–1895) who, for the first time, emphasized logical and syntactic organizations as a necessary prerequisite for the acquisition of knowledge. While previously the agreement on communicable concepts was stressed, Avenarius pointed to the need for consensus about logical and linguistic structures. To Avenarius these structures are arbitrarily selected in about the same way in which rules of a game, such as chess, are being set up. There is neither intrinsic nor extrinsic validity in these systems; their value is solely dependent upon criteria such as internal consistency, simplicity, and comprehensiveness.

Constructivism

Avenarius's interpretations failed to have a major effect upon the philosophy and the execution of the behavioral and social sciences. His ideas gained considerable importance, however, through the extensions by the early Carnap (1928). Accepting the shift from substantive to functional conceptualization (Cassirer, 1910), Carnap elaborated structural interpretations with a strong nominalistic and constructivistic emphasis. He traced his interpretations to Russell's (1903) theory of relations and to the "reduction of 'reality' to the 'given' (1928, p. 7)" as successfully performed by Avenarius, Mach, Poincaré, Külpe, Ziehen, and Driesch. The "givens" have to be sought in the unmeditated, phenomenal experience. Carnap, rather than halting at such contemplative state, asks that out of these experiences we take constructive steps. Knowledge does not so much consist in introspective apprehension as in active construction. At the beginning, he would agree with Cassirer (1910), we do not find sensory impressions but the sentence (*Satz* as related to *setzen,* "proposing") that alone generates knowledge by making it communicable, social, and human.

Individual and scientific knowledge is based upon two basic components: property description and relation description.

> A *property description* indicates the properties which the individual objects of a given domain have, while a *relation description* indicates the relations which hold between these objects but does not make any assertion about the objects as individuals. Thus, a property description makes individual or, in a sense, absolute, assertions while a relation description makes relative assertions. (Carnap, 1967, p. 19)

While the present author would take exception to the notion that property descriptions are nonrelational, Carnap's main attention, anyhow, centers around the relation descriptions. Construction of knowledge consists in transforming relation descriptions according to *construction rules* or *constructional definitions.*

> . . . . to *construct a* out of *b* (and) *c* means to produce a general rule that indicates for each individual case how a statement about *a* must be transformed in order to yield a statement about *b, c.* (Carnap, 1967, p. 6)

The development of constructivism has been prepared by Poincaré's emphasis that knowledge cannot be based upon the "givens" alone, e.g., sensations, but that "only relations between the sensations have an objective value" (Poincaré, 1902, p. 198). For Carnap, this move, although in the right direction, does not go far enough. Scientific knowledge becomes possible only through the systematic explication of the interrelation of relations, i.e., through the study of structures. Ultimately, all knowledge is structural and is removed and separated from its base, the property descriptions or, in Poincaré's sense, the relations with objective value.

Within a system of structural description, Carnap distinguishes two kinds of definitions: *ostensive definitions* and *definite descriptions.* The former resemble property descriptions but are stated in relational terms.

> Here, ". . . the object which is meant is brought within the range of perception and is then indicated by an appropriate gesture, e.g., 'That is Mont Blanc' . . . definite descriptions . . . list . . . essential characteristics, but only as many . . . as are required to recognize unequivocally the object which

is meant within the object domain under discussion," e.g., "Mont Blanc indicates the highest mountain in the Alps," or . . . "the mountain so many kilometers east of Geneva." (Carnap, 1967, p. 24)

While empirical sciences have to incorporate ostensive statements in order to relate to their specialized fields of observations, science will, untimately, remove itself from this basis through purely formal, structural descriptions. Scientific disciplines differ in the degree to which such transformations have been accomplished. Physics, in certain areas, can be removed from its ostensive basis. Psychology has not reached such an advanced status. According to Carnap, such "de-subjectivization" will always result in formal structural descriptions. "Each scientific statement can in principle be so transformed that it is nothing but a structural statement." (Carnap, 1967, p. 29)

An Example of Structural Description

Carnap provides a simple demonstration of structural descriptions, the example of a railroad network. From such a record sufficient specifications can be deduced in regard to any point (in this case, station) without going outside of the system. My own analysis of language and meaning, I believe, represents an equally strong demonstration (see Riegel, 1970b, 1970c).

Contrary to common as well as to scientific conceptions, meaning is a relation (or rather a set of relations); concrete experience consists of such relations; elements and words are abstractions. Early in life and in unfamiliar situations, meaning is introduced through ostensive or, more generally, extralingual relations, i.e., by pointing toward labeled objects and qualities, or by directing or performing requested actions. These extralingual relations represent, however, exceptional circumstances for depicting the meaning of objects, events, or qualities. Regularly, such information will be substituted by intralingual relations. We will, for example, explicate the meaning of ZEBRA by saying that it "is an ANIMAL, has STRIPES, is found in AFRICA, is like a HORSE, etc." rather than by pointing at one.

Such explications presuppose that the listener has already acquired a repertoire of relational expressions so that he may insert the new information into the network available to him. This is achieved, for instance, by both relating and differentiating ZEBRA from other ANIMALS, by grouping ZEBRA into its spatial location, by recognizing criterial attributes of ZEBRA, etc. Undoubtedly, the meaning of ZEBRA, as explicated through these relational statements, is incomplete (e.g., for zoological purposes) and subjective both in regard to the speaker and the listener. There is no assurance, but in principle doubt that both will imply precisely the same understanding of the term. ZEBRA for one might denote a dangerous beast, for the other a handsome creature.

Despite these idiosyncratic interpretations, communication is possible as long as, within a limited group of speakers, major sections of such a relational structure are being shared. Individuals will communicate within the boundaries of such networks by attending to subsections, such as those included in our example above. Under still more limited conditions (e.g., if only the information "ANIMAL with STRIPES" is transmitted, leading in turn to multiple interpretations such as ZEBRA, TIGER, or HYENA), the need may arise to extend the subset within the relational network by including references to specific locations, i.e., AFRICA or INDIA, to types, i.e., HORSE or CAT, etc. In other words, the domain of the relational structure will vary along numerous dimensions, such as individuals (abilities, age), groups (language, sex, occupation), situations (school, job site, cocktail party), etc. Theoretically, the structure can always be extended to make a disambiguation possible. The repertoire of linguistic expressions is rich enough or can always be enriched to make identifications possible.

My last remarks call attention to the fluctuating and shifting state of relational structures. Such conditions are characteristic, in particular, of languages. The example used by Carnap (1968, pp. 25–27), i.e., that of a railroad network, is less convincing in this regard, because it seems unreasonable to consider this structure, i.e., the system of railroad tracks, as anything but fixed. Moreover, to depict this structure by activities, i.e., by the moving trains, would be unusual. Language, however, might well be regarded as a system of activities. Its underlying neuroanatomical organization is known only in its grossest features and any particular nervous impulse may reach a cortical destination simultaneously along many alternative tracks. Moreover, neither the source nor the destination; e.g., neither the tracks (relations) nor the intersections (elements) are firmly fixed. In most psychological and sociological interpretations, however, the notion of fixed structures has been given preference. Traditionally, language too has been regarded as a system of elements (words) and connections (associations), but rarely as a system of transformed energies. Language has always been regarded as an objectified product but not as transformational labor. With our example, we are thus led, once more, to our earlier contrastive comparison between the major trend in Gestalt psychology and Piaget, the former emphasizing the priority of organized structure, the latter the transformational activity.

SOCIOLOGY AND ANTHROPOLOGY

French Sociology

The contributions of the three positivists of the late 19th century have supplemented one another. Mach, in his analysis of sensory impressions, explored the foundation of the experimental psychology of Helmholtz, Wundt, Külpe, and Titchener. His French counterpart, Poincaré, in following the tradition initiated by the founder of positivism, Auguste Comte, emphasized the conventional and communicative basis of knowledge and thus gave main attention to sociology and linguistics. Finally, Avenarius explored the logical structure of knowledge and thereby synthesized the trends explored by Mach and Poincaré. In the present section, I elaborate further the contributions by French sociologists and anthropologists.

Because psychic processes could become an object of scientific explorations only with observation of the objective conditions that cause their occurrence and progression, Comte, in his classification of the sciences, did not assign a separate place to psychology. The requested observations would either have to focus upon the anatomical and physiological basis of the organism or upon the conditions and development of the social milieu. During his later years Comte paid increasing attention to these sociological aspects. This tradition was continued by Poincaré and led to the foundation of the French school of sociology.

In contrast to their British counterparts, who, like Tylor and Frazer, would insist on the universal permanence of human traits, French sociologists, led by Durkheim (1912), regarded psychic functions as a product of social conditions and therefore as variable. Perhaps even more important than such a sociologization of psychology, sociology became psychologized. This trend is most clearly expressed in Durkheim's concept of "collective images" and "collective mind," both of which are psychological terms generalized to sociology. Everything social consists of images or is the product of images. Although these images cannot be reduced to physical conditions, the individual exists, at the same time, as a physical being. Thus, Durkheim supports a distinct dualism: The human being is both an individual physical and a communal social being. If one were to approach a study of psychology at all, it would have to consist either of psychophysiology or of psychosociology. The object for sociology, the collective mind, is independent of the individual and his consciousness.

Durkheim, together with Mauss (1903), applied this conceptualization to the study of intellectual functions. Logical categories were seen as originating from social relations. The concept of space, for example, was derived from the notion of social territory and forces. Smilarly, Halbwachs (1925, 1950) analyzed the social conditions of memory by explaining that in recall we reconstruct past events by connecting them with conditions of the social life. Blondel (1928), finally, combines interpretations of the collective mind with Bergson's idea of an individualistic *élan vital.* In his analyses of such psychological constructs as volition, affects, and perceptions, he transcends Durkheim's formulation. Instead of eliminating psychology in favor of biological and, especially, sociological interpretations, he proposes individual psychology as a third approach. For example, the study of perception has to be concerned with collective aspects insofar as it deals with general concepts, such as "books," "table," etc. On the other hand, it has to be concerned with neurophysiological and anatomical conditions, equally general and common to all human beings. But, finally, the study of perception also has to be concerned with experiences that are unique for an individual. It is on this last issue that Blondel deviates from Durkheim's dualistic conception and reintroduces psychology as a third form of exploration.

Blondel's deviation from Durkheim was criticized by Halbwachs (1929) for failing to recognize sufficiently the formative role of social customs, habits, and concepts. An individual outside of society, Halbwachs maintains, would not be able to function generatively. The disagreement between Blondel and Halbwachs becomes most apparent in the former's analysis of volition. On the one hand, volition originates from biological reflexes; on the other, it represents an act that is distinctly social in nature. Although genetic connections do not exist between these two forms of volition, there does exist an individual will that is psychological in nature and free. Of course, most people do not develop such a tendency; they are solely directed by collective volition, to which they subject themselves "obediently," and by their biological drives, to which they submit themselves in an equally "obedient" manner. Only the intellectual "elite" is capable of developing individual volition.

Blondel's interpretations share basic features with the cultural anthropology of Lévy-Bruhl (1922) and, although nongenetic, they are similar to the cognitive developmental psychology of the early Piaget (1928).Lévy-Bruhl adopts from Durkheim the concept of the "collective images." But while Durkheim postulates a "collective subject" as the carrier of these images, Lévy-Bruhl rejects such a metaphysical construct. For Lévy-Bruhl collective images, although they are determined by society, are concepts of and located in the individual. Closely in line with Blondel's distinction, Lévy-Bruhl investigates different levels of the "collective mind." He is known for his study of the "primitive mind," which he contrasts sharply with that of modern man without emphasizing, as Durkheim did, the continuity in the development of the human race and human consciousness.

As convincingly shown by Leach (1970), these different trends, represented by Lévy-Bruhl on the one hand and Durkheim on the other, converge in anthropology upon the functionalism of Malinowski (1926) and the structuralism of Lévi-Strauss (1958). It is also at this juncture that one of Piaget's (1928) early contributions attains significance. Piaget tries to resolve the conflict between Durkheim's emphasis of the continuity in the development of man and Lévy-Bruhl's emphasis upon qualitative differences by elaborating his famous distinction between functions and schemata. Functions remain the same throught the stages of human evolution and individual development; schemata change like organs in the evolution of species or forms of logical operations in the development of the individual. In both cases, functions and schemata complement one another; functions do not exist without schemata and schemata do not exist without functions.

In Piaget's early writings (especially 1923, 1924) he reveals the influence of the social psychology of Blondel and the anthropology of Lévy-Bruhl. Indeed, he succeeded in fusing the sharp dichotomy created by Durkheim between the inner biological and the outer cultural nature of man. These were also the years when he contributed his interpretations of the development of language functions in terms of egocentric and socialized speech, which were rebutted by Vygotsky (1962). In his later writings, Piaget abandoned his emphasis upon the impact of social conditions, however, and increasingly focused his attention upon psychic structures. Thus, the opposition to the viewpoints emerging from the followers of Vygotsky grew stronger. The latter came to represent the new interpretations of Soviet psychologists discussed in chapter 6.

Dialectical Anthropology

Recent thinking in the Soviet Union about the philosophical foundation of the behavioral and social sciences seems to follow the viewpoints expressed by French sociologists. In regarding psychic activities as the joint outcome of inner biological and outer sociocultural conditions, they too reject a central and independent role for psychology. In contrast to the reductionism of French sociologists, they do not merely split these conditions apart but emphasize interactive processes through which psychic activity and consciousness emerge. Moreover, they consider these interactions in their temporal dependencies and thus provide dialectical interpretations. Similar to Piaget, changes in psychic activities may produce changes in inner biological conditions and these, in turn, may change psychic activities. In contrast to Piaget, there exist also active interventions from the outer sociocultural to the psychic conditions and vice versa.

Soviet psychology has its roots in two separate movements: the reflexology of Sechenov, Bekhterev, and Pavlov, and the dialectical materialism of Marx, Engels, and Lenin. In contrast to the behaviorists, however, who mechanistically split the reflex arc into its superficial external components, i.e., the stimulus and the response, Pavlov regarded the reflex as a functional unit. Only an extended conditioning history will enable the organism to separate the stimulus from the response. In the Soviet conception, the response becomes a *reaction* to the stimulus, but at the same time the response *reflects* upon the stimulus. This antimechanistic notion became a fundamental ingredient of the Soviet interpretations and is referred to by Rubinstein as constitutive relationism. Interestingly enough, the same viewpoints were expressed in one of the founding articles of American functionalism, i.e., in John Dewey's (1896) treatise on the reflex arc, which, often misunderstood, was soon discarded from consideration by American psychologists.

The first foundation of Soviet psychology relates psychic activities to their inner biological material basis. The second foundation relates them to their outer cultural–historical material basis. This conceptualization builds upon the historical and dialectical materialism of Marx and Engels that was injected into Soviet psychology through the posthumous publication of Lenin's (1929b) *Philosophical Notebook*. The discussions emerging after this event elaborated, in particular, two notions, the dialectical interpenetration of opposites and dialectical leaps.

By emphasizing the interaction between psychic and cultural–historical activities, Soviet psychologists recognized the social dependency of the former. As psychic activities emerge (and their emergence is, of course, co-determined by their interaction with biological activities), the social conditions are being changed as well. As Marx stated, man, through his own labor, transforms the conditions around him, which in turn will change him (or at least the generations following him). Thus, man creates himself through his own labor. For instance, by inventing a tool, by generating new conceptual or linguistic expressions, man produces a lasting effect that "backfires" upon him and the following generations of individuals, who thus will emerge under changed conditions. At least in regard to its psychosocial implication, the notion of dialectical interpenetration explains the superficiality of the thesis that ontogeny recapitulates phylogeny. Both sequences are bound to coincide because both are the products of interactive human efforts.

The principle of progression by qualitative leaps is closely related to that of dialectical interpenetration. It resembles Piaget's description of cognitive development, though it emphasizes the interaction between psychic activity and outer, material cultural–historical conditions rather than intrapsychic shifts captured by Piaget's dialectical contrast of assimilation and accommodation. As our previous examples imply, dialectical leaps are brought about by human activity. Thus, the invention of tools, of linguistic expressions, or of language in general, changes dramatically the sociocultural conditions under which human beings are growing up. Inversely, as these sociocultural conditions have come into existence during the history of mankind, they will induce upon the organism stepwise changes, each reflecting basic reorganizations of the operations that the individual will be able to perform, e.g., to speak, to write, to formalize, etc.

My last statements indicate, once more, the intimate connections between functional changes produced by human activities and the structural shifts representing the products of these activities. Thus, my discussion returns to the interpretations advanced by Piaget. The interactive process of shifts is not restricted to the activities of the individual, however, but embraces all other individuals in his or her social world; nay, all individuals who through their ceaseless efforts over generations have created the cultural–historical conditions under which any present-day descendant grows up and lives.

During the most recent period in the short history of Soviet psychology, a double interaction theory has been proposed by S. L. Rubinstein (see chap. 6) that deviates from the dichotomizing attempts of French sociologists. He agrees with them, however, in assigning to psychology a secondary role. Both biology and sociology, because of the material foundations emphasized by Soviet psychologists, rest upon more fundamental bases. Psychology is a construct and could not exist without the former. Of course, these evaluations also indicate an intrinsic strength of psychology. Psychology, more than biology and sociology, is or ought to be concerned with activities rather than with products. This conclusion, once more, returns our attention to the comparison of function and structure. Rubinstein agrees with Piaget by emphasizing the mutual dependence of both; he disagrees with him (at least with Piaget's writings during the forties and fifties) by emphasizing that the function–structure relationship ought not to be limited to the activities of the separate individual but ought to be extended to the interactions within his cultural–historical world. He disagrees further with Piaget by trying to trace the two interactions to their material foundations.

CONCLUSIONS

In the preceding section, Piaget's developmental structuralism was submerged within Rubinstein's double interaction theory. Such an interpretation seems to handle all issues that have been proposed in opposition to the traditional mechanistic viewpoints of American psychology, i.e., issues that focus upon the active organism in an active environment. However, in contradiction to their dialectic foundation, Soviet psychologists consistently emphasize the material bases of psychic processes. Thus, they emphasize the products rather than the activities that generate them. In concluding this chapter, I will direct our attention to alternative interpretations and review, once more, the trends and options of structural–transformational psychology.

Western psychology found one of its most authentic representations in William Stern's (1935) *Psychology on a Personalistic Basis,* which has been criticized by Vygotsky (1962) as individualistic and intellectualistic. Stern exemplifies a trend that derives from the British philosophy of Locke, Hume, and Berkeley (especially the latter) and continues to dominate Western thinking in the behavioral and social sciences. In extension it led, as we have seen, to the positivism of Mach, to the psychologism of Wundt, Helmholtz, and Külpe and to the phenomenologism of Husserl. Despite their wide differences, all of these scholars built their interpretations upon the sensory-perceptual basis of knowledge. The world around us came to be regarded as a mere outward projection of the mind. Psychology became the most fundamental of all sciences.

While for this group of scholars knowledge was to be gained through sensory experience and contemplations based upon them, a second school of thought, associated with the advances in the natural sciences, began to emphasize the constructive aspects of knowledge. According to Russell and Carnap, physics and astronomy represent prototypes of constructive sciences whose founding components, unlike psychological sensations, are not directly accessible to us but are intellectually generated. From this point of view, knowledge is founded upon the "sentence," in its German sense of *Satz* and *setzen*. Knowledge is gained by proposing sentences rather than by receiving sensory information in a passive state.

Although related viewpoints were expressed early in psychology—for example, in Brentano's *Act-Psychology* (1874)—they never attained an appreciation comparable to that accorded those based upon a sensory basis of knowledge. However, philosophers have paid increasing attention to this issue, as revealed in the work of Russell and Carnap as well as in such anti-scientific movements as existentialism. More recently, Holzkamp (1972) has interpreted sciences in general and psychology in particular as activities, and therefore as movements concerned with and dependent upon social conditions and historical relevance. Most influential, however, is Piaget's (1963) notion of the individual's intellectual development and of the growth of knowledge in society, of genetic epistemology, based upon the premise that progress can only occur through spontaneous, generative activities of the organism.

Aside from its sensory-perceptual and its operative–constructive bases, science and knowledge represent forms of organization and structure. Again, these organizations may either be seen as existing outside the individual and recognizable through sensory experience, or as generatively produced by the individual and imposed upon the outside world through his interpretations. Regardless of this choice, organizational aspects have received increasing attention through the work of Avenarius, Russell, Carnap, Piaget, and finally, Rubinstein. Because of the complexity of the structures, these theories have shown a strong tendency toward formalism, at least among the Western scholars. This trend is clearly exemplified in the progression of Piaget's research and theory. He advanced, in terms of his own theory, from an operative to a figurative psychology. His early studies of early developmental periods consist of rich but ambiguous interpretations of children's operations. Next, he produced equally rich displays of imaginative—though less than fully standardized—experiments, coupled with formal descriptions of the children's logic. In discussing the highest stage of development, he provides little else than an abstract model of intellectual operations, essentially a theory of what these operations logically ought to be. Supportive evidence is not supplied and, apparently, not intended to be supplied. All that such evidence would provide are some superficial demonstrations that neither sufficiently confirm the consistency of the theory nor suggest important extensions.

Piaget's theory ties structuralism to the perceptionism of the earlier psychologists. Structures are confirmed by observations; structures organize experience. Soviet psychologists go beyond such a perceptionism and consider their evidence as originating from the material world outside of the observer. In contrast to earlier materialistic interpretations, they insist, however, that these conditions are not independent of the human organism; they are as much the product of human labor as they are forces impinging upon the human being. While Soviet psychologists opt for constructive theories, they abandon these theories all too soon by emphasizing the objectified material products rather than the activities by which these products are generated. Piaget, on the other hand, while emphasizing activities rather than material products, restricts himself to the developing individual under exclusion of the cultural–historical activities within which the individual grows.

A synthesizing extension would have to emphasize perception, action, and organization both in the individual and in the society. By emphasizing the products, this theory would be structural; by emphasizing the activities, it would be transformational. This theory would relate psychic activities both to their inner biological and their outer sociocultural foundations without exclusive emphasis upon their material nature. These foundations become material if the products and structures are emphasized; they remain psychological if the activities and transformations are emphasized. Development proceeds through dialectical interactions between psychic activities and their inner biological and outer sociocultural foundations. Again, if we look at the objectified conditions, development represents, both for the individual and for the society, a sequence of temporarily stable schemata; if we look at the activities, development represents a constant flux of transformations.

CHAPTER 9

Historical Comparison of Monetary and Linguistic Systems

The relationship between goods or merchandise and the labor or activities necessary to produce them has been regarded, at least since Marx (1891), as dialectical: Labor that does not produce something is futile; goods that are not produced by labor are miracles. In the following discussions I equate labor with the acts of producing or perceiving speech; and merchandise, with speech products such as sentences, words, or speech sounds. Through acts of speech a person increases the individual and collective repertoire of linguistic products. This repertoire is comparable to capital in the economic sense. Capital is only useful for the individual and society when it is productive, i.e., when it is transformed into new labor, speech acts. Traditionally, linguists have regarded language as commodity but not as labor.

THE BARTER SYSTEM AND THE PROTOLANGUAGE

Our monetary system originated from the one-to-one bartering trade in simple hunting and farming societies. A social situation in which one participant exchanges, for instance, a sheep or a pig for a certain amount of grain or wool seems to have few similarities to a situation of linguistic exchanges. The items traded do not have any representational or symbolic

A more extended version of this article was published under the title, "Semantic basis of language: Language as labor" in K. F. Riegel and G. C. Rosenwald, (Eds.), Structure and transformation: Developmental and historical aspects, New York: Wiley, 1975, pp. 167–192.

value, they serve to satisfy direct needs of the persons participating in the exchange. Basic similarities become apparent, however, once we realize that language also is a system of social interactions in which not the objects but rather the labor that leads to their creation and possession is exchanged. Strictly speaking, objects do not play an essential role in such an exchange. Where would they come from, how would they be generated, except through the efforts of the participating individuals? It is the labor involved in raising or catching the animal, in the seeding, tending, and harvesting the crop that is being exchanged. The exchange value is determined by the amount of efforts, the quality of the required skills, and the scarcity of the available resources (which, in turn, need to be acquired and secured through the individual's efforts).

Many linguists and, especially, psychologists look upon sentences, words, or speech sounds as building blocks or objects of language. But language is basically an activity that, in turn, serves to induce or provoke activities in others. This comparison is similar though not identical to de Saussure's distinction between *la langue* and *la parole*. The former, characterizing the universal properties of language, represents the total repertoire of forms and the structure that has emerged through the efforts of mankind. Surprisingly, as Labov (1970) noted, *la langue* has been studied by relying on the "linguistic intuitions" of one or a few individuals. A science of *parole,* though never developed, would have to deal with various speech acts in different social contexts.

Language as an activity reveals itself most clearly under primitive conditions comparable to those of the barter trade. Through grunts, cries, gestures, and manipulations, i.e., in Bühler's (1934) terms, through "signals" and "symptoms," one participant might induce the other to recognize a danger, to give assistance, or to coordinate activities. The sounds and movements might be recorded as objectifications of such a primitive language by the linguists, but these transcriptions provide only a distorted picture of the needs and intentions or the activities involved. These activities are meaningful in a given situation and in an immediate manner. In the linguist's description, their meaning is bleached; they become abstract and rigidified (see Malinowski, 1923).

Already, at this level, language as well as commercial exchanges rely on basic rules. The barter system presupposes property rights. If it is not granted, for example, that the sheep belongs to person A and the grain to person B, no stable exchanges, not even thievery, can take place. In Piaget's sense, this type of commerical activity is comparable to the level of sensory-motor operations. One item is exchanged against another item, regardless of the particular shapes in which they happen to be found. Trade does not yet require a knowledge of conservation.

Similarly, protolinguistic communication presupposes the validity of expressions, which, once given, cannot be undone. In this sense they have immediate, existential meaning. Language at the protolinguistic level is bound to a given situation of high survival but of low symbolic value. Its increase in representational character can be compared to that occurring during the change from a barter to a coinage system.

THE COINAGE SYSTEM AND THE TOKEN LANGUAGE

1. When changing from the barter to the coinage system, communities select one of their major commodities as a standard for exchange. In agricultural societies a certain quantity of grain might serve this function; and in stock-farming societies, the horse, the cow, or the sheep. (In ancient Rome, the word for money, *pecunia,* derives from *pecus,* denoting "livestock.)

Shifts in standard commodities indicate the growing diversification of societies. This growth is determined by variations in geographical and climatic conditions. It has to be brought about, however, by the activities of generations of paticipating members. Through these activities, society progresses toward more advanced forms of manufacturing and industrial production, and, at the same time, toward a division of labor. Such developments increase the significance of natural resources other than food crops, stone, wood, wool, coal, for example, and most important, metals. Because of their scarcity, compactness, and endurance but also because the resources can be easily controlled by the dominating classes of the society, metals soon became the exclusive standard for monetary systems.

The transition from the barter system to a coinage system is not necessarily abrupt (see Cipolla, 1956). After one or a few items have been selected as standard commodities, the exchange continues to proceed as before. When metals are introduced to serve as standards, they continue at first to fulfill basic needs of everyday life. For instance, metals such as copper, bronze, or iron are not only used as currency but the coins also serve as standard weights as well as they provide the material for the production of tools and weapons. As the society advances, these common metals are replaced as standards for exchanges by others that are less readily available. Subsequently, smaller and lighter coins can be introduced, whose mining, melting, and minting are more easily controlled and which do not serve essential functions for toolmaking but serve rather those of luxury and extravagance. For example, in the Roman Empire, bronze coins. with a standard wight of 327.45 grams were substituted by much smaller silver and gold coins. Whereas the amount of metal of the bronze coins had a direct, nonmediated value for the receiver, rare metals, such as silver and gold, lacked such utility. Therefore, refined rules about their use had to be established by the community; the value of the coins had to be guaranteed by the state through laws that set the standards, determined the metal composition, and regulated their distribution. At the same time, classes of persons who succeeded in controlling the processing of these rare metals could set themselves apart as the rulers of their society.

As coins lost their foundation upon the concrete value of commodities but gained in symbolic value, the economy expanded rapidly. At the same time, through the reckless manipulation of a few and through the uncritical trust of many, the changed conditions were selfishly exploited. The emerging histories represent an unending sequence of catastrophes, inflations, and devaluations (Gaettens, 1955). Imperialistic expansions (from the Punic Wars to the war in Vietnam) always outpaced the growth of the economic and monetary systems. Since not enough metal could be secured, the silver or gold content of coins was drastically reduced. Subsequently, coins lost rapidly in value until the system had to be replaced at the expense of the working, wage- and salary-earning population. Despite these dire consequences, the coinage system, in comparison to the barter system, offers many advantages that, in particular, shed some light similar implications for language systems.

2. Coinage systems, especially those based upon symbolic rather than pragmatic standards, allow for delayed exchanges, sequential exchanges, and multiple distributions. *Delayed exchanges* provide the possibility that the seller does not need to convert immediately the items he receives into other merchandise but may store coins of corresponding value until a better opportunity for a purchase arises. Such delayed reactions are of equal significance in the development of language systems. While the nonlanguage-using organism is closely bound to the here-and-now of a given situation, the use of a language, corresponding in abstraction to the coinage system, does not only allow for more efficient communication but also for better storage, especially once a written code of the language has been invented.

In contrast to the barter trade, exchanges do not need to be limited to two persons interacting at a particular location, but *sequential exchanges* are bound to result. A person who wants to buy a sheep but has no commodities that are of interest to the seller might reimburse him in coins; the seller, in turn, might approach a third person who is willing to dispose of the desired item. Frequently, the chain will extend over many more than three participants. Coins serve as efficient intermediary, provided that their value is sufficiently safeguarded by social agreements and rules.

The social exchange of goods made effective through the invention of coins has similar implications as the invention of verbal codes for linguistic systems. Once a coding system has been adopted messages can be more reliably transmitted across long sequences of communicating persons than under the more primitive conditions in which utterances are spontaneously and idiosyncratically produced. In a more remote but also more significant sense, the composition of the messages themselves becomes sequential in nature. Linguistic tokens, such as sentences, words, or speech sounds, are ordered into strings. Nonlinguistically encoded action sequences are hard if not impossible to transmit.

Once a coinage system has been introduced, *multiple distributions* of goods can be arranged easily. A person who has sold his sheep does not need to spend his earnings at the place of the trade but can distribute them across many vendors and purchase a multiplicity of items. Again the improvements of such operations in comparison to the one-to-one exchanges of the barter-trade are comparable to those brought about through the development of language systems. In the most direct sense, a language user can transmit his message simultaneously to a whole group of listeners; in a remote sense, he has multiple ways of expressing his wishes or intentions and can partition his message into smaller chunks that are presented separately. This possibility is especially important for safeguarding the transmission when individuals with varying linguistic skills are involved in the communication process.

3. The linguistic system that we have compared with the coinage system might be called a token language. It is founded upon basic forms or elements, such as words, syllables, letters, morphemes, or phonemes. Aside from determining its elements, the main goals in the analysis of such a system consist in the description of its syntagmatic and paradigmatic, i.e., temporal–diachronic and spatial–synchronic properties.

A token language system lies halfway between the manifold of phenomena of the experienced world and the single token coinage system of the economy. Both systems are reductionistic. Languages use a large set of tokens, e.g., words, to denote the many different objects, events, or qualities. However, every token denotes a whole array of similar items. For instance, the word CHAIR denotes many different objects. Moreover, the relations between tokens and the items denoted are of several different types, indicating actor–action, object–location, part–whole, object–class name, and many other relations. The corresponding monetary systems consist, in general, only of one token, e.g., the dollar, which designates (relates to) every possible item and condition in the same manner. Because, thus, a large manifold is reduced to just a single element, elaborate forms of operations need to be implemented. This is done by relying on complex numerical properties of the system that capture the large variety of items and conditions by assigning to them corresponding variations in the quantity of tokens, e.g., dollars. The emerging structure represents an arithmetic formalism.

In comparison to such a single token system, languages consist of many different tokens (frequently called types) and of many different kinds of relations between tokens and between tokens and the denoted items. Manipulations with these tokens do not include operations of addition or multiplication but only those of order. By applying order rules recursively, a multitude of expressions can be generated; by applying them to different types of relations, this multitude is enriched much further. The emerging structures are topologically rich. Such systems rely on cognitive operations that are mastered by older children only, e.g., on decentration and reversibility. They remain concrete because the tokens, e.g., the words, are thought of as building blocks reflecting directly the conditions of the real or phenomenal world. Just as with coins, these tokens, rather than the commodities that they represent or the labor that produces these commodities, may occasionally come to be regarded as the true objects of the world.

Tokens are selected and retained through social conventions that, moreover, determine the permissible rules of operations. They fail to express the activities and efforts that lead to their creation. As much as the further development of the monetary system advances to a full realization of the transactional character of economic operations, so does modern linguistics emphasize the interactional character of language. Whereas, traditional linguistics consisted, essentially, in the delineation of linguistic forms and of the rules of their combinations, units such as words, syllables, or letters lose their significance in modern interpretations. What attains significance are clusters of relations representing the activities within and between language users.

THE DEBENTURE SYSTEM AND
THE INTERACTION LANGUAGE

1. Economic history resembles a progression of catastrophes in which, due to ceaseless expansions and lack of constraint, one monetary system

after the other has been wrecked. At the terminal points of these progressions, the metal value of coins was reduced out of proportion to its original designation, the confidence in the system was lost, prices skyrocketed, and people were forced to return to the barter system in order to secure their daily needs. Since the beginning of the 18th century at least, autocratic rulers began to make a virtue out of the pitiful state of their financial systems by abandoning the backing of the currency through silver or gold and by substituting paper money for hard coins.

The first well-documented case of such an innovation is that of John Law upon whose advice Louis XV introduced paper money in France. After a few successful years, the confidence in the financial system was lost, leading the nation one significant step closer to the French Revolution. At about the same time, George Heinrich von Görtz financed the military adventures of Charles XII in Sweden through the issuing of state certificates. After the king's defeat and death the financial manipulations were violently attacked and Görtz was executed. Nevertheless, all leading nations have since introduced paper money and, more recently, most industrialized nations have abandoned the full coverage of their currency by gold or silver or at least do not guarantee full convertibility. This shift represents the third major step in the development of monetary systems, which we will call the debenture system.

It would be misleading to think of paper money only in terms of the common bills issued by national banks. Of course, these documents are of greatest utility for everyday commerce in comparison to all other certificates and, except for changes affecting the economy as a whole, remain fixed in their values. Similar in kind are certificates and bonds issued and guaranteed by national governments, states, and communities as well as by larger industrial and business organizations. Since their values fluctuate with the condition of the economy in general, and with the ups and downs of the money market in particular, these risks need to be compensated for by the payment of interests. Next in line, stocks fluctuate stronger than bonds. They are backed by commercial or industrial companies but rarely by the government itself. The last extension in the development of paper currencies consists in the utilization of personal checks. Here, each individual attains the role that formerly only a stable government was able to attain, namely, to guarantee the value of such transactions.

The last steps in the history of monetary systems, thus, represent another stage of operations and symbolic representations. Written statements become substitutes for standard units of rare metals, which in turn serve as substitutes for the items to be exchanged or, at first, as direct objects of trade. During the earliest stage in the history of trade, exchanges were tied to the given items and to the persons interacting in a particular locality. With the introduction of coins, exchanges could be temporally delayed, could be executed along extended chains of participants, and could reach simultaneously an array of different vendors. Although this increase in flexibility led to advances in the volume of trade, the expansion remained limited because the total amount of rare metals backing the economic transactions increased only slowly. With the shift toward various forms of paper money, this limitation was abandoned and the monetary system was explicitly tied to the sum total of activities in which a whole nation, an industrial complex, or, lastly, a single individual was, is, or was to be engaged.

The explicit return to a standard set by the activities and labor of an individual or groups of individuals represents only a superficial shift. As exphasized before, the objects of trade have always been the efforts necessary for producing particular goods rather than the merchandise itself. Even the gold and silver accumulated in the treasuries of states represents, basically, the efforts and work by the people. Because of the static character of these financial units it appears, of course, as if the wealth attained had been once and for all removed from the activities that produced it. The deteriorations of such financial systems whenever the growth in productivity failed to keep pace with the increase in monetary volume show, however, that such a stability is rather fictitious.

The apparent accumulative and static character of economies based on coins makes them closely similar to linguistic systems that emphasize linguistic elements, such as words, syllables, letters, morphemes, or phonemes, those that failed to consider language as a system of activities and interactions. While the protoeconomy of the barter trade implies too little symbolization to make it closely comparable to language, the intermediate system of coins, because of its elementalistic notions, is about equally inappropriate for such a comparison. An adequate understanding of language can be achieved only through comparisons with the debenture system, which is based upon matrices of transactions rather than upon classes of fixed elements.

The power of commercial and industrial operations in modern economic systems is not so much determined by the amount of hard currency or cash, but by the diversification and the speed with which limited assets are transformed and retransformed. The worth of money is determined by its owner's ability to utilize it productively. Stored money is of lesser value and, indeed, lessening in value as a function of continuing inflation. While such operations also characterize the more advanced stages of the coinage system, such a system remains more firmly anchored to the amount of cash available to the operator. The opportunity for obtaining loans upon written declarations, for investing them immediately in new financial ventures, for transferring the profit to cover commissions, and for obtaining new resources for investments characterizes the effectiveness of the debenture system. In the extreme—and there exist numerous documented cases of this type of operation, many bordering on illegality—a finanacial operator might gain large profits without much or without any firm financial basis, only through quick transactions of fictitious capital. In this extreme form, the debenture system, through the transactions that it facilitates, has lifted itself from its foundation. It has become a pure system of interrelated activities. The cash that, presumably, buys these activities and the products that they generate have become of negligible importance.

2. In modern linguistics, beginning with Sapir, Jesperson, and the Prague School, the study of transactions, likewise, has overpowered the study of forms. Already Jesperson emphasized that the purpose of a linguistic analysis is "to denote all the most important interrelations of words and parts of words in connected speech. . . . Forms as such have no place in the system" (Jesperson, 1937, pp. 13 and 104). More recently, this idea has been expressed in the transformational grammar of Chomsky (1965), in Piaget's (1963, 1970) cognitive developmental psychology, and in the structuralism of Lévi-Strauss (1958). In Chomsky's theory, transformations relate deep structure components to the surface structures of languages. As for Piaget, the language-using individual is actively participating in these transactional processes. These operations are confined, however, to the organism. An interaction with external, e.g., social forces, is deemphasized if not disregarded in both theories.

Undoubtedly, Chomsky's theory has profoundly shaken the traditional, elementalistic, and parallelistic views of linguists and psychologists with their undue emphasis on external physical stimuli and mechanical physical reactions by essentially passive organisms. Piaget, like Chomsky, has strongly emphasized the transactional character of psychological operations. He, indeed, seems to draw the final conclusion of such an interpretation by stating, "Transformations may be disengaged from the objects subject to such transformations and the group defined solely in terms of the set of transformations" (Piaget, 1970, pp. 23–24).

Both Chomsky and Piaget have stated their theories in mentalistic and idealistic terms. While such an orientation has set them clearly apart from most American psychologists, they have failed to assign an appropriate role to the cultural–historical conditions into which an individual is born and within which he grows. The environment is regarded as passive. All learning and development is initiated and directed by the organism. To attain his goals, the individual needs, of course, information and material from the outside. There is no place in these theories for an active role of the environment and for a co-determination of an individual's development by other active organisms. It is at this juncture that a comparison with economic theories becomes most pertinent because these theories bypass and advance far beyond modern interpretations of language and cognitive development.

For a complete understanding of cognitive and linguistic operations, we have to consider two interaction systems. One relates these operations to their inner basis, to their physiological, biochemical foundation. The other represents the interactions with the cultural–historical environment into which an organism is being born. While the latter system is realized in theories of economic operations and in the symbolic interactionism of Mead (1934), the former system is expressed in the theories of Piaget and Chomsky. An advanced synthesis of both interaction systems as proposed by Rubinstein (1958, 1963; see also Payne, 1968; Wozniak, 1972, 1975) has been discussed in chapter 6.

Rubinstein extended, on the one hand, the first interaction system by relying on Pavlov's work. He introduced the second interaction system by relying on Vygotsky (1962) and, thereby, on the historical materialism of Marx, Engels, and Lenin. The psychic activities of an organism are seen as the changing outcome of these two interaction systems, one tying them to their inner material, biochemical foundation described in terms of relations within the nervous system and sensory and motor organs, the other tying them to their outer material, cultural–historical foundation described in terms of relations between and within the physical and social world of individuals. Behavior is seen as an activity continuously changing in the process of interactions. It is not a thinglike particle that can be separated from these transactions. Language, likewise, is an activity, founded through the two interactions that, in particular, serves to integrate nervous activities and cultural–historical functions. It should be studied as such a process rather than as a conglomeration of particles or forms that are the rigidified products of relational activities.

CONCLUSIONS

In this chapter we seek to demonstrate that a purely transactional analysis has been successfully implemented in economic operations. Language, likewise, ought to be regarded as an activity and not merely as a system of particles or tokens, products or commodities.

At the protoeconomic level, trade consists in the exchange of particular items on a one-to-one basis and is bound to a given situation. Such a system is concrete, with little symbolic representation. But the items exchanged are not to be viewed as having thinglike, substantive character; what is exchanged are the activities and the labor necessary to produce them. Similarly, linguistic operations at this level involve extralingual relations between labels and objects, internal states, or—most important—actions. If a comparison with Piaget's developmental levels is attempted, the protoeconomic and the protolinguistic systems are characterized by sensormotor activities.

The next economic system is comparable to the level of concrete intellectual operations. It relies on standard commodities represented by concrete materials or objects, for example, gold or silver, and allows for a wide range and much more flexible operations, such as sequential and multiple distributions of traded goods, as well as for storage and delayed actions. The conceptual danger of a system of this kind lies in the tendency to regard its basic monetary unit as a fixed, universal entity. History has repeatedly shown that this apparent stability is easily shattered when the basis of activity, representing the labor and efforts by the participating people, is brought at variance with the standards of the system.

Traditionally, similar viewpoints have dominated psychology and linguistics, namely, the view that language consists of sets of basic units, such as words, syllables, letters, morphemes, or phonemes, from which the more complex forms are derived. Thereby, the view of language as an activity and a process is either disregarded or lost. Just as different currencies represent different monetary systems, so do different sets of linguistic elements represent different languages or dialects. Thus, there exists variability and (linear) convertibility or (nonlinear, transformational) translation. The universal basis of different linguistic systems is represented by the protolanguage of the preceding level with its notion of the identity of operations. Correspondingly, the protoeconomy of the barter system represents the universal features of the more advanced trading operations. It is based on property rights. At the second linguistic level, more specific lexicological conventions and syntactic rules of order and restitution are required.

Only at the third stage of development does an analysis of the economic system advance our understanding of linguistic systems to a significant degree. Monetary forms characteristic for this stage and represented by certificates, bonds, stocks, and checks are symbolic units of exchange. They help us to realize that it is not the objects or any particular material, such as rare metals, that are exchanged but the labor and activities of people producing these objects and operating with these documents. Transactions on such elusive bases require explicit rules of conduct, of which only a minor portion concerns the specific relationship of these certificates to the objects of trade. Most of them deal with intraeconomic relations.

The conditions are similar in linguistic operations. Only when we realize that linguistic units, such as words, syllables, or letters, are mere abstractions from the stream of operations that characterizes language, do we gain a full understanding of linguistic systems. These operations constitute the information immediately given through the interrelating activities of communicating individuals. An understanding of these interactions can be gained only if these activities are studied as they are produced and perceived. The products of these interactions are rigidified objectifications that do not capture the constituting activities of languages.

CHAPTER 10

Structural Analysis
of the History of Early
Greek and Early European Philosophy

In this chapter history will be regarded as a dialogue. In a dialogue one person proposes a statement and another person reacts to it by either proposing an alternative or a modification of the first statement. If the second person disregarded the statement by the first person, no true dialogue would take place. After two alternate statements have been made, the first person may modify his original statement or propose a third one. In each case, he would try to consider the statement made by the second person and at the same time would have to remain consistent with his own earlier statements. If he were always to disregard the second person's statement, no true dialogue would take place.

In the dialogue of history, the first two participants may belong to the same generation or cohort, providing a thesis and an antithesis, but the third person who synthesizes the former interpretations may belong already to the next cohort. Alternatively, a statement that during the time of the first cohort was integrative and embracive may be split into two contrastive viewpoints by the following cohort. These two alternative forms of development have been described as the root and the branch structural progression (see chap. 4).

In the following discussion of early Greek and early European philosophy, I rely on the branch structure model and regard history as a process of stepwise differentiation. It would be another task and quite beyond the present scope to enter into a discussion of the integrative philosophies of the cohorts following those to be described. In Greece, this cohort produces the philosophical systems of Plato, Aristotle, and the Skeptics; in modern Europe it represents Kant, Hegel, and the positivistic–phenomenological efforts during the 19th and 20th centuries (for discussion of the latter, see chap. 8).

As in a dialogue between contemporary participants, no statement made is ever annihilated or lost. All statements continue to co-exist, both as historical representations of the past and within the modified statements of the present built upon them. Thus, in terms of the progressions described in chapter 5, I am implying the complex sequence model, which allows for differentiation of pathways as well as for accumulative transfer of information across historical cohorts (see also Van den Daele, 1969).

While, thus, early historical development (with which I will be exclusively concerned) is characterized by successive differentiation of more and more divergent viewpoints, the period of integration (with which we will not be concerned) is not only characterized by the manifold of all of the earlier viewpoints, but also by the integrative systems proposed that—as in Gestalt psychology—are more than the sums of all their parts and therefore begin to dominate most of the following historical periods.

Later stages in history are characterized by all the earlier plus the integrative viewpoints of the Classical period and by renewed attempts of differentiations (which, now, appear as specializations), or by partial integrations (which in their extreme form represent eclecticism). The amount of knowledge to be handled seems to surpass the integrative capacities of single contributors; therefore, selective preference is increasingly given to topics such as ethics, aesthetics, epistemology, logic, or to philosophical boundary areas such as those of physics, biology, psychology, and sociology, which sooner or later come to divorce themselves altogether from their origin and contribute to the solution of concrete problems in engineering, medicine, economics, politics, etc.

The scope of the present chapter prevents me also from discussing at any length the developments that took place after the great integrative systems had been proposed. This topic will be mentioned only once, i.e., when I describe the transition from Greek to modern Western philosophy.

EARLY GREEK PHILOSOPHY

Some roots of modern philosophy date back to the mystical beliefs of the ancient world; others, to the Egyptian and Babylonian sciences of physics, astronomy, cosmology, and mathematics. In Greece, the cults of Dionysus and Apollo provided the affective–spiritual bases from which philosophy emerged. Since no separate class of priests existed, early Greek philosophy remained largely independent of religious, moral, and ethical considerations. However, religious beliefs were exemplified in studies of nature; if there was any god and religious determination in the world, it had to be reflected in the order of nature and in the order of the human mind, a conviction that is a basic postulate of Greek philosophy.

The ordinary early Greeks, like people elsewhere and of other times, took part in religious activities but nevertheless did not drown themselves in questions about the genesis of the world and life, about essential characteristics and substances, or about knowledge and the individual's acquisition of it. They took the socially accepted beliefs for granted and remained preoccupied with their daily activities of work and entertainment. The philosopher, on the other hand, began to reject such an attitude, and began to raise questions on how we learn about the world, how we distinguish between truth and appearance, and how we come to know ourselves. But the overriding theme for Greek philosophy remained the ontological search for the essence and the essential cause, for the reason and the origin of the existing things.

The Philosophy of Cosmologism—Generation I

The first philosopher who searched for systematic answers to these questions was Thales of Miletus (625–545 B.C.).* He called water the essential substance of the world, possibly because of his observation that there is an organismic need for this "element," based on the phenomenal impression that all things contain water, water evaporates into clouds that bring rainfall and life to plants, water shapes the beaches of rivers and the sea, and water erodes land and even mountains. Sharp distinctions between the inorganic and the organic, between dead and living matter, were unknown. Every object was regarded as organic, vital, and forceful. Water was not merely material but the cause and germ for everything else.

Thales became equally renowned for his contributions to astronomy and mathematics. He predicted with great accuracy a solar eclipse, relying probably on Babylonian timetables. A geometrical theorem bears his name, but it is again uncertain whether he derived it on his own or whether he in-

---

* There is a good deal of uncertainty about the dates of birth and death of the early Greek philosophers. In the following, I am relying on H. Schmid, *Philosophisches Wörterbuch* (11th ed.), Stuttgart:Kröner, 1951.

troduced it from Egyptian sources. Taken together, these contributions reflect his broad interests and the universality of his concern.

While Thales was the first to propose a philosophy of the universe emphasizing both observations and deductions, his views were elaborated by his student Anaximander (611–545 B.C.). Anaximander denies that one particular element, such as water, could form the essential substance of all things. Rather, the source of all being, the *arché*, is the *apeiron*, i.e., an infinite, inexhaustible, and qualitatively indeterminate substance that, thus, is antithetical to all observable things. This substance can only be described in negative terms, and can only be characterized by the absence of all qualities of known objects.

Stating the quality of the apeiron in such a way seems to result in a mere reformulation of the original question; it does not yield any definite answer. However, according to Anaximander, this formulation made the problem of a universal substance more definite and clear because this substance cannot be identified by means of any of the known qualities or things; it has to have abstract, nonobservable characteristics.

Anaximander emphasized the genesis of all observable things out of the apeiron, a conception that would later be elaborated by Heraclitus. For Anaximander the manifold of existing things developed through a differentiation into polar opposites, such as warmth and cold, vagueness and distinctness, sky and earth. During the process of differentiation, first the fire sphere of the sky emerged, then the fluid spheres of the oceans, and finally the solids of the earth. These statements indicate his return from abstract thought to naturalistic observations.

The last of the three wise men of Miletus, Anaximenes (585–525 B.C.), accepted more decisively than Anaximander the earlier sensualistic notions of Thales. By regarding the air as the essential substance of the universe, he relied on sensory observations, but he also proposed two abstract principles. The first reveals the distinction between the observable matter of nature and the laws that govern the processes of change to which matter is subjected. Anaximenes regarded air as the singular substance that underlies all other qualities of nature, and stressed the idea of a living force. This force prevails over all matter. Matter has merely passive functions and is thus dependent upon the first. This argument leads to Anaximenes' second principle, which deals explicitly with the question of how different forms of nature emerge out of the basic matter, the air: They emerge through compression and attenuation. Fire is attenuated air; clouds, water, mud, stone are compressed air; air itself is the one persisting substance from which all others are derived. More explicitly than his predecessors, he thus promotes the idea of a single unchanging element, the real essence of the cosmos. Thereby Anaximenes prepares a concept for which, decades later, Democritus would become widely known.

These early half-sensual, half-rational interpretations were followed by two general trends that characterized the thinking of subsequent generations of philosophers who, on the one hand, increasingly emphasized a reliance on the observables and a dependency of all knowledge on the flux of natural events. On the other hand, the rationalists began to alienate their interpretations from the phenomenal experiences emphasized by the sensualists, and elaborated means of logical, deductive inferences and constructed abstract ideas about the world. Both forms of thinking are inherent in the interpretations proposed by the three early philosophers of Miletus. Their immediate successors, Heraclitus and Pythagoras (generations IIA and IIB), did not deviate very strongly from their early views. It remained the task of Democritus and Leucippus (generation IIIA), on the one hand, and for the philosophers of the Eleatic school (generation IIID), on the other, to expand the ideas to their full breadth. The Sophists (generation IV) would carry them to their outer extremes.

The Philosophy of Order—Generation IIB

Pythagoras (580–500 B.C.) still represents, like his contemporary Heraclitus (544–483 B.C.), the old prototype of a philosopher. He exemplifies the competence of a mystic, a preacher, a theoretician, and a keen observer of nature. Pythagoras's interest in mathematics determined not only his philosophical notions about nature but also his ethics and his attitudes toward life.

Numerals offered to Pythagoras a welcomed form of expression and a compromise that seemed to reunite the diverging forces of the changing events of nature and the unchanging character of ideas. Pythagoras believed that everything exists in quantity and consists of a number of parts. Relationships between objects, such as the lines and angles in geometrical figures, the configurations of the stars in the sky, or the wave lengths of tones (as inferred from the length of the strings that produce them), can be expressed by numbers. Numbers are not merely symbols but attain ontological status, and, thus, represent the essence of the universe. For example, he viewed one-ness as expressing the essence of all things (because all other quantities are multiples of one), five-ness as expressing friendship and marriage (because it is composed of the smallest odd and the smallest even number), four-ness or nine-ness as expressing justice (because they are composed of equal factors), etc.

Today we regard numbers (as well as geometrical elements) as abstract entities and as constituting parts of ideal systems that may be superimposed on observables and may, thus, bring order into a manifold of unordered details. In popular beliefs and superstitions, however, the above symbolic and mystical interpretations are still preserved.

Anaximenes may well have been the first philosopher to promote the distinction between passive matter and those active forces that govern its interactions and changes. Similarly, Pythagoras may well have been the first philosopher to discuss the relationship between mathematical ideas and observable events. He avoided a distinct separation of both by declaring that numbers are the essence of being and by subsuming the latter under the first.

The Philosophy of Being—Generation IIID

Pythagoras's concept of numbers is a compromise between an extreme rationalism and a philosophy based on sensory observations of the changing nature. This compromise was soon abandoned by the Eleatic school, represented by Parmenides (540–480 B.C.), Zeno (490–430 B.C.), and, to a lesser degree, by their predecessor Xenophanes (577–480 B.C.). According to the Eleatic philosophers, truth can be attained through thinking only; any reliance on sensory data and observations is misleading in principle.

The sensory basis of knowledge was not rejected by simply calling attention to fallacies, illusions, hallucinations, or dreams, but also by means of logical inferences. Only reasoning could demonstrate sensory fallacy. Best known are the "antonomies" attributed to Zeno through which the inherent contradictions of sensory observations were supposed to be revealed. Thus, Zeno demonstrated on logical grounds that Achilles could not possibly pass a turtle that had started a short distance ahead of him. Whenever Achilles would reach the spot where the turtle had been at the preceding moment of observation, the turtle would also have made a certain advance. Then, during the next time interval, which admittedly was shorter than the preceding one, the same judgment would recur. Relying, thus, on accepted but not yet formalized ways of thinking, the Eleatic philosophers tried to undermine the faith in sensory observations.

In extension to the early cosmologists and to Phythagoras, an interpretation of the universe was attempted. Since sensory information had to be discarded, the essential substance could not possibly be revealed by processes and objects that we observe in nature. Nature is characterized by a constant change and flux, by becoming. In contrast, the real being had to be characterized as not moving or growing but as remaining unchanged throughout the times. Such a substance could not possibly consist of parts either, it would have to be indivisible.

The Eleatic view of the essence of the universe was a far step from the earlier concrete perceptualizations of nature. As a consequence of their rejection of sensory data, the Eleatic philosophers had to admit that they could describe the universal substance in negative terms only; they could state only those qualities that the true being did not possess. And these qualities were precisely those used for describing objects and processes of nature; except that all of these qualities had to be denied.

The Eleatic philosophy received high recognition for its rigor and consistency. Its abstractness, however, not only contradicted common sense notions of nature but also approached the limits of intellectual tolerance among the educated people during this period of Greek history. For what, after all, is this world and our knowledge if the most obvious things and observations are so intimately confounded by errors and misconceptions? The growing doubt about the value of philosophy was further strengthened. The Eleatic philosophers were not the only ones who were then providing explanations to the truth-seeker. There existed at the time several other schools of philosophy, some of which were diametrically opposed to the Eleatic views. Foremost among these were the philosophies of Heraclitus, Democritus, and Leucippus, each of which stressed the sensory and experiential basis of knowledge.

The Philosophy of Becoming—Generation IIA

Heraclitus was the most distinguished opponent of Eleatic philosophy. In his teaching, he closely followed the cosmologists and Pythagoras, and was as much a philosopher as he was preacher and mystic. His contemporaries, it seems, had difficulties in understanding Heraclitus's philosophizing; they called him "The Dark."

In his search for a unique substance and moving force of the universe, Heraclitus turned his attention to fire. Thus, three of the four "elements" that a few years later Empedocles (483–424 B.C.) would distinguish were alternatively considered as the essential substances. Not accidentally, the remaining "element," earth, was the only one that did not attain this distinction in early Greek philosophy, although it had been so considered in prephilosophical Greek mythology as well in those of other civilizations of the Mediterranean and the Near East. For instance, in the Bible, God is reported in Genesis to have created Adam from earth. Heraclitus's reason for regarding fire as the universal substance lies in his recognition that its motility and vitality represent best the moving forces of nature.

At least two propositions have been attributed to Heraclitus. Because of their profundity and the difficulties encountered in explicating them, they continue to retain a rather indefinite place in present-day thinking. Heraclitus succeeded in expressing these propositions with extreme simplicity but without transmitting to us a detailed analysis of their implications. These propositions are the notions that "strife is the father of all things" (of all inventions, as we might say today), and that "you can never enter the same river twice."

As implied in Heraclitus's first proposition, development and change represent processes of continuous differentiation through the effectiveness of opposing forces. These forces have been described by Heraclitus as love and hate, day and night, the humid and the dry, birth and death, etc. The development of Greek philosophy itself may be regarded as an example for Heraclitus's interpretation. The holistic philosophical position of the cosmologists is subjected to continuing differentiation through disputes, disagreements, and contradictions, with each participant in this dialogue overemphasizing his particular point of view in order to reveal it clearly, to show the other philosophers' shortcomings and contradictions, and to attract new scholars effectively. However, productive growth, e.g., of the idea of a universal substance, can succeed only if each philosopher also realizes and adapts to all of the earlier statements. Such a condition will prevail in any meaningful discussion and shows that reason, *logos* (a concept introduced by Heraclitus), governs the cosmos throughout. Otherwise, interaction would cease. The notion that continuous adaptations have to be made by any person throughout the whole course of his life is also implied in Heraclitus's second proposition, i.e., in his statement that no one can enter the same river twice.

With his second proposition, Heraclitus provided the first theory of development and history or, at least, pointed to the major implication of the concept of growth. By emphasizing that no system can ever attain the same, namely, an earlier state again, he characterized nature as being in a constant change and flux. In complete opposition to the Eleatic philosophers, the notion of an unchanging being is regarded as an illusion and an empty abstraction. Growth and "becoming" are the essential principles of the cosmos. Since it is the observables, the objects of nature, that are continuously changing, his philosophy accepts, in principle, sensory information as the basis for knowledge. There are illusions, hallucinations, and misconceptions to guard against, but despite these limitations, observations provide the main and true route to knowledge. Again, in this line of reasoning, Heraclitus finds himself in juxtaposition to the Eleatic philosophers. He is to be followed and succeeded by Democritus and Leucippus.

The Philosophy of Particles—Generation IIIA

Heraclitus led a hermeneutic life, isolated from social interactions. Although he emphasized the observable nature as a basis for knowledge, i.e., although he insisted that the essential qualities of nature are not hidden but are revealed as they appear in our perceptions, he did not overevaluate observations at the expense of reasoning and introspections. His moderate position was to be challenged by the most outstanding early students of nature, Democritus (c460–371 B.C.), Leucippus (460–? B.C.), and Empedocles. In many respects, Empedocles resembles the earlier cosmologists, whose varying viewpoints he synthesized in his theory of the four "elements," i.e., fire, air, water, and earth. This classification was firmly accepted far into modern times. The same holds true for his descriptions of bodily constitutions, the humoral bases of temper and emotions, and types of human diseases. These ideas were not fully elaborated, however, until several centuries later when a group of empirically minded physicians headed by Galen (131–201 B.C.) engaged in their systematic investigations. The classification of choleric, sanguinic, stoic, and phlegmatic tempers is attributed to these scholars and still attracts some personality psychologists and psychiatrists.

The mechanistic theory of the cosmos proposed by Democritus is based upon the notion of a smallest particle, the atom. Paradoxically, this unit shares most properties of the essential being described by the Eleatic philosophers. Also atoms do not resemble in any known manner the manifold of phenomena observed in nature: they are indivisible and unchangeable. But although both theories resemble each other in rigor and consistency, there are major differences. In contrast to the Eleatic philosophy, the theory proposed by Democritus is not of the logical–inferential type but is inductive and empirical. Its main properties are derived from experiences. Even though the resulting system is highly abstract, it serves primarily the purpose of explaining and incorporating known observations about nature.

The atomistic explanations proposed by Democritus resemble common viewpoints in physics. Atoms are the smallest particles that differ from each other only in their size, form, and location within an "empty" space, i.e., the "nonbeing," a concept again congruent with Eleatic viewpoints. At the onset, before the observable objects of the universe were formed, all atoms were moving on random paths. Occasionally, some would collide and either push each other aside or become attached to one another, thus forming larger units. Finally, the observable objects would emerge. Despite its random source, the genesis of the universe and its objects were regarded by Democritus as a completely determined process, representing the *logos* of the world. However, single movements could not possibly be recognized as reflecting this order.

Democritus also proposed a theory of perception substituting the simple notions proposed by Empedocles. According to the latter, perception consists in assimilation and is possible because both the object perceived and the perceiver are composed of the same four elements, i.e., earth, water, air, and fire. Thus, perception rests upon ontological similarity of the object and the perceiver, a view that has been surprisingly well retained through history and was revived, for instance, by Goethe's statement that "the eye could never apperceive the sun unless it was 'sunlike' by itself." Similar views are also inherent in theories of space perception that emphasize the transformation of the spatial dimensionality and the structural similarity of both the perceived object and the perceiving eye.

In his perceptual theory, which is known as the eidola theory, Democritus revealed most clearly his materialistic attitude. The soul, as any other object of nature, consists of material atoms, though the most flexible ones. Faint copies are emitted from the objects and transmitted through the empty space that fills the room between the many separate atoms. While these copies constitute the mechanical stimulation for the sensory organs, the colors, sounds, warmth and coldness do not exist objectively in nature but are *nomoi*. They are postulated by the perceiver and represent his interpretations of nature. In Locke's terminology, they are not primary but secondary qualities.

The Philosophy of Direction—Generation IIIB

The philosophical notions proposed during the course of Greek history eventually began to exceed the limits of intellectual tolerance of the average as well as of the better educated persons. Whereas the Eleatic philosophers developed some notions about the essential being that were in complete disagreement with common sense observations and knowledge they, at least, promoted an appreciation for religious and theological problems. Such dedication also characterizes Heraclitus's philosophy, although his concept of nature and its blind forces that determine the course of the universe with unrestrained necessity contradicted common theological thinking. It excluded any concern for purpose, meaning, and direction.

Despite impending changes in public reaction, two further developments took place. On the one hand, the Sophists introduced subjectivism into philosophy by degrading knowledge into a status of relative validity and by acknowledging the subject as the judge of truth, or rather of his preference for any particular "truth." On the other hand, different compromises were sought, aiming at synthesizing the diverging views of philosophical inquiries. As representatives of this attempt, Anaxagoras and Socrates thereby prepared the way toward the period of the greatest achievements in Greek philosophy, the period of Plato and Aristotle.

Historically, Anaxagoras (500–428 B.C.), a contemporary of Empedocles, preceded Democritus. His contributions formed a connecting link between these two philosophers. He deviates from both, however, by introducing the concept of *nous,* a teleological principle. This concept reveals his opposition to the mechanistic and materialistic theory of Democritus, his inclination toward Eleatic thought, and his preparatory influence leading to Aristotle.

Like the earlier sensualists, Anaxagoras is concerned with the question of the basic elements that in their complex compositions make up the objects of the natural world. Like Empedocles he points out that these elements must be qualitatively different and do not submerge into each other. The observables consist of various mixtures of these basic substances. But within these compounds they remain separated units and do not lose their identity. In contrast to Empedocles, four elements are not considered to be a set large enough to account for the manifold of observable objects. How can flesh develop from anything that is not flesh itself? Anaxagoras concludes that there must be as many different elements as there are different kinds of matter.

Although this view is by no means congruent with the theory subsequently proposed by Democritus, it shares with it the notion that differences between matter have to be located at the level of imperceivable small particles, whose distributive emission characterizes the deterioration of things and whose synthesizing unification characterizes growth. In these processes, the elements do not change, they only unite or separate; flesh comes to flesh, stone to stone, water to water. In sharp contrast to Democritus, the guiding factor, nous, which determines changes in the universe, is an intellectual principle; it guarantees that the development proceeds in a rational manner toward a universe that reflects logic and order. The nous is, however, material in nature. It is the most subtle and motile of all matters and is the only substance that does not mix with other forms of matter during the original, chaotic state of the universe.

The Philosophy of Knowing—Generation IIIC

As much as Anaxagoras's philosophy can be regarded as a deviation from materialistic and mechanistic viewpoints and as a rapprochement of rational thought and purposes, the philosophy of Socrates can be regarded as a deviation from rational philosophizing toward a theory that places greater emphasis on observations and experiences in the concrete world. Anaxagoras's views lead into Aristotle's dualistic philosophy of form and matter, actuality and potentiality; Socrates' views led into Plato's dualistic philosophy of ideas and observables, thought and perception. Socrates' maxim that "knowing is virtue" is considered to be his only authentical quotation; no written scripts have been handed down to us through history.

Socrates attracted a great many students, some of whom became recognized philosophers or political leaders. His intellectual and personal power, despite an unattractive appearance, has been attributed to his drive not only to talk about his philosophy but also to live by it, which proved to be irresistible to others. This attitude was revealed in his firm rejection of escape or clemency during his trial, in the course of which he was accused of misguiding the youth, of promoting atheism, and of encouraging blasphemy. He accepted his verdict because he wanted to show that any individual who had enjoyed the benefits and hospitality of a community should also submit himself to its consensual judgments under less fortunate circumstances.

In his philosophy, Socrates leans toward the Eleatic views but deviates from almost all earlier interpretations by trying to detect the *logos* or the laws of the universe within the human being and not in outer nature. In these attempts, he reveals an affinity toward the Sophists although his explorations are directed toward more abstract and higher epistemological and, especially, ethical goals. For Socrates the human mind takes part and has its origin in the logos. Teaching, accordingly, is hermeneutic; it is comparable to the art of the midwife. The acquisition of knowledge is a rediscovery of previously perceived truth, i.e., truth already acquired in an earlier life.

Several students of Socrates, namely, those of the Megaric and Elic schools, engaged in similar attempts to develop further a theory of knowledge and nature. The majority, however, remained concerned with ethical problems. These were the Cynic and Cyrenaic philosophers. Some of their ideas led directly into the great ethical schools of the post-Aristotelian period, the Stoics and the Epicureans.

The Philosophy of Subjectivism and Relativism—Generation IV

Contemporaries of Socrates, the Sophists, took the last step that was left after the philosophical systems of Pythagoras, Elea, Heraclitus, and Democritus had been proposed. While all these philosophers tried to discover the logos of the universe by analyzing nature, the Sophists declared that the human individual was the sole standard for such knowledge. Thus, they also deviated from Socrates, who maintained that the human mind is but a representation of the universal logos in which it had part in an earlier life. The Sophists shared the Eleatic view that reasoning is the only means of attaining truth, but they did not direct their search toward universal knowledge. For the Sophists, truth was a personal matter and not dependent on universal conditions. In their views about nature, the Sophists were inclined to accept the material, mechanistic notions of the universe proposed by Democritus.

For a long time in history, the contributions by the Sophists were evaluated in negative terms. Primarily, this was due to the overshadowing influence of the following generation of Greek philosophers, to Plato and Aristotle, whose philosophies represent a firm and conservative reaction against the Sophists. Since their influence has remained significant, the contributions by the Sophists are still underevaluated. Nevertheless, there can be little doubt that they greatly accelerated the development of philosophy and the general education of the public. They introduced philosophy into everyday life. Being splendid orators, lawyers, teachers, and politicians, they promoted the general understanding of social and historical events, criticized repression, slavery, warfare, social injustice, and aided the common man to gain and defend his individuality. Because they engaged in so many diverse activities, they did not present a uniform system of philosophy, and their names, e.g., Protagoras (480–410 B.C.) and Gorgias (483–375 B.C.), may well have been lost to us had they not been preserved through their fictitious or actual participation in the Platonic dialogues.

According to Plato, Protagoras derived his well-known proposition that "man is the standard of all things" on the basis of such trivial evidence that an object may appear cold to one person and warm to another. Subsequently, truth was seen as dependent upon the public consensus dominating at any particular time and upon the ability of any proponent to present his views persuasively. But besides these simplistic conclusions, a more general change in perspective was introduced through these examples. Thus far in the history of Greek thought, the fate of the individual was regarded as determined by eternal and divine laws. Through the influence of the Sophists, the responsibility for one's own life was handed over to the individual. With this attitude the Sophists accelerated one of the most important social changes in Greek history. The state and its social hierachies were no longer regarded as divine and reasonable institutions, but rather as arrangements founded upon a contract in which all human beings, including the slaves, had an equal right to participate. The state and its laws, religion, and the gods had to be regarded, according to Critias (460–403 B.C.), as man-made creations. Other Sophists presented their views more cautiously, but all of them agreed in their doubts about the perfection of human institutions and the existence of their gods. Although their movement represents one of the most daring steps toward problems we still confront today, most of them still wait for appropriate recognition.

EARLY EUROPEAN PHILOSOPHY

By about A.D. 500 the tradition of Greek-Roman philosophy, science, and technology had fallen into oblivion, and if renewed inspiration had not been provided by the Islam, might have been lost forever (see chap. 6). The last centuries of ancient philosophy generated a wealth of diversified viewpoints, specialization, eclecticism, and tendencies toward scientism and application. The Christian Church, which was rapidly gaining dominance, either disregarded or condemned these movements. When renewed interest in philosophy was generated through exchanges with the Near East, north Africa, and southern Spain, primary attention was given to the integrative systems of Plato and Aristotle. The revival of learning lead to Scholasticism, which culminated in the monumental work of Thomas Aquinas (1225–1274). Scholasticism can be regarded as the early blueprint for the philosophy of western European.

The downfall of the Roman Empire and the rise of the Christian Church are political–spiritual events that devastatingly interrupted the growth and even the preservation of knowledge. For these reasons it is justifiable to regard Greek philosophy on the one hand and modern western European philosophy on the other as distinct periods of history. However, such separation does not mean that modern philosophy did not depend and build upon the earlier developments. In terms of the models described in chapters 4 and 5, a general accumulation and transfer from the first to the second historical system indeed took place and was made possible through Arabic intermediaries.

In view of this transfer, the two historical progressions appear similar in structure but different in topic or theme. Like the openness, clarity, and brightness of their world, Greek philosophy asked unmediated direct questions about nature: What is the world? It is primarily ontology. Modern Western philosophy, like the landscape of mountains, meadows, and woods, is plagued by dimness, profusion, shadows, and doubts. It does not dare to ask immediate questions about the nature of the world but restricts itself to the preparatory question of how we might gain knowledge in this world. Primarily, western European philosophy is epistemology.

Also from the perspective of our own structural–developmental methodology, the analysis of the history of ancient philosophy provides for clearer contrastive interpretations than the analysis of its modern counterpart. This variation stems from the difference in historical distances. The farther back we look into the past, the more distinct become the viewpoints of the few philosophers whose contributions survived the ages. The closer in time these interpretations are, the more diffuse and overlapping they appear to the observer and the larger is their number. Thus, a contrastive comparison of early periods is easier to derive and might be more convincing to the reader than one for later periods. This limitation does not only hold true for the general comparison between the early Greek and the early western European philosophies, but also within each structural progression, and provides a major reason why I have restricted my discussion to the early periods of each of the two historical movements. The postintegrative periods, especially, i.e., those following the contributions by Plato, Aristotle, and the Skeptics, by Kant, Hegel, and the Positivists–Phenomenologists, respectively, are characterized by a multitude of viewpoints that lend themselves only selectively to the kind of structural–developmental interpretation that I am attempting.

The stronger intellectual contrast during the earlier periods is due, on the one hand, to the greater limitations in the amount of knowledge available. This makes the various schools appear as distinctively different. On the other hand, the contrast may be due to the loss of intermediate viewpoints that, lacking distinctness, did not survive the selective overinterpretations of generations of historians. The differences are quite similar to those of personal evaluations: We know ourselves least well because we experience ourselves closely in too many different situations. We are better able to judge other persons because we observe them only in a few and, perhaps, highly critical situations.

In view of all these difficulties, we might come to question the significance of the present interpretation. Undoubtedly, I overgeneralize where traditional historians demand detailed differentiations. However, the analysis of knowledge and science itself and the traditional historical interpretations have often assigned quite inappropriate places to historical figures and historical contributions (see chap. 11). In many cases, outstanding philosophers and scientists have suffered under the selective emphasis (distortion) and the selective disregard (neglect) by their fellow scholars and by historians. Only a structural systematic interpretation will enable us to correct such distortions. Much like the astronomers who were searching for a missing planet in the planetary system and much like the chemists who were succeeding in filling the gaps in their periodic system of elements, it might even force us to search for contributors in order to fill a slot disregarded by traditional and more eclectic interpretations.

In negative terms, the critics will say that I overgeneralize, a crime that they weigh more heavily than the selective disregard and lack of concern for holes in the fabric of historical progressions. In positive terms, history has to be generated through the constructive efforts of systematic interpretations. We should not shy away from this task.

The Philosophy of Individualism—Generation I

The Middle Ages were terminated by an awakening of the individual. Luther rejected the outer religiosity manifested by the belief in dogmas and institution. He substituted for it an inner faith and an inner responsibility of the individual that alone would lead to his salvation. In the philosophy and sciences of the 15th century, a great variety of different viewpoints had been proposed, many of which revived some Greek and Roman interpretations. Within the blooming diversity, we can recognize some general trends.

First, all Renaissance thinkers were united in their opposition to the systematic philosophers of Greece, especially to Aristotle, who by now had attained a narrow and dogmatic status through the interpretations by the Scholastics. Renaissance philosophers, in trying to liberate thinking from dogmatic restrictions, rebelled against his authority and the authority of the Church. Much of the Western philosophy that followed has remained in this state of rebellion, which subsequently put Aristotle in a rather narrow spot instead of recognizing the dialecticism of his original philosophy undistorted by Scholastic categorizations.

Second, Renaissance thinkers pointed to the unity of the universe, which they regarded, like the Greek cosmologists, as a unity of activity and not merely as a unity of substances. Moreover, their interpretations emphasize the human being, humanism, and the beauty of the universe as much as they tried to dissect it into component parts and forces. Again, quite similar to their Greek counterparts, Renaissance thinkers presented their views in the form of poems or eulogies of man and nature.

Third, the role of the individual in the universe became of particular concern to Renaissance thinkers. Generally, the world was seen as being constituted of different domains or spheres: the outer nature in its universality, perfectness, and aesthetic lawfulness, the *macrocosm;* and the inner nature of man, which reflects and represents the outer nature in form of the *microcosm* and, thus, makes its apprehension possible. Finally, and in sharp contrast to the Greek mentality, the infinity of the universe and of the human potential was emphasized and hailed in ever more enthusiastic exclamations.

These uniform tendencies should not be overemphasized, however. Indeed, their sparkling diversity makes it quite difficult to select a set of persons who represent best the multiple range of Renaissance philosophy. For the present purpose, I arbitrarily picked three persons who indicated fairly clearly the emerging trends of modern Western philosophy and who in their contrast of approach reflect a structural diversification quite similar to that of their Greek counterparts, the cosmologists.

First, Giordano Bruno (1548–1600) represents the early transition from medieval to Renaissance philosophy. He was concerned with questions of what we might call macrocosmology and microcosmology. The outer world is infinity and unity. Any distinctions, such as between above and below, center and periphery, heaviness and lightness, are only perspectives of the perceiver. The universe itself is unity and continuously strives toward such unity. The organism partakes in this unity of which it constitutes, of course, only a diminutively small part. In turn, the organism is composed of a multitude of *monads,* which through their intrinsic activities and their tendency toward self-preservation and balance are able to apprehend and to participate in the infinity and harmony of the universe.

Giordano Bruno retained his enthusiasm until his tragic end at the stake in Rome during the Counter Reformation. This "hot" philosophizing found its "cool" counterpart in the French philosopher Michel de Montaigne (1533–1592), with whom the sequence of brilliant French essayists has its beginning. In contrast to Bruno, Montaigne is concerned with human self-recognition and epistemology. In rejecting the overburdening systems of Plato and Aristotle, he felt closest to the Skeptics and like his great French intellectual descendant, Descartes, begins his inquiries with a systematic doubt of accepted knowledge.

In this attitude, Montaigne is supported by the philosopher who opened most distinctly the tradition of British empiricism, Francis Bacon (1561–1626). More strongly than his contemporaries, Bacon questioned the categoricism of Aristotle handed down and rigidified by the Scholastics. He began his inquiry by questioning and rejecting all of these metaphysical systems and instead emphasized an unbiased and ceaseless empiricism that, he was convinced, through the accumulation of more and more information would eventually produce all possible knowledge. Knowledge is, thus, based on induction rather than on speculations deduced from traditionally accepted systems of knowing. In contrast to Montaigne and Bruno, Bacon was primarily concerned with the acquisition of knowledge in the natural world rather than with critical interpretations and with inquiries of the role of man in the sociohistorical world. He expressed an early utilitarianism by stating that knowledge is power. The pragmatic natural science approach to knowledge, on the one hand, and the logico-deductive approach, on the other, were to determine firmly the future developments on the British Island and the Continent, respectively.

The Philosophy of Consciousness—Generation IIB

Like Pythagoras and the Eleatic school, the following philosophers increasingly rejected the reliance on sensory data and tried to derive knowledge through reasoning and abstract inferences. Descartes (1596–1650), the first philosopher representing this trend, resembled his Greek counterpart, Pythagoras, in many important ways. For example, he shared his interest in mathematics. Descartes did not regard numbers and other mathematical elements as ultimate substantial entities, nor as having a part in these entities, but rather as functional means for describing in universal terms the conditions and relations of objects and situations. He did not deny that numbers and mathematical elements belong to the realm of ideas but denied their ontological character. Numbers serve to translate empirical observations into the abstract and precise language of mathematics. In particular, Descartes must be credited with equating the geometry of the Euclidean space with the algebraic system of numbers by means of the Cartesian coordination system.

Like Pythagoras, Descartes regarded mathematics as prototypical system for all other scientific inquiries. The general difficulty for these disciplines consisted, of course, in that they had to deal with the ambiguous concepts derived from experience, whereas mathematics dealt with imaginary and ideal units. Descartes applied the axiomatic approach of Euclid in order to clarify the field of philosophical speculations. In this manner he derived those notions that were clear and distinct and could fulfill the same functions for philosophy as Euclid's axioms fulfilled for mathematics. Accordingly, Descartes argued that one may in principle doubt all knowledge, especially that which is dependent on sensory observations, because a demon may willfully or by chance misguide our observations as in dreams, illusions, hallucinations, and other misperceptions. However, during all these elaborations one notion always remains certain to the critical observer, namely, the notion that he himself has doubted and thus has experienced his own experiencing and his own self. Stated in Descartes's terms, by thinking about oneself and one's own valid or nonvalid perceptions, one gains the notion of one's own being: *cogito ergo sum.*

Since it is impossible to develop a philosophical system based on the single notion of self-doubt, Descartes analyzed the consciousness for other ideas with respectable degrees of certainty. Immediately he detected the idea of God. In contrast to our ideas about ourselves, God exists outside of our consciousness and ultimately has to be considered as the force that determines and guarantees all our notions about ourselves. Having opened the way for knowledge outside of ourselves, it is now possible to discuss the degree of certainty attributable to different perceptions. According to Descartes, ideas with high degrees of certainty are the logical principles, the ideas of substance, space, causality, and of numbers. Moreover, our certainty about God allows us to regard all other perceptions of the external world with greater confidence. After all, it was God Himself who created this world and our consciousness. Why should He have introduced any grossly misleading perceptions?

Descartes draws a distinction between conscious ideas, *res cogitans,* and extended matter, *res extensa.* In particular, he followed Democritus in insisting on the phenomenal characteristics of extended objects and attributes such as their colors, temperatures, forms and surface qualities. These are subjective interpretations by the perceiver and not features of the objects themselves. The only distinct and clear characteristics of bodies are their extendedness and their submission under the law of causality. All other qualities are in our consciousness only.

Descartes's system is dualistic. Both the *res cogitans* and the *res extensa* are qualitatively different and not reducible to each other. We know about the first through our conscious self-reflection; we have to rely on God's intervention for our knowledge about the second. Both substances function independently from each other. Both interact only in the human organism, namely, in the pineal body of the brain. The soul whose functions are volition and thinking may activate movements. The functions of the body are perceptions and passions, both of which are determined mechanically and become conscious only to humans through the interactions between body and soul. All other organisms are guided by perceptions and passions only. They function like automata by reflexes.

The Philosophy of Universal Knowing—Generation IIID

Spinoza (1632–1677), one of the major successors of Descartes, applied deductive methods not only to obtain a clear and distinct basis for his theory of knowledge but also to resolve questions about nature, the human mind, and ethics. He claimed that, like the mathematician who elaborates his definitions and axioms one should analyze without prejudice and passion the maxims of ethics and the essence of the human being. In opposition to Descartes's dualism, Spinoza proposed a single universal substance. His pantheism resembled the Eleatic philosophy and cultivated Giordano Bruno's idealism, with lesser zeal and greater coolness.

Like the Eleatic philosophers, for Spinoza there is only one independent substance that is infinite, eternal, and can be apprehended by rational thinking only. This substance is identical with God. The *res extensa* and the *res cogitans* of Descartes are nothing but attributes of the universal substance, the changing conditions of God. Thus, God is body and mind and every unique physical condition parallels a unique condition of the mind. Body and mind do not cause each other, as Descartes had maintained, and do not interact. Although physical conditions may be linked by causal chains, the ultimate cause for both, mind and body, is God.

In clear opposition to Hume's psychological and genetic theory, ideas are related by logical bonds. The world is logos. In regarding objects as real, Spinoza opposed, furthermore, Hume's nominalism. Ideas are attached to these objects and differ in their degree of perfection. Ideas are forms of thinking and objects are forms of matter; both are attributes of the one substance, of God. The real substance is a self-sufficient whole; the attributes are its property or quality. Ultimately, the universal substance has an infinity of attributes. However, only two are known to us: consciousness and extension. Both are related to each other; every perception, feeling, or thinking represents a knowledge about an extended object; it also represents a bodily state by itself.

At first we know about our bodies only. The soul is the consciousness of the body or of the effects of other objects on the body. Thus, the whole of our mental lives are composed of acts of consciousness and images. Our souls may attain a high degree of freedom in a striving for consciousness. To the extent that our actions arise from passions, we are slaves; to the extent that they are products of thinking, we are free. If we would see our actions as God sees them, we would act like God. To gain knowledge is the greatest joy and virtue, as it had been for Socrates. The right use of reason will lead humanity to harmony and agreement in a world that is, in its very basis, a closed and balanced system of aesthetic beauty. The changes and modifications that we observe are only incomplete representations of a logical–mathematical order of the infinite and divine being.

The Philosophy of Motions—Generation IIA

As Spinoza may be regarded as the historical analogue to the Eleats, Hobbes (1588–1679) may be regarded as the counterpart of Heraclitus. He shared his interests in developmental and historical processes but did not become involved in a controversy as dramatic as that between Heraclitus and the Eleatic school. Rather, such a confrontation developed between Descartes's rationalism and Locke's sensualism. In accepting this controversy as the decisive choice point in the development of modern philosophy, a shift from rationalism toward a greater emphasis of the sensory basis of knowledge is revealed. However, the conceptual distances between the opposing philosophers shown in Figure 13, i.e., between Heraclitus and the Eleats on the one hand, and between Locke and Descartes on the other, have remained about equally large for both periods of historical development.

For Hobbes, as for his predecessor Bacon, sensations are the basis for all knowledge. He rejected any teleological explanations in favor of the mechanistic and materialistic views Descartes had proposed for explaining only the conditions of the extended matter. Hobbes rejected, however, Descartes's dualism and his view of the soul as an immaterial substance. Everything that we know is material in nature, or more specifically, everything can be explained as matter or as movements of matter. Mind is a brain substance. Images and ideas are motions in the brain, just as the universe is composed of motions of its particles.

In regarding motion as the most basic principle, Hobbes's philosophy

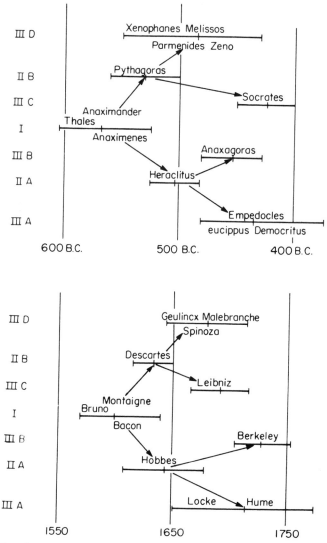

Figure 13. Branch structure representation of the history of early Greek and early European philosophy. (*Note:* The First 20 years of the life of each philosopher have been omitted.)

resembles closely that of Heraclitus and is opposed to the Eleatic and Descartes's notion of a unique, indivisible, and unchanging substance, *res cogitans*. To Hobbes, ideas are mere names. Thinking is an operation with these names, symbols, or signs, just as mathematics is the art of manipulating numerals or geometrical elements. Mathematics is for Hobbes an ideal system into which he tried to translate his philosophical and scientific concepts. This application represents a synthetic approach; that is, it proceeds from universal propositions or principles that are manifest in themselves to concrete conclusions.

Whereas for Descartes the synthetic approach is the primary means for attaining knowledge, Hobbes gives greater attention to the second, the analytic approach, which proceeds from sensory experiences to general principles. Also, for this approach mathematics serves important functions. On the basis of mathematical and logical formulations (in particular, on the basis of axioms that are accepted as assumptions but not as inborn and self-evident facts), inferences and predictions may be made and subsequently tested for their accuracy. This type of approach represents the methodology of the natural sciences that, during the time of Hobbes, were beginning to emerge. The limitations and possibilities of this approach are still being discussed by students of the philosophy of science in almost the same manner as suggested by Hobbes. According to this view, two types of truth exist: "True" can be a conclusion if it is consistent with the logical-deductive system, and "true" can be a conclusion if there is enough agreement between an inference or prediction and the empirical information gathered.

Finally, there is close similarity between Hobbes and Heraclitus in their concern with social processes, history, and development. To Hobbes, the first stage in the development of social institutions is characterized by complete dominance of the egotistic interests of the individuals, which necessarily leads to a fight of everyone against everyone (*bellum omnium contra omnes*). The quest for security forces the human beings to give up some of their power and to cooperate with one another on the basis of a social contract. Accordingly, the emerging institution, the state, is nothing over and above the group of individuals who constitute it; the state has no right and justification of its own. Mankind has to select new social arrangements during the course of its history. Social arrangements vary between the original barbaric state and that of submission under an authoritarian rule. Hobbes favored such a conservative and authoritarian arrangement. In this choice he followed Plato and Aristotle as well as the Renaissance politician and philosopher Niccolò Machiavelli (1469–1527). His choice may partly reflect his disappointment in the social conditions during his lifetime and his desire for a firmer political order.

The Philosophy of Sensations—Generation IIIA

Unlike Hobbes, his successor Locke (1632–1704) became the admired spokesman for the liberal democratic ideal. Entering early into the service of the Earl of Shaftesbury, he followed this family into exile in Holland, returned to England after the disposal of James II, and afterward held several important public offices. In relying on induction and analytic thinking, Locke supported many of Bacon's and Hobbes's philosophical notions but regarded all experiences as experiences of consciousness.

There are also many similarities between Democritus and Locke. But while the former, and the Greek philosophers in general, tried to explain nature, Locke and the modern European philosophers tried to explain the way we attain knowledge about it. The first are primarily ontologists; the latter, epistemologists. In particular, ideas were for Locke what the atoms were for Democritus.

According to Locke, all knowledge has to come through the senses; there are no inborn ideas in the mind. He distinguishes between two sources for the ideas: sensations and reflections. The first are the origin of the ideas; the latter represent the intellectual processes of perceiving, thinking, believing, etc., by which they are arranged. The newborn child perceives only concrete and simple ideas, such as pain, sounds, colors, odors, etc. By means of induction the child, then proceeds toward abstract and more general conceptions. Simple ideas are combined by acts of the mind as numerals or symbols are combined in mathematical reasoning and thus yield complex ideas, such as beauty, mankind, universe, etc. Ideas may be classified into three groups: modes, substances, and relations. The first are dependent on other things; thus, the color is the mode of a colored object. Substances refer to self-dependent things: to a particular man, chair, etc. Frequently, particular modes are associated with particular substances, such as the golden shine of the coin with its shape, weight, etc. Finally, relations refer to ideas such as "greater than," "equal to," etc. To Locke knowing, ultimately, meant the recognition of relationships and, in the narrower sense, the recognition of congruencies and incongruencies. When we know that "gold is yellow" we realize a particular relationship between a metal and a color and, furthermore, between both and many other metals and colors as well as other substances and modes.

Locke did not restrict his analysis to sensory impressions but referred (by means of his notion of substances) to objects in the physical world that have their existence independent of the impressions in our mind. More specifically, knowing that "there is a God" or "that there are atoms" does not merely refer to some judgments about relationships of ideas in our mind, but such knowledge characterized by an instinctive certainty reveals something about the reality outside of our mind.

In particular and quite similar to Democritus, Locke distinguished between primary and secondary qualities. The former reflect the qualities of the things as they really are, e.g., their substance and extension in space and time; the latter are merely projections of our sense impressions into the things and are generated in our mind, e.g., colors, sounds, odors, temperatures, etc. Locke's viewpoint has become known as *critical realism*. It differs from the *naive realism* of most of his predecessors, who took, without much questioning, the existence of an external world for granted, and subsequently argued that the existence of the external world is the necessary prerequisite for all of our perceptions (not only for those based upon the primary qualities). If we set out to explore the criteria for perceptions, Locke would suggest two to us. There are, first, the objects in the outer world that determine that we agree with each other about the primary qualities. However, we should also have to rely on criteria for the secondary qualities. Do all persons perceive red, for instance, in the same way? This question is impossible to answer since all perceptions are subjective. However, Locke points out that people have come to agree to call a certain sensation red. This is merely a convention, a name assigned to secondary qualities.

Already Hume (1711–1776) extended Locke's thoughts and carried them vigorously to their logical conclusions. Thus, he stands in relation to Locke as Democritus does to Leucippus. According to Hume, all knowledge is obtained through sensory impressions, inner and outer feelings (such as colors, sounds, pain, pleasure, etc.) or ideas (which are faint copies or images of impressions and represent the immediate experience as it appears in thinking and reasoning). Impressions are first in occurrence. Because they are so vivid, they often force upon us the belief that they are caused by real objects in an external world. But even the knowledge that an object will reappear if we redirect our senses toward it does not reveal anything else but a high expectancy caused by the vividness of our impressions. In contrast to impressions, ideas are less vivid, are memories, and are originally dependent upon impressions. After sufficient experience, both impressions and ideas may occur simultaneously. In this case, they are denoted as perceptions by Hume. Perceptions are what the world consists of. We cannot possibly know whether there are real substances, causes, minds, etc.; we do not even know with certainty whether there is a God. Thus, Hume surpassed Locke in rigor and rejected the notion of external substances that have an existence independent from our senses. By applying the same notions to the perception of the self, Hume went yet a step further in his analysis. If we introspect we are not led with certainty to the perception of a unique self or ego as particularly Descartes had suggested; all that we observe are again sensations, feelings, and volitions. The self is nothing but a cluster of perceptions.

Hume rejected the notion that substances and causality are primary qualities. Causality, for example, is the perception of events in time. While this view had been suggested before for causal relations between physical events, Hume applied it to psychological processes as well. The experience that we have, for instance, when the caloric content of a substance is increased by heat does not lead to the necessary conclusion of a causal determination and is not apprehended by immediate insights. We perceive only the sequence of events, and since we may perceive this sequence frequently and regularly, we may become quite certain about the outcome. However, we should never regard the relationship between cause and effect as one of logical necessity. Induction does not lead to logical conclusions.

Hume's analysis is an attempt to formulate philosophy in psychological–genetic rather than in logical terms. The opposite has been true for his opponents, especially Descartes, Leibniz, and Kant. According to Hume, mental associations are formed between two ideas if the corresponding impressions occur frequently in the same temporal order. The frequency of their associations determines the certainty of our causal interpretation as well as the certainty that the second idea will appear in our mind soon after we have experienced the first. All knowledge is based on induction and our notion of causality, being acquired through experience, is no exception in the development of habits and thoughts.

As much as Hume carried the theories of Hobbes and Locke to their conclusion, so did he extend their views about history and social institutions. Whereas Hobbes represented a conservative political attitude and supported the hierarchical social structure of his time, and whereas Locke favored individualism and democratic ideals, Hume subscribed to the social philosophy of the *laissez-faire laissez-aller* best represented by his friend Adam Smith. The institution of the state was not created in order to put an end to the continuous fight between man (Hobbes), nor as a social contract based on reasoning (Locke), but was the reaction toward outer threats and dangers. After our submission to sociopolitical rules had lasted for a certain period of time, we became accustomed to the institutions that then continued to persist even after the conditions that had led to their creation had disappeared. In other words, the established institutions and social order are unnecessary burdens whose influence ought to be eliminated.

Perceptual Idealism—Generation IIIB

During the first half of the 18th century a number of diverging trends characterize the field of philosophy: those proposed by Descartes and Spinoza on the one hand, and by Hobbes, Locke, and Hume on the other. The ideas proposed were rather incompatible and, as in the history of Greek philosophy, two forces emerged: one aiming toward a consolidation of the diverging views and preparing the way for the great dualistic systems; the other reaching toward still more extreme positions by turning philosophy into subjectivism, relativism, and skepticism. The latter type of philosophy is represented by the French and German movement of the Enlightenment; Berkeley and Leibniz aim toward moderating compromises and prepare the way for the synthesizing systems of Kant and Hegel.

Much like Anaxagoras in comparison to Democritus, Berkeley (1685–1753) preceded Hume by a few years. Like Hume, he extended Locke's views and maintained that objects or substances are nothing but complex perceptions, their existence is in our consciousness only, *esse est percipii*. In rejecting the criticism that according to his philosophy objects would have to dissipate as soon as they disappear from perception, he insisted that we would be able to claim the possibility of their renewed perception but not of their existence. Indeed, it is the major task for natural sciences to study the laws of the succession of perceptions and ideas, i.e., the laws that Hume had called the laws of association. The aim of our inquiries is to study the interrelations between ideas and, possibly, to make predictions about their occurrence but not about external, physical causes of perceptions.

Thus, Berkeley, on the one hand, agreed closely with Locke and particularly with the nominalistic view of Hume. On the other hand, he proclaimed an active agent, the subject or the soul. Perceiving and thinking are not passive states but active processes. The mind of the individual is confronted with and embedded in the universal spirit. Ultimately, God is the cause for all our perceptions. Thus, Berkeley, after all, does not restrict the task of philosophy to a description of the interrelationships of our ideas, as in Hume's psychological–genetic theory, but as in Spinoza's pantheism, it is the metaphysical task of philosophy to interpret perceptions and thoughts as messages of a divine being. As we interpret or understand these ideas, we are perceiving; as we produce them, we are revealing the activity or the will of our soul. And, finally, much like Descartes, because we take God's existence for granted, we may also proceed in accepting an outer world. The universe consists of spirits and ideas that we conceive as substance, matter, causes, or forces and generally as God's nature. With this turn, Berkeley does not only approaches Spinoza's pantheism but prepares the way for the idealism of Fichte, Schelling, and Hegel.

The Philosophy of Organismic Rationalism—Generation IIIC

By founding his philosophy on the rationalism and the mathematico-deductive method of Descartes, Leibniz (1646–1716) tried to synthesize the diverging views of his time and prepared the way for a universal philosophy that was to be realized by his successor, Kant. There exists at least a superficial similarity between Leibniz and his Greek counterpart, Socrates: Both left few written notes, they preferred to express themselves through teaching and personal interactions, and led the lives of wanderers. Socrates would become engaged in any inspiring discussion in the streets of Athens; Leibniz would travel from court to court, enter into the service of several important rulers, and engage in many social, political, and diplomatic activities. Since there has not been an interpreter for Leibniz as there has been for Socrates, i.e., Plato, the task remains undone. Most discussions of his work rely on files of his personal correspondence. This leaves much room for inconsistencies and an impression of far-stretched speculations.

Leibniz's philosophy attempts to harmonize many diverging lines of thought. One important dichotomy consists of the physical–mathematical explanations of nature as proposed by Democritus and Descartes, on the one hand, and the theories about substances and purposes, on the other, in which ultimately the individual was to lose his identity and be subsumed, as for Spinoza, under the one universal substance, under God. Inspired by the scientific discovery of the living cell and by preformation theory, Leibniz rejected Descartes's view of all lower organisms as automata and insisted that there is purpose not only for humanity but for lower organisms as well.

Leibniz, furthermore, rejected Descartes's notion that extension is the only attribute of matter. Rather, it is the attribute of a mathematical space that can be indefinitely divided and, therefore, does *not* represent matter. As for Spinoza, matter is characterized by substance that is not extended but is intellectual in nature. Matter is the totality of perceptions and images of the reflecting being, the *mundus sensibilis*. The soul cannot perceive itself but can only think about itself; it is the *mundus intelligibilis*. The terms in which we think, i.e., substance, cause, identity, and activity, are objectively valid because we have *a priori* knowledge about them. We know about substance, for instance, because we ourselves are substance. All perceptions and images differ from each other; they represent different points of view of the world. One particular point of view of a reflecting being represents its body; that perception is most distinct and clear to him. However, this being also perceives everything else in the world and it does not only perceive everything in space but also everything in time, everything that has ever happened. Commonly, these perceptions are not recognized; they are unconscious, they are *petites perceptions.*

Since there is no external world conceivable for Leibniz that gives rise to perceptions and images, the soul is the only source and cause for them. How is it possible then that the images and perceptions of different souls fit each other and seem to represent one external world seen from different points of view? In his explanation, Leibniz introduces the notion of *preestablished harmony.* God has created the souls with such perfection that from the very beginning all their perceptions and images correspond to one another. Also God himself is in harmony with this world. However he always perceives everything distinctly and clearly and does not need to rely on our space–time conceptualization.

Leibniz's system can be regarded as the translation of an atomistic model of the material world (similar to that proposed by Democritus) into the scientific and philosophical domain that deals with living organisms and active minds. In contrast to Locke and Hume, Leibniz tried to find a synthesis between atomistic theories of matter and those of ideas. He regards the universe as composed of innumerable individual things that are indivisible and unextended but, at the same time, full of energy. These *monads* are vitalized atoms. Each has perceptions of the world and the potential for infinite developments. In its perfect actualization, the monad would perceive and understand the whole universe as God does.

Monads have eternal existence but change their internal states. The changes are directed toward perfection. Monads are found in different degrees of perfections. In air, water, and stone, their perceptions are feeble and obscure; they reveal themselves as chemical actions. In plants, monadic perceptions appear as vital energy. In animals, experiences are associatively operative. At the levels of the plants, the monad sleeps; in animals, it dreams; in man, it is awake. The higher the intellectual and energetic level of the monads, the more likely they appear as complex units. However, life lies in each individual monad. Thus, unlike Spinoza, Leibniz regards the universe as consisting of an infinite multitude of substances, not only of one.

Some of the most significant contributions of Leibniz lie outside of philosophy. Like Descartes and Pythagoras, he was a highly creative mathematician and elaborated, independently of Newton, the differential calculus. Like Descartes and Spinoza, he regarded mathematics as an ideal conceptual system that philosophy should follow and adopt. He objected, however, to Descartes's notions that errors are mostly introduced by false assumptions and that mathematical rigor should help to eliminate these errors. On the contrary, we may obtain greatest certainty in our conclusions if we continuously try to derive assumptions from more general theorems. Thus, Leibniz suggested an approach that only recently attracted appropriate interest among philosophers and scientists. This approach promotes the unification of logic and mathematics as well as the development of an applied logic similar to applied algebra. Leibniz went so far as to suggest that we should analyze and reduce all terms of the natural languages to some basic concepts, that we should develop a universal system of simple concepts, a *metalanguage* that would substitute for all natural language and would be of universal generality and precision.

Thus, Leibniz provided some of the most modern views about scientific and philosophical matters but also introduced numerous metaphysical speculations that are unacceptable from a modern perspective, for example, his theological justification of the imperfect state of the world, his proof for the existence of God, i.e., his theodicy, or his attempt to show that the present world as a creation of God is the best of all possible worlds. Nevertheless, even these contributions shed new light, and stimulated and supported a free intellectual attitude in a society that was still dominated by spiritual and scholastic concerns, that had deteriorated during centuries of political struggle and religious warfare, and that subordinated the people under ecclesiastic and secular powers who stripped them of their rights.

The Philosophy of Enlightenment—Generation IV

Leibniz's aims prepared the way for intellectual freedom and progress and are shared by the contributors to the philosophical movement known as Enlightenment. This movement can be regarded as the last step beyond Spinoza's pantheistic rationalism and Hume's nominalistic sensualism. Like the philosophy of the Sophists, it led to subjectivism, relativism, and materialism as much as it led to the removal of social and political biases. Two lines of thought can be distinguished within this movement, the French and the German schools of Englightenment.

At first, the German school closely followed Leibniz, whose philosophy was translated by Wolff (1679–1754) into plain, common sense rationalism. Other philosophers tried to derive a new rational basis for religion, law, the state, and social institutions. But opposition to their rationalism also began to emerge, leading to the rejection of theological orthodoxy, to a new emphasis on history, the equality of man, and intellectual tolerance. Two of the leaders, Reimarus (1694–1768) and Lessing

(1729–1781) proposed a religion of reason in which lawfulness and purpose, as recognized by the thinking individual, were its sole foundation, not irrational events such as miracles and revelations. By regarding the Christian faith as a developmental stage leading to universal religion, they were among the first to propose an historical analysis of Christianity and to reject Leibniz's idealistic notion of the best of all possible worlds. Reflecting the unceasing experience of warfare, hunger, hate, and intolerance, they developed rather pessimistic and skeptical views about the world.

In contrast to the German movement, French philosophers of the Enlightenment followed more radical lines. Their philosophy and social theories directly supported and prepared the way for the French Revolution. They were strongly influenced by the English sensualists rather than by Spinoza and Leibniz. They firmly believed in the power of the human intellect and in scientific progress demonstrated by the many discoveries during the second half of the 18th century. Among these philosophers, Condillac (1715–1780), Lamettrie (1709–1751), Helvetius (1715–1771), and Holbach (1723–1789) fostered extreme forms of sensualism, materialism, and mechanism, by means of which they tried to reduce all processes of the mind and consciousness to activities in the nerve and brain cells. While these notions were consistent with Descartes's philosophy of the *res extensa,* the introduction of Locke's philosophy into French intellectual circles by Voltaire (1694–1778) accelerated this development further.

Voltaire, the fighter for intellectual tolerance and social justice, remained closely linked with a life-style that originated at the court of Louis XIV and that accepted a disregard for the powerless and uneducated masses. The demand for social justice and equality was more forcefully expressed in Montesquieu's (1689–1755) rejection of the monarchy as a God-given institution and in his insistence on the separation of the legislative and executive functions of the state. The most powerful proponent of these ideas was, however, Rousseau (1712–1778), who, in following Locke, regarded the state as a contract between individuals that, thus, may be abandoned if this institution begins to function to the disadvantage of some of its participating members. A striving for equality and tolerance was reflected also in his analysis of educational principles: Education ought to be governed by the idea that the original and natural state of the child (as well as that of "primitive" people) is peaceful, harmonic, and innocent. These conditions ought to be the goal toward which reason should guide us. This romantic idealization did not prevent Rousseau from condemning those powers that have led us astray, the powers of the political and religious establishments. They have created the social institutions that are the main cause for the inequality of people and the resulting social injustice. Subsequently, Rousseau came to regard the creation of a new state as an educational question rather than an organizational one.

CONCLUSION

The history of knowledge does not end with the Sophists nor with the philosophers of the Englightenment. To many, the history of philosophy seems only to begin at these points in time. The stage is prepared for the synthesizing, dualistic system of the classical periods, for the philosophies of Plato and Aristotle, on the one hand, and of Kant and Hegel, on the other. These philosophers, in turn, set the stage for the diversification not only of knowledge but of education and social arrangements as well. Although I will not discuss these developments in detail, at least three implications have already been emphasized in some of the preceding sections.

First, in astounding similarity, two of the classical philosophers, Aristotle and Hegel, attained profound influence upon divergent cultural developments. Aristotle's philosophy was sanctioned as the theory of knowledge in Christian theology during the time of Scholasticism. Scholasticism, as shown in chapter 6, provided a blueprint for modern European philosophy. Similarly, Hegel's dialectical idealism not only served as a blueprint but in its left-wing extension by Feuerbach, Marx, Engels, and Lenin became the accepted dogma for the new cultural conception of the individiual, society, and their development elaborated in the philosophy of the Soviet Union.

Second, after the great synthesizing systems had been proposed, philosophy shifted toward specialization and eclecticism. Thus, selective emphasis was given to ethics, aesthetics, epistemology, or logic. In chapter 8 I traced these contributions to the elaboration of the concepts of structure and transformation in modern European philosophy.

Third, also during the postclassical periods, various scientific disciplines divorced themselves from philosophy. With psychology as the focus of our attention, I elaborate in chapter 11 a structural analysis of the history of experimental psychology. The conceptual model and treatment of the material will be closely similar to the present analysis of the history of philosophy and, therefore, supplements closely my present efforts.

Structural Analysis of the History of Experimental Psychology

Although one could extensively debate the origin of modern psychology, we will settle this question quickly by deciding that psychology began with G. T. Fechner (1801–1887). Undoubtedly, due recognition has to be given to J. F. Herbart (1776–1841) and his quixotic attempt to refute Kant's dim views about psychology by proposing a "Psychology as Science, Newly Founded on Experience, Metaphysics and Mathematics." What is so attractive about Fechner is his deeply felt striving for a synthesis between a naturalistic–physicalistic approach to psychology and his engagement in mentalistic–spiritualistic explorations.

FECHNER—GENERATION I

Fechner was a physicist by training. He published also, under the pseudonym of Dr. Mises, on such topics as *Life after Death, The Souls of Plants,* and *Proof That the Moon Consists of Iodine.* There is, now, increasing agreement (see Marshall, 1969; Woodward, 1972) that these spiritualistic–satyric essays are more than eccentric trips but characterize the other side or the antithesis of knowledge, which throughout his life Fechner tried to integrate with the natural science approach for which he had gained considerable renown.

Historically, the synthesis can be pinpointed with disturbing precision. While still recovering from a "breakdown" that had paralyzed his intellectual activities in 1840, he envisioned the synthesis while lying in his bed on October 22, 1850. The following years saw a burst of activity; he executed a comprehensive program of research, elaborating in detail a methodology for study, that led to the publication of his *Elements of Psychophysics* in 1860.

His vision entailed the synthesis between scientific observations along physical dimensions, as already explored by E. H. Weber (1795–1878), and the apprehension of mental units, sensations. Later critics have maintained that Fechner merely continued to measure physical stimuli but, beyond Weber, introduced some rather questionable assumptions for equating these measurements with mental units. Nevertheless, this turn provided a basis strong enough to generate an extensive body of research that, in large part, still remains fundamental for our present understanding of the functioning of the sensory-perceptual systems.

While Fechner contributed much to establish this body of knowledge, he was soon overshadowed by such scientific giants as H. von Helmholtz (1821–1894) and, to a lesser extent, E. Hering (1834–1918). Von Helmholtz, a surgeon by training, became only tertiarily affiliated with psychology. His main contributions lie in anatomy–physiology and in physics. In his psychology, he resembled Fechner closely although, like his counterpart, E. Hering, he shifted the emphasis of investigations toward physiology. It is for this reason that I do not assign an independent slot to him in my analysis of the history of psychology but consider his contributions as systematic and ingenious extensions of the foundation laid by Fechner.

During his later years, Fechner reemphasized his mentalistic roots by aiming toward a scientific study of aesthetics. These efforts did not find the same recognition as his seminal work in psychophysics. It is only recently that psychologists have begun to appreciate these contributions (Berlyne, 1971).

In summary, we can distinguish three periods in Fechner's scientific career. During the first he felt and expressed a profound conflict between the natural science approach and mentalistic–spiritualistic inquiries. During the second period, for which he gained exclusive acclaim in the history of psychology, he proposed his synthesis of psychophysics and engaged in extensive research and methodological explorations. During the third period he shifted toward the study of aesthetics but received due recognition neither from his contemporaries nor from several generations of younger psychologists. Fechner was not the only psychologist whose work became one-sidedly interpreted by future generations. In his case, exclusive attention was given to the middle years of his active academic life, i.e., to the period between 1850 and 1870.

WUNDT—GENERATION II A

The second generation of psychologists is characterized by professionalization, institutionalization, and systematizations, on the one hand, and by the reestablishment of philosophical ties, on the other. While both of these tendencies are characteristic for W. Wundt (1832–1920), the second is specifically represented by his antagonist, F. von Brentano (1838–1917). Although the conceptual separation had not been dramatized by these two opponents themselves but rather by their students and followers, this split had far-reaching consequences upon the further development of psychology. It has been described as the split between the content and the act of experience (Boring, 1957). More specifically, Wundt was concerned with sensory-perceptual phenomena, whereas Brentano emphasized processes and operations not only of perceiving but of judging, thinking, feeling, and believing as well.

Historians of psychology have given predominant attention to the contributions by Wundt and his many students. This selective emphasis is understandable because Brentano did little for the establishment of psychology as a profession and science. Few experimental studies were done under his direction and psychology began to slip back into philosophical discussions. Nevertheless, his impact upon psychology was strong, primarily, through the work of his students and associates.

In contrast to Brentano, who was a deeply religious and committed man, Wundt has often been characterized as somewhat narrow-minded, stubborn, and without personal warmth. Recently, several scholars have questioned such descriptions (Blumenthal, 1970; Balance, 1973; Bringmann, 1973). Wundt promoted very broad and universal conceptions. He was the first to systematize the field and to give psychology not only a distinct place among the sciences but also to institutionalize it through the arrangement of a laboratory, conventions, professional organizations, publications, journals, etc. In all these efforts he was as much a psychophysicist as he was a physiologist, anthropologist, sociologist, linguist, and philosopher. Historians of psychology, for example Boring (1957), have attended only to his role as an experimental psychologist who followed rather closely the leads of Fechner and von Helmholtz (under whose supervision he found his first appointment). But, as for Fechner, though not as dramatically, Wundt's professional career reveals shifts in emphasis of which only the first period, between 1870 and 1890, has received focused attention.

The first period characterizes Wundt as an elementalist who initiated numerous studies mainly on visual and auditory perception, searching for mental atoms that he came to call sensations, images, and simple feelings.

Although during the second half of this period, Wundt began extensive writings in logic and ethics, historians found it more appropriate to regard the early parts of this period as the most decisive ones in Wundt's career. While such an interpretation fitted well the dominant patterns of historical description, Wundt himself quickly moved away from these early viewpoints toward explorations of internal states of the organism as well as toward studies of language, customs, and culture and toward ethnopsychology (see Riegel, 1975a).

WÜRZBURG SCHOOL—GENERATION IIIB

Wundt's first period of elementalism began to be more forcefully executed in the United States through one of his staunchest followers, E. B. Titchener (1867–1927), and less clearly, by one of his first students and first assistants, J. McK. Cattell (1860–1944). The selective interpretation of Wundt as an elementalist seems to have also originated through Titchener's influence upon one of the most prominent historians of psychology, E. G. Boring.

Wundt had already become engaged in exploring internal states of the organism during his first intellectual period. Apperceptions were considered as occurring when sensations were evoked either in states of attention or, alternatively, when accompanied by feelings. The latter viewpoint was more closely related to his earlier work and led him to propose a system of elements of feelings, simple feelings. This theory is closely congruent with Osgood's distinction of three basic dimensions of connotative meaning, evaluation, potency, and activity (Osgood, Suci, and Tannenbaum, 1957). Experimentally, this interest was not carried much further by the third generation of psychologists and was only revived by the work on motivational and social influences on perception leading to the so-called New Look in psychology during the early 1950s.

Wundt's alternate proposal of regarding apperception as occurring in states of attention found some immediate appraisal, though not approval, in the work of the Würzburg school founded by Wundt's second assistant, O. Külpe (1862–1915). During his studies and work with Wundt at Leipzig, Külpe was one of the staunchest proponents of elementalism and rigorous experimentation. As soon as he had accepted the chair at Würzburg, however, he became committed to the study of thought processes, which thus far had evaded the scrutiny of the Leipzig laboratory. Külpe's own work and that of his students and associates (Mayer, Orth, Marbe, Watt,

Ach, Messer, and Bühler) soon brought him into conflict with Wundt. Even more extensively than his teacher, he began to explore the internal conditions of subjects, liberally using introspective methodology. This led to the well-known explorations of unconscious attitudes, task, sets, determining tendencies, or, in German, *Aufgabe* and *Einstellung.* In addition to methodological differences, scholars at Würzburg disagreed with Wundt on his additivity assumption, according to which sensations plus feelings would account for apperception. In contrast to Wundt's position (which was also promoted in Holland by Donders's work on psychomotor reactions and performances), the research at Würzburg led to the conclusion of the nonadditive nature of these intervening conditions.

While, thus, Wundt's interest during his second intellectual period found expression, though not approval, at Würzburg, there still remains another of his major preoccupations. During the later decades of his life, Wundt became strongly committed to the study of culture, customs, habits, and last but not least, language. The analysis of the "objectified" products of the human mind, Wundt proposed, should serve as a second route for scientific psychology, the first being that of experimentation. Although Wundt devoted not less than ten large volumes to this topic, two of which dealt with language, his work was not appreciated by contemporary and successive generations of psychologists. Only one of his late students, the successor to his chair in Leipzig, F. Krüger (1874–1948), carried these ideas further.

Krüger's interest in ethnopsychology is not so much revealed by his early cooperation with C. Spearman, resulting in their joint exploration of structural methodology (1907), as in his attempt to cast structural interpretations into a framework of developmental interactions both in the individual and society. Like the ethnopsychological interpretations of his teacher, Krüger's work did not receive any appreciable recognition. Only during the most recent years have these topics entered into the consideration of a few developmental psychologists and sociologists (see chaps. 2 and 5).

EBBINGHAUS—GENERATION IIIA

During the first period of his career, Wundt aimed at detecting a set of basic psychological elements. This interest continued during the second period with the emphasis, now, shifted from sensations and images to simple feelings. After these elements were firmly established, it was argued, complex phenomena of perception, cognition, and thought could be explored. The necessary bonds between the elements were to be furnished by associations. While students in Wundt's laboratory devoted most of their efforts to this analytical task, they were rarely able to venture beyond these elements in order to study the laws of association, the formation of percepts, concepts, and thoughts. These explorations remained a goal rather than feasible and concrete achievements.

Given these circumstances, it is not surprising that the publication of Ebbinghaus's work on memory (1885) was immediately hailed as a major breakthrough. With the stroke of a genius, Ebbinghaus (1850–1909) bypassed the tedious analytical work of finding the basic elements; he simply invented the elements, his infamous nonsense syllable, and was now able to study the "laws" by which these elements would combine.

Almost single-handedly, Ebbinghaus explored many of the major issues that are still of concern to students of human learning and memory. Although he had not been directly influenced by Wundt, his work supplemented and extended the former achievements so clearly that, justifiably, we can list him as a direct intellectual descendant of Wundt. In comparison to the scholars at Würzburg, he carried the elementalism and associationism of the early Wundt to great perfection and to a greater extreme. Thus I have placed him toward the outer fringe of our diagram. The work at Würzburg proceeded in opposition to Wundt and established close ties with various intellectual descendants of Wundt's major opponent, F. von Brentano.

BEHAVIORISM—GENERATION IVA

Ebbinghaus's work was to be surpassed by the behaviorists' movement, initiated and popularized by J. B. Watson (1878–1958). Introspectionism was well controlled in Wundt's laboratory and consisted essentially in yes–no or larger–smaller judgments. Its control was much weaker in the Würzurg laboratory, and Watson rejected it vehemently. But as methodological rigor was increased by the behaviorists, their epistemological sophistication regressed to naive realism of the pre-Lockian period. Indeed, nothing else was accepted but the reality of the physical stimulus and the physical response. No attention was given to the sensory and phenomenological basis of knowledge. Knowledge itself was, thus, stripped of its critical character and replaced by a blind faith in a world of things and movements. As methodological rigor (M) grows, epistemological rigor (E) declines; one can do well only one of the two at the same time. In a formula: $M + E = \text{constant}$.

In view of these limitations it is justifiable to place behaviorism at the lower end of my chart. Behaviorism carried the associationism of Ebbinghaus and the elementism of Wundt to their extremes. In particular, we locked behaviorism into the time period from 1910 to 1930. Its impact lasted, of course, much longer and behaviorism came to dominate most of the major psychological developments, at least in the United States.

BRENTANO—GENERATION IIB

Wundt did not regard psychological elements as particle substances but rather as smallest energetic units. The notion of activity and processes was more firmly expressed by F. von Brentano (1838–1917). Linked to the philosophy of Leibniz and Berkeley, his psychology precluded the rigorous application of experimental procedures. Instead, Brentano supported an open-minded empiricism, introspection, and inquiries by means of discussion and argumentation. He criticized Wundt and most of the other psychologists for investigating the objectified content of experience, such as colors, sounds, smells, and tastes, but not the psychic process of sensing, judging, thinking, etc. The latter, however, are the necessary psychological foundations, and in turn, lead to the recognition and discrimination of the content of experience.

Brentano taught in Würzburg and Vienna but did not form a coherent group of followers. Nevertheless, some of his students attained influential positions and determined decisively the future course of psychology.

One of these students, C. Stumpf (1848–1936), was eventually appointed to the chair of psychology in Berlin. In promoting a phenomenological approach, for example, in his studies of music, he became a well-known antagonist not only to Wundt but also to Helmholtz and their analytical explorations of sounds and music.

While in Berlin, Stumpf was the teacher of Köhler and Koffka and earlier (as was Brentano) of E. Husserl (1859–1938). Husserl, in turn, founded philosophical phenomenology, a movement that both his teachers, Stumpf and Brentano, had well prepared. Together with the historian W. Windelband, Husserl exerted considerable influence upon the philosophers and psychologists W. Dilthey and E. Spranger. The first is known for his contrastive comparisons of nomothetic and idiographic sciences, of explaining and understanding (see chap. 4); the second, for his phenomenological interpretation of development (see chap. 7). Husserl also influenced the existential philosophers M. Heidegger and J.-P. Sartre.

The phenomenological emphasis in the psychology of Brentano and

Stumpf revitalized some earlier trends, most notably expressed in the arguments about color perception by Goethe, Purkinje, and Hering in opposition to Newton, Young, and Helmholtz. The notion of exploring psychic conditions and processes as they appear to the unadulterated mind of the keen observer, rather than studying psychic phenomena by breaking them into component and, thus, abstract parts, became most influential in Gestalt psychology. Before these Gestalt psychologists adopted their outspoken stance, however, two intermediary positions made themselves felt and known.

FUNCTIONALISM—GENERATION IIIC

In his criticism of the analytical psychology of (the early) Wundt, Stumpf received support from W. James (1842–1910), whom Boring considers one of the founders of functionalism. The term *functionalism* was used by Titchener (1898) to elucidate his own type of psychology, structuralism, rather than to point at a distinct group of scholars, a set of ideas, or a conception of the psyche (see chap. 8). Titchener's distinction draws upon medicine. Subsequently, his own structuralism might best be compared with anatomy and functionalism with physiology. From modern viewpoints, however, Titchener's own work lacks some of the main features of structuralism, namely, an emphasis upon organization and totality. In comparison, the Austrian school as well as Gestalt psychology promoted the concept of structure much more forcefully and radically than Titchener. He, indeed, represents best the systematic atomism (or anatomism) initiated by Fechner and the early Wundt.

Functionalism in psychology, to which Titchener in his opposition contributed more delineating clarity than most of its participating members, is said to include scholars such as W. James, J. Dewey, J. R. Angell, H. A. Carr, G. S. Hall, J. M. Baldwin, and J. McK. Cattell. All of them share a dislike for the academic, scientific atomism of the early Wundt. It is much harder, however, to state in positive terms what concepts and ideas all of them embraced. In contrast to the laboratory psychology, they promoted a healthy concern for the adaptation and changes of the real individual in the real world. Subsequently, many of them are concerned about the process of education. Some of them showed a distinct dislike for experimentation. However, Boring insists that the functionalists' movement prepared the way for behaviorism, which also was concerned with the concrete changes in organisms (even though this concern soon degenerated to the study of the white rat in the laboratory maze). Although several functionalists received their training in Wundt's laboratory, i.e., F. Angell, G. S. Hall, and J. McK. Cattell, most functionalists preferred a phenomenological rather than an analytic approach to psychology. This preference relates them to Brentano and Stumpf. The students of Wundt became known for their attempts to introduce individual variation into the laboratory situation, which until then dealt with the ideal subject under ideal conditions.

All in all, functionalism left multifarious marks upon psychology. In part, it redirected the scientific efforts toward philosophy (as was also the case for Brentano and Stumpf); in part, it emphasized education and social considerations; in part, it prepared the way for behaviorism by criticizing the introspective atomism of academic psychology.

AUSTRIAN SCHOOL—GENERATION IIID

The act psychology of Brentano and the phenomenology of Stumpf hardly influenced functionalism. The influence of these two men was established in two further steps leading to the Austrian school and ultimately to Gestalt psychology. Already some supporters of Wundt's early psychology, for example, E. Mach (1838–1916), had questioned the concept of psychic elements. Thus, Mach would contemplate how small a sensation would have to be in order to be conceived as singular. Unhesitatingly, he proposed that there might well be sensations of triangularity, circularity, etc. Although it was regarded as one of the main tasks in the early laboratories to determine, for instance, how closely two points of stimulation could be brought together until they would be experienced as unitary, Mach's proposition raised the fundamentally different question of organizational relationships among those stimuli. Organizational properties could not possibly be explained by the summation of an array of stimuli unless either their interrelationships were preserved externally (and, thus, added into the stimulus condition); or one assumed that the perceiver himself would impose these organizational aspects upon the world (see chap. 8).

The psychologists of the Austrian school, such as E. Mach, A. Meinong, H. Cornelius, S. Witasek, V. Benussi, and C. von Ehrenfels, took varying positions in regard to this question. In general, they tried to compromise by retaining whatever they felt was good from the laboratory of the early Wundt and adding to it new components that would account for the organizational as well as transformational aspects. Among the various members of this informal group, C. von Ehrenfels (1859–1932), a student of von Brentano, became most influential. While some of his colleagues engaged in conceptual distinctions between such entities as founding content (the basic elements) and founded content (the organizational attribute), he proposed two basic observations that were to become known as the first two "laws" of Gestalt: (1) that such a pattern represents more than the sum of its parts; and (2) that it is possible to transpose all parts in a lawful manner without destroying the pattern.

GESTALT PSYCHOLOGY—GENERATION IVB

It remained the task of von Ehrenfels's student, M. Wertheimer (1880–1943) in cooperation with W. Köhler (1887–1965) and K. Koffka (1886–1941) (both students of Stumpf), to elaborate the concept of Gestalt to its full strength (and ambiguity). Whereas members of the Austrian school still searched for accommodations with the dominant elementalism of the late 19th century, Gestalt psychologists rejected this attempt by placing the Gestalt ahead and atop of its component parts and by questioning the psychological usefulness of breaking up such a pattern in the first place.

Like Brentano, Gestalt psychologists opted for a phenomenological approach that led them to accept all concrete experiences, including imaginations and dreams, as the only real basis for psychological inquiries. To speak of illusions is possible only if one has developed some other means, such as those of physics, by which one recognizes discrepant results. What matters originally and basically, however, are the experiences as they occur in the form of the immediate impressions upon the observer.

Following earlier arguments, for instance, by Kant, Gestalt psychologists had to decide where to place the focus of organization. Again in a radical turn, Köler proposed that these patterns are to be found in the real organization of the physical world. These outer patterns would then be transformed within the sense organs and within the nervous systems until they are to be found in equally real patterns of cortical exitation. Although Köhler was never able to demonstrate the "real isomorphism" of outer and inner gestalts, his interpretation resembles in certain ways that of the other contemporary radical movement, behaviorism. In both cases, the intervening and/or introspecting individual is successfully eliminated. Behaviorists study physical stimulations and physical movements of the organism. Gestalt psychologists study physical patterns in the outer world and their inner physical representation in the nervous system. Later critics were justified in saying that the "Gestalter was left out of the Gestalt analysis."

While Köhler's point of view was not shared by all Gestalt psychologists, it sheds light upon the competitive movements, especially upon the Würzburg school. Here the organization was sought in the state of the mind or in the personality of the introspecting observer rather than in outer nature; it was the subject's contribution to the sensory input received. These contributions could, at least in part, explain the organization of perception and other psychological processes.

In deviation from Köhler's preference for real-isomorphism, other scholars of the Gestalt movement explored conditions that could not be located in outer or inner physical configurations. Gestalt psychologists contributed successfully to the study of nonphysical conditions of personality and social organization. Goldstein applied the concept of Gestalt to the study of personality; personality too was seen as being more than the sum of its parts, e.g., traits or skills. Lewin extended the Gestalt concept to social psychology and, it is appropriate to say, Werner to developmental psychology.

COMPARATIVE ASSESSMENT

In the present chapter I have tried to delineate the historical progression of experimental psychology in terms of a branching tree diagram (see chaps. 4 and 5). I started with Fechner, who in his psychophysics synthesized the natural science ideal of experimentation and theorizing with spiritualistic and mentalistic views of the soul and the mind. The second generation of psychologists revealed a split between the analytical approach of the early Wundt, on the one hand, aiming at the detection of a system of psychic elements and focusing upon the content of perception, and on the other, the synthesizing phenomenological approach by von Brentano, aiming at the exploration of the acts of perceiving, judging, and feeling rather than the content of these activities.

The dichotomy of the second generation was kept alive and led to further subdivisions within the third generation. Among Wundt's followers the psychologists at Würzburg analyzed the internal states of the perceiving or performing individual and, thereby, approached the study of those internal processes that, according to Brentano, Wundt had neglected in his analytical work. On the other hand, Ebbinghaus and students of verbal learning completed the task outlined by Wundt by exploring the laws under which elements are combined or associated and, in particular, acquired, stored, and retrieved. Thus, Ebbinghaus too was concerned with clarification of the inner working of the mind, for which Brentano had asked without providing the necessary tools or means for systematic explorations. Both the Würzburg psychologists and students of human learning remained, however, much more analytical in their approach than those influenced by Brentano.

The generation of psychologists following Brentano had only indirect connections with him. This holds true especially for the American functionalists who promoted the exploration of concrete adaptations in real life and thus were interested in learning, development, education, and social processes. They relate to Brentano via the middleman, C. Stumpf, and through their shared opposition to the introspective, academic psychology of Wundt, which in America was represented by the structuralism of Titchener. The other group of psychologists decending from Brentano, the Austrian school, had much closer connections with him, especially through their main spokesman, von Ehrenfels. The Austrian psychologists prepared the way for Gestalt psychology with which they shared (as they shared with Brentano) a phenomenological orientation. Since, unlike the functionalists, they devoted their attention to perceptual processes, they maintained an active interest in Wundt's studies and especially those of his former disciples, O. Külpe and the Würzburg psychologists.

In crosscomparisons of the descendants of Wundt and Brentano, both the functionalists and the followers of Ebbinghaus were concerned with learning and concrete achievements rather than with epistemological and experiential-perceptual problems. It is, therefore, not surprising that both groups related to one of the most powerful movements of the fourth generation, to behaviorism, whereas the Austrian psychologists and those at Würzburg related to the other major movement at the fourth generation, to Gestalt psychology. In within-comparisons, both the functionalists and the Austrian psychologists share Brentano's emphasis upon psychic processes (rather than the content of experience) and his phenomenological approach, whereas the generation of psychologists, following Wundt, i.e., the Würzburg psychologists and Ebbinghaus, remained committed to an analytical approach and laboratory investigations.

The two groups of the fourth generation of psychologists relate to each of the two extreme positions attained at the third generation, i.e., the Gestalt psychologists to the Austrian school and the behaviorists to Ebbinghaus. In a crosslinking manner, the Gestalt psychologists also relate to Würzburg and the behaviorists to the functionalists. Both the Gestalt psychologists and behaviorists are joined in their opposition against the introspectionism and mentalism of both Wundt and Brentano. Thereby they

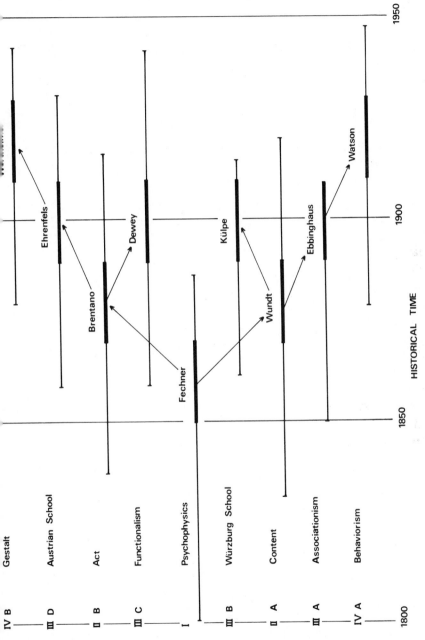

Figure 14. Temporal interrelationships of major figures in experimental psychology.

promoted physicalistic viewpoints, the behaviorists studying the relationship between physical stimuli and physical movements of the organism and the Gestalt psychologists the isomorphism between physical patterns in the outer world and in the activity patterns of the cortex. Both differed, of course, in their preference for either analytical–elementalistic or phenomenological–organizational descriptions.

Both behaviorism and Gestalt psychology influenced significantly the development of psychology during the following decades. The behaviorists dominated almost single-handedly the experimental work in the United States. The Gestalt psychologists did not gain a direct influence of similar strength. However, they contributed profoundly to the spread of psychology within other areas of psychological inquiry. They exerted a strong impact upon the theorizing and study of personality, development, social behavior, and thought processes. Thus, they shared various node points of other historical structural progressions that were emerging in psychology. Instead of turning our attention to approaches lying intermittently between the extremes of behaviorism and Gestalt psychology, I conclude my discussion with a few comments on the crosslinkage of various structural progressions that could be derived if one were to depict the history of subdisciplines in the behavioral and social sciences other than that of experimental psychology.

CONCLUSIONS

Figure 14 represents only one topic in the history of psychology, i.e., traditional, experimental psychology. The schema is equally well suited, however, for describing the early developments in other areas, for example, those discussed in chapters 7 and 13. As these fields of inquiry mature, various alternate pathways become recognizable. In trying to identify these pathways, we were faced with the following problems: (1) Famous psychologists, e.g., Fechner and Wundt, became recognized only for selective contributions but not for topics to which they themselves attributed great significance. (2) Various crosslinking connections were observed that relate, for instance, Wundt's influence to both groups of the generation immediately following him, i.e., the Würzburg school and Ebbinghaus, as well as to others, not directly connected with him, i.e., the functionalists. (3) Some of the direct descendants revealed their connections primarily through their opposition to some ideas of their predecessors, i.e., the Würzburg psychologists to Wundt; others had no direct connections, i.e., Ebbinghaus to Wundt, but nevertheless follow their predecessor closely in spirit. (4) Some ideas promoted by representatives of a particular generation, e.g., the Gestalt psychologists, had a more significant effect upon movements lying outside the topic of our analysis and diagram, e.g., personality, social, and developmental psychology. (5) The contributions by some psychologists received delayed recognition and are not represented in our diagram, e.g., Fechner's work in aesthetics, Wundt's work in psycholinguistics.

All these qualifying statements make us aware that my structural description as well as its diagrammatical representation have described a subsection of the history of psychology only. It would be desirable to prepare complementary reports in which the history of other subareas of psychology would be analyzed, e.g., of psycholinguistics, personality theory and research, developmental psychology, social psychology, etc. The procedure, I maintain, could be of the same systematic structural type as the present one. In such analyses, many other scholars, presently not mentioned, will have to be considered and relations to outside disciplines will have to be explored.

Once such descriptions have been completed, some outstanding scholars will appear as node points or knots in several of these networks. They are the persons through which the various structures become interconnected. Eventually, the history of the behavioral and social sciences would be represented by a complex system of such structures, not all of which originate at the same historical time: some progress at faster rates of differentiation than others, some are intertwined with other substructures, and some develop in relative isolation.

Of course, the structural system that I am proposing is not realizable at the present time. It characterizes the temporal interrelations between the histories of various subdisciplines. Its presentation may also renew some doubts about the promotion of schematic overgeneralizations at the expense of concrete differentiations. But it has not been my intention, of course, to claim that the few aspects presented in this essay and represented by the scholars named in the schema of Figure 14, would sufficiently characterize the history of the behavioral and social sciences. Many others inside and outside our disciplines need to be considered. If we could handle all these topics, the description of several historical structures in conjunction will allow us to generate a powerful transformational system that does more justice to the multiplicity of ideas expressed. Undoubtedly, such a system cannot be condensed into a two-dimensional display but represents a multidimensional transformational matrix, the fabric of historical changes.

PART III

Research Reports

CHAPTER 12

Structural Analysis of the History of the Department of Psychology at the University of Michigan

Although scientific psychology has existed in the United States for almost a century, a comprehensive and detailed treatise on its historical development has not yet been written. In particular, reports on the history of the various departments of psychology are either nonexistent or inaccessible. The following study proposes a methodology that will enable any interested person to generate parts of such information, and applies this methodology for a structural historical analysis of the Department of Psychology at the University of Michigan.

Some revealing records on the growth of university departments are those on dissertations and PhD committees. Such records, undoubtedly, characterize the overall activity of a department but, more important, the overlapping compositions of the PhD committees allow for an analysis of the organization of the department, of the various subgroups and their historical changes. An analysis of these records would be similar, though more complete than the Master–Pupil studies by Pledge (1947), Boring and Boring (1948), Wesley (1965), and Wesley and Hurtig (1970). Of course, dissertations are only a part of what departments are concerned with and not all that they produce. Moreover, the topic with which an individual candidate has been concerned in his dissertation, unfortunately, may not char-

The original article was published under the same title in Human Development, *1970, 13, 269–279.*

acterize the direction of his professional career. Despite these and other reservations, the data on the dissertation committees are most readily available at the record offices of universities and through commercial services such as University Microfilms, Ann Arbor, Michigan.

Explorations such as the present one might lead to the development of instructional routines that untrained assistants could apply for the treatment of the records, which then would be submitted for analysis to electronic computers. Once such instructions and programs are available, one might use them for an analysis of any department. Eventually, these data might be pooled and a data bank developed on the dissertational history of psychology in general, of any other area of science, or of any university. At the present time not all of these steps are completed. Therefore, in the following presentation we will have to rely on a technically less sophisticated analysis of our data.

THE PRODUCTION RECORDS OF THE DEPARTMENT

From an inspection of the detailed idiographic history of the Department of Psychology at the University of Michigan by Raphelson (1968), we learn that in 1901 Walter Pillsbury became the director of its psychological laboratory. He had come to Ann Arbor in 1897. His first PhD student was John Shepard, who took his degree in 1906. Until 1929 psychology remained a part of the Department of Philosophy. By the end of 1969 a total of 795 PhDs had been granted, including degrees in the joint programs of Social Psychology, and Education and Psychology. My analyses will be based on 636 PhD committees, omitting about 50% of the degrees in the two joint programs and 11 of the early PhDs, whose complete records were unavailable to me. The growth of the department on the basis of the dissertations can be accurately described by three linear equations shown in Figure 15.

The excellent fit between the numbers of degrees granted per five-year intervals and the numbers predicted on the basis of these equations is highly significant ($\chi^2 = 10.78$, $dF = 12$; $p > .50$). The first linear equation extends up to 1924, i.e., about the length of one full graduate education beyond the end of the First World War. The second linear equation has a markedly increased slope, and extends up to 1949, i.e., about the length of one full graduate education beyond the end of the Second World War. This

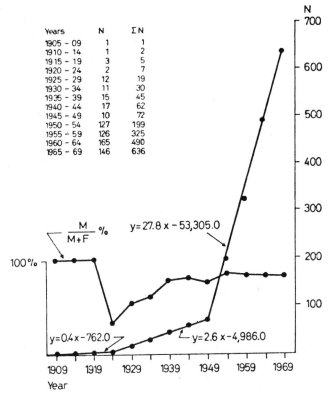

Years	N	ΣN
1905 – 09	1	1
1910 – 14	1	2
1915 – 19	3	5
1920 – 24	2	7
1925 – 29	12	19
1930 – 34	11	30
1935 – 39	15	45
1940 – 44	17	62
1945 – 49	10	72
1950 – 54	127	199
1955 – 59	126	325
1960 – 64	165	490
1965 – 69	146	636

Figure 15. Number of PhDs in psychology at the University of Michigan and sex-ratio (M/M&F %) as a function of historical time.

period might be called the emancipation or liberation period since unusually large percentages of PhDs were granted to women. During the first period no advanced degrees were given to female students. This period might be conceived of as the period of the patriarchs. The third linear equation, with a strong further increase in slope, extends up till 1970 and shows toward the end the only noticeable inconsistency, i.e., a decline in the numbers of degrees granted below the predicted values. Most likely, this deviation is caused by the present dropout of students and by lower admission quotas due to increased financial difficulties. During the third period, the number of degrees granted to women dropped below 20%. This observation, coupled with considerations of the enormous increase in size and the decline in structural distinctiveness, might justify calling this a period of identity confusion.

DISTRIBUTION OF COMMITTEE CHAIRMEN
AND MEMBERS

With the increase in the number of PhDs the staff of the department had to increase as well. The burden of the increased output has been placed upon a limited number of younger staff members. If we compute the number of participations in PhD committees over the number of active staff members in the department (i.e., those that served on more than 10 committees) we find a ratio of 0.84 per year for the first two periods. For the third period (after 1949), this ratio increases to 2.98 per year. These ratios vary greatly over time and between persons. At one extreme, we find Lowell Kelly, who served as chairman on 36 committees during a period of 21 years, and Ed Walker, who served as a member or chairman on 103 committees during a period of 20 years (not including those established by departments other than psychology), i.e., on the committee for about every sixth or seventh degree granted. At the other extreme, we find 40 persons serving only once as chairman and 198 serving only once on a committee (including many outside members from departments other than psychology). Altogether, there are 116 different chairmen for the 636 dissertations analyzed.

Figure 16 lists the persons who served as chairmen on 10 or more committees and presents a comparison between the number of staff members and the corresponding frequencies with which they served as chairmen of committees. (For further explanations, see note to Fig. 16.) When plotted on log-log paper, this comparison reveals a straight-line relationship and thus is open to the numerous interpretations suggested by Zipf (1949). Discussing the multiplicity of meanings of words, for instance, Zipf compared the selection of particular meanings with that of tools and their usages: There are a few universal tools (such as the monkey wrench of the bad mechanic) that are used for doing almost all jobs; on the other hand, there are many special tools (such as those of a desk calculator repairman) that are useful for very specific jobs only. Similarly, there are a few universalists who serve on many different committees and, thus, keep the department together; there are also many specialists (as well as younger staff members who have not yet become effective) who serve narrower functions. Both groups are necessary and important for the proper and effective functioning of a department.

As also shown in Figure 16, a similar Zipf-distribution was obtained when the number of different committee members (including the committee chairmen) was plotted against the frequencies with which they served on committees. Altogether there were 436 different staff members serving a total of 2,901 times on the committees.

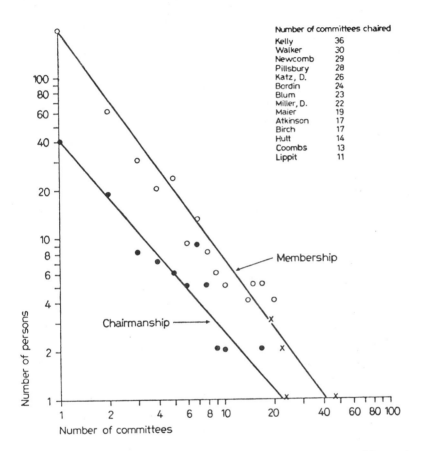

Number of committees chaired	
Kelly	36
Walker	30
Newcomb	29
Pillsbury	28
Katz, D.	26
Bordin	24
Blum	23
Miller, D.	22
Maier	19
Atkinson	17
Birch	17
Hutt	14
Coombs	13
Lippit	11

Figure 16. Logarithm of the number of persons plotted against the logarithm of the number of times these persons served as chairmen or members of PhD committees (X = averages over numbers of committees). Regarding chairmanships, Figure 16 should be read as follows: There are 40 persons who served only once as a chairman, 20 who served twice, 8 who served three times, etc. Crosses indicate averages. Thus, there is one person who served as chairman on 26.3 committees on the average. As shown in the list of Figure 16, there are actually 9 such persons who served as chairmen on 19 to 36 committees. Similar interpretations are to be derived for the distribution of memberships on dissertation committees.

STRUCTURAL CHANGES IN THE DEPARTMENT
OF PSYCHOLOGY

Staff members serving repeatedly on committees with one another are likely to share interests and orientations. Joint membership might be used to determine clusters within a department, and, subsequently, for studying their emergence and change over a period of time. Since the University of Michigan requires that each committee include one member outside of the department, the total list of committee members is rather long, i.e., 436 names, only a few of which interact often enough to be of interest for the present analysis. By selecting only those 64 persons who served on more than 10 committees, we focus upon the core members of the department but have to realize that membership in this group is also determined by age. Young staff members may not have had enough time to serve on many committees.

By pairing all 64 members with one another, we determined the number of times they served on the same committees. We then transformed the obtained numbers into distance measures and submitted the 64×64 matrix to Johnson's hierarchical cluster analysis (1967). Some of the results are summarized in Figure 17.

As the number of staff members in the department increased with historical time, the seven clusters delineated decreased in clarity. The first cluster emerges very strongly and early, representing the original members of the department led by its chairman, Professor Pillsbury. It persisted in an undiluted state for a considerable period of time. The last three clusters, on the other hand, are ambiguous and weakly defined. Here, most members are also connected with persons from several of the older clusters but, especially, with those staff members not included in the present analysis, i.e., those that served on fewer than 10 committees.

The cluster of the first nine members of the department is denoted as P. It lasted up to about 1950 with several members, notably Norman Maier and Carl Brown, overlapping with the second departmental generation (F'). At the second generation, three clusters can be distinguished. The first (F'A) includes the new chairman, Donald Marquis (since 1945), and seven other members, mainly in the areas of clinical psychology and personality research and methodology. At the same time, with the founding of the Institute for Social Research (in 1949), a cluster of six social psychologists emerges (F'B). The third cluster of the second departmental generation (F'C) includes five experimental psychologists with broad interests, i.e., in noncognitive variables and mathematical psychology.

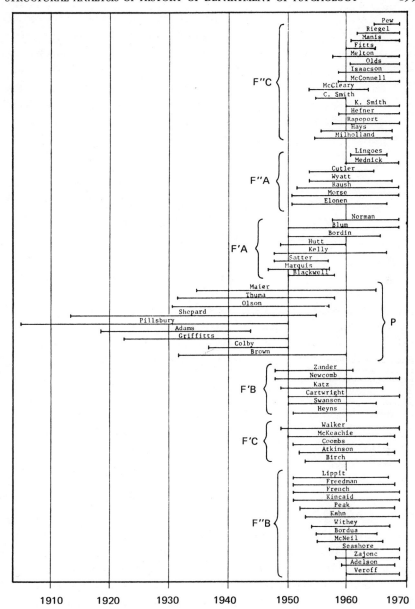

Figure 17. History of the Department of Psychology at the University of Michigan based on shared PhD committees and analyzed by Johnson's hierarchical cluster analysis (P = first, F′ = second, F″ = third departmental generations; F′A = experimental–clinical (core of new department), F′B = social–psychological I, F′C = experimental–personality, F″A = clinical–educational, F″B = social–psychological II, F″C = mathematical–physiological–experimental).

The separation of a third departmental generation (F″) from the second one is somewhat arbitrary. While most of its members became active participants in PhD committees during the sixties only, several of them overlap in time with staff members of the second departmental generation. This is especially true for the seven members of cluster F″A, representing clinical and educational psychologists, and for the 13 social psychologists of cluster F″B. The remaining cluster, F″C, is the youngest and includes a mixed group of methodologists, physiological psychologists, and persons interested in human performance and cognition.

INTERACTION BETWEEN THE AGING
OF THE DEPARTMENT AND THE AGE
OF ITS MEMBERS

The interaction between the growth of social organizations and the growth of individuals has only recently attracted sufficient attention among social and behavioral scientists, especially among psychological gerontologists (see Schaie, 1965; Riegel, 1965a; Baltes, 1968). While the conceptual and technical details of this topic cannot be discussed here, a general recognition of the problem is necessary and can be demonstrated on the basis of our data.

Although younger staff members were added over the years, the department, during its first period, aged mainly with the aging of its members. This statement pointedly suggests that the interests and activities in the department changed with historical time; however, these changes were primarily dependent upon the developments of the constituent staff members. With the appearance of the second and, especially, the third departmental generations, changes were primarily brought about through selective appointments. As groups of younger psychologists were hired, they actively pushed their older colleagues into the background, for instance, by considerably higher participation in PhD committees. This statement is congruent with the well-documented observation that with the accelerated growth of a scientific discipline, the span of effective participation of the scientists shrinks continuously and extends for present-day physicists over a period of less than five years (Price, 1961).

Shown in Figure 18 are the adjusted numbers with which members of the seven clusters participated in committees, plotted against the age span of active participation in committees. The scores had to be adjusted because each group included a different number of members, spread over different periods of time. The scores were adjusted to 100 man-years per group.

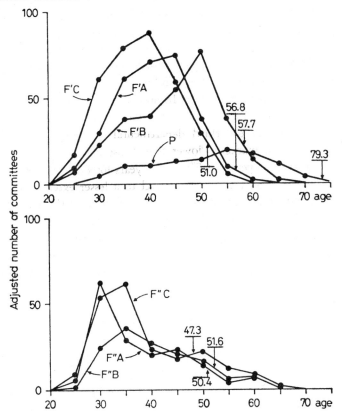

Figure 18. Adjusted number of committees served as a function of the age of the committee members from seven departmental clusters (see Figure 17). (The underlined numbers indicate the average age that members of these clusters have or would have attained in 1970.)

The activity of the first departmental generation were spread rather thinly over a period from 25 to 75 years with a peak at 55. The average participation of these staff members in PhD committees equaled only .84 per year. (This figure underestimates slightly the productivity of the first departmental generation because some incomplete records of this group had to be excluded from the computations). In sharp contrast, the members of the F'C cluster of the second departmental generation participate on the average in 3.37 committees per year with individual variations going up to 12 committees per year (Ed Walker in 1962). Their participation in committees excelled that of the first departmental generation (P) already early in their career, i.e., at an age of 25 years, and reached its preliminary peak at an age of 40 years. The members of the cluster F'A participated on the average in 2.70 committees per year and reached their peak at 45 years.

The members of the cluster $F'B$ participated on the average in 3.15 committees per year and reached their peak at 50 years.

Figure 18 makes it also apparent that the more recent clusters (in the order $F'C < F'A < F'B < P$) were composed of members with lower chronological ages. The average ages that had been or would have been attained at the year 1970 are listed in Figure 18 and increased in the expected order from 51.0 to 56.8 to 57.7 to 79.3 years. The present average ages attained within the clusters of the third departmental generation are lower yet, though they are not markedly lower than those of the second generation. They amount to 51.6 years for $F''B$, 50.4 years for $F''A$, and 47.3 years for $F''C$. Both the clusters $F''A$ and $F''C$ (and to a lesser extent $F''B$) attained peak productivity levels at younger ages than those of the second departmental generation, namely at 30 and 35 years, respectively. Only the future development of these groups (as well as that of the second departmental generation) will show whether they succeeded in pushing the productivity (in terms of PhDs) to still higher levels at still earlier ages.

CONCLUSIONS

The history of the Department of Psychology at the University of Michigan was analyzed by relying on the number of PhDs granted and on the changing compositions of the PhD committees. Beginning with the first PhD of 1906, there was a slow, linear increase in the number of PhDs until 1924. Thereafter the increase was much steeper, though still linear, with large proportions of women receiving their degrees. A still steeper linear increase occurred after 1949.

With the increase in the number of degrees granted, the departmental staff expanded. An analysis of the composition of the PhD committees allowed for the delineation of seven partially overlapping clusters. Although in recent years the subareas in psychology are less clearly distinguishable, definite shifts in focusing were noticed. These were introduced through selective hiring of staff members. During the earlier years changes in orientation of the department paralleled those that occurred during the life span of individual staff members.

The above data and methodology are not expected to provide definite answers to complex problems. Their presentation is mainly intended to open the discussion of interdepartmental and interuniversity projects for the analysis of such histories. Special emphasis has been given to technically simple and mechanized means for these comparisons.

CHAPTER 13

Cross-Reference Analysis of the History of Psychological Gerontology

This chapter will present a quantitative analysis of the history of psychological gerontology based upon the reconstructed flow of written information in reference networks. The large amount of wasted research efforts and the concurrent lack of investigations of significant issues leads us to question our concepts of research and theory, communication, and education, and more generally, our concept of the individual, society, and their development.

QUANTITATIVE ANALYSIS

With the exception of recent reports by Birren (1961) and Munnichs (1966) on psychological gerontology and those by Charles (1970), Groffmann (1970), and Reinert (1970) on life-span developmental psychology, there have been few systematic inquiries into the history of this discipline. Most reviews, textbooks, and handbooks provide, however, brief sections of historical reconstructions. Moreover, nearly complete listings of the publications have been prepared under Shock's supervision and have been published regularly in the *Journal of Gerontology*. The following analysis is based, in part, upon this bibliography.

The original article was prepared for the American Psychological Association Task Force on Aging and was submitted to the White House Conference on Aging, 1971. An extended version of this article has appeared under the title, "On the history of psychological gerontology," in C. Eisdorfer, and M. P. Lawton (Eds.), The psychology of adult development and aging, Washington, D.C.: American Psychological Association, 1973, pp. 37–68.

Method

The reference files of the present author on the literature of psychological gerontology prior to 1958 (Riegel, 1958b, 1959) were supplemented by adding all entries that appeared under the heading "Psychological Processes" in Shock's classified bibliography of gerontology (1951, 1957) or in the *Journal of Gerontology* up to the last issue of 1970. Attention was given to journal articles. Abstracts of proceedings and unpublished reports were eliminated as well as articles on selected topics, especially those dealing with the statistics of suicides, employment, financial support, and the pathology of aging. The overriding criteria for inclusion were the occurrence of such terms as "age," "aging," "adult development," etc. in the title of the article and/or publication in appropriate journals, such as *Journal of Gerontology, Geriatrics,* or *Gerontologist.*

In an attempt to sample some divergent topics from the contemporary field of psychological gerontology, only three recent publications were originally chosen as lead articles. It soon became evident, however, that even a complete retrieval of the citations originating from these three publications would go far beyond the scope of the present investigation and the means available to the investigator. For this reason, only the single article listed below was retained at the top node, that is, at the most recent point in the publication network from which the search would start (see Figure 19). It would be desirable, of course, to extend the search process to articles representing several other topics.

Blum, J. E., Jarvik, L. F., and Clark, E. T. Rate of change on selective tests of intelligence: A twenty-year longitudinal study of aging. *Journal of Gerontology,* 1970, *25,* 171–176.

The article by Blum, Jarvik, and Clark (1970) represents a top node point of a root structure going backward in historical time. In order to explore this structure, all the references made to earlier publications that met the criteria mentioned above were coded and transcribed onto the file card for the article by Blum *et al.* Notations to the node publication of the following generation were made on all the reference cards of the preceding (parental) generation. Some of the concepts used are demonstrated in Figure 19.

After the first generation of references was recorded on the file cards, each of the references became a new node point and the second generation of references was transcribed. This process was continued until the earliest period of retrievable references was reached, that is, the compounded period prior to 1919. Review articles, books, chapters in books, and dissertations

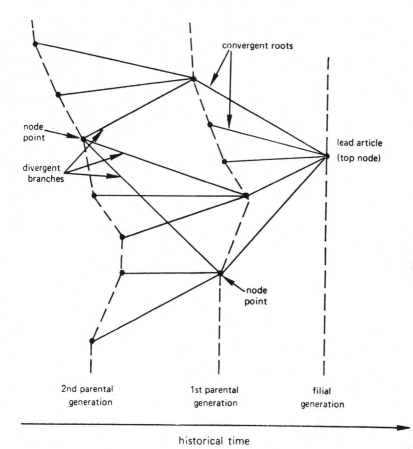

historical time

Figure 19. Subsection of reference network for the description of technical terms. (*Note:* The denotations "convergent" and "divergent" hold only when the progression is considered as moving from left to right, i.e., forward in historical time. In case of a retrospective analysis, the terms become "divergent roots" and "convergent branches." In other words, these denotations are dependent upon the interpretation applied.)

were listed only as terminal points in the retrieval system; that is, references made in them were not transcribed onto the cards; their own cards were retained in the file, however, and the source referring to them was recorded.

Results

A first and rather simple finding describes the increase in the number of publications in psychological gerontology with historical time. These data, plotted in averages for two-year intervals, are shown in Figure 20 and

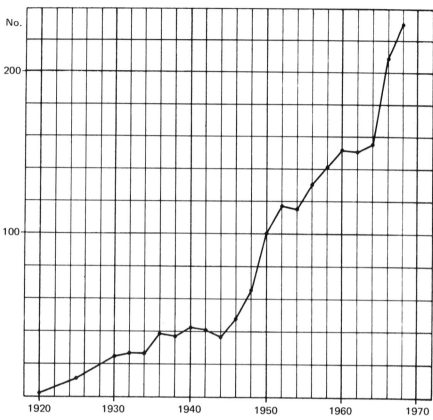

Figure 20. Number of publications per year in psychological gerontology.

Table 4. The period covered begins at the turn of the century. Some publications during the second half of the 19th century do exist along with others, spread unevenly over several preceding centuries. However, because of the small number involved, these references are not suitable for our analysis. Moreover, the approaches used in these publications differ markedly from our present-day orientation and are either medical, philosophical, thelogical, or belletristic in nature.

Beginning at the turn of this century and continuing until 1940 a steady increase in the number of publications occurred. During a short period thereafter, further acceleration was halted, but with the end of the Second World War there occurred a steep increase that has not yet faded away. In 1968, the last year for which (at the time of the analysis) a rather complete estimate of the number of publications can be obtained from Shock's listings, a total of 235 publications in psychological gerontology

Table 4. Number of Reference Cards, Number and Percentage of Cards Retrieved, and Number of Retrievals as a Function of Time

Year	Reference cards	Cards retrieved	Percentage of cards retrieved	Number of retrievals
1968–69	460	10	2.2	10
1966–67	418	14	3.4	22
1964–65	310	27	8.7	43
1962–63	299	49	16.4	104
1960–61	307	63	17.3	146
1958–59	282	91	32.3	261
1956–57	263	79	30.3	176
1954–55	230	62	27.0	187
1952–53	236	70	29.7	161
1950–51	200	47	23.5	155
1948–49	130	31	23.8	107
1946–47	94	28	29.8	79
1944–45	76	26	34.2	132
1942–43	82	22	26.8	60
1940–41	85	25	29.4	79
1938–39	76	19	25.0	29
1936–37	78	16	20.5	30
1934–35	58	11	19.0	36
1932–33	58	13	22.1	57
1930–31	55	11	20.0	32
1920–29	110	28	25.4	68
Before 1919	43	6	14.0	9
Total	4,310	738		1,983

were recorded that met the criteria for inclusion. The number of reference cards placed in the file totaled 4,310.

A second question concerns the percentages of items picked up through the retrieval analysis. Starting with only one lead article in 1970, we should expect a marked increase in percentages during the preceding decade. The farther we go back in time, however, the more likely it should become that several writers converge upon the same source. The detection of these key nodes and their sequential dependences represents one of the major goals of my analysis. Within the present corpus of data, the convergence upon a limited set of such node items implies that the expansion in the number of references retrieved by going backward in historical time is limited within distinct boundaries. After an initial burst in the number of items retrieved from the latest decade, these percentages attain a level of a steady state characteristic for the topic of the lead article at the top node of the retrieval system. In other words, we should not expect a continued increase in the number of references retrieved the farther we move back in time because not enough publications exist for the earlier periods to which an early author could refer and which would enter into the retrieval network under the criteria specified. As long as unrelated publications are excluded, the retrieval analysis should finally lead us to a few key papers representing the origin of psychological gerontology.

As shown in Figure 21 and Table 4, the whole decade of the 1960s represents the period during which our retrieval networks shows a rapid expansion. A total of 261 references are made to 91 of the 282 publications of the two-year period of 1958–1959; that is, many references are made to the same sources repeatedly. Fewer references are made to publications of the earlier years; that is, the curve is distantly skewed to the right. However, these findings and elaborations require some further modifications.

The shape of the curve shown in Figure 21 is dependent upon the citation habits of psychological gerontologists. For instance, we might expect that present-day behavioral scientists lack historical perspective and/or are forced by the editorial policies of some journals to make only a few and superficial references to closely related publications, most of which might precede the author's own publications only by a few years. In contrast, earlier behavioral scientists are often thought to have been familiar and concerned with large portions of the literature and to be inclined to explore these sources throughly and exhaustively. Consequently, the average citation span might be longer for early authors and might have shrunk with historical time. As a further consequence, the length of the survival period, the "half-life" of publications (Price, 1965), might have decreased with historical time. Thus, while much more is being produced than in former days, large proportions of our recent products are being disposed of after a short period of time. It is not unlikely then that a good deal of our efforts are being wasted and, at the same time, our channels of communication are being polluted.

A tentative answer to these issues can be obtained by computing the percentages of retrieved items per total items as a function of historical time. As shown in the upper section of Figure 21, these percentages fluctuate slightly around the overall average of 23% during the period from 1920–1960. Thus, our lead article of 1970 directs us toward less than one-fourth of the total literature in psychological gerontology. The study of retrievals originating from other lead articles would show whether additional portions of the unaccounted 77% of the literature will be brought into the retrieval system, or whether this portion represents publications that either

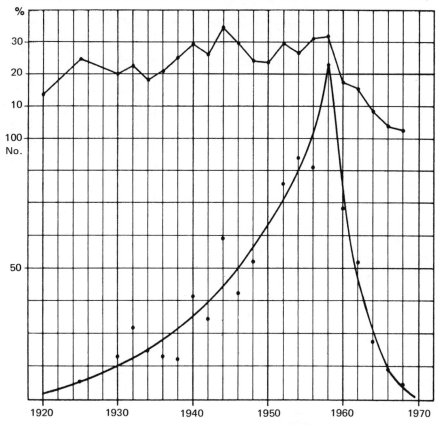

Figure 21. Number and percentage of publications retrieved from the reference file as a function of time (average numbers per year, not per 2-year periods as shown in Table 4).

never linked up with the mainstream of the reference network or did so for a short period of time only.

In order to analyze the present and past citation habits of psychological gerontologists, I determined the average number of references (meeting our criteria) and the average year of these citations per publication. When computed for two-year periods, the results of Figure 22 and Table 5 were obtained.

Contrary to my expectations, the number of citations per scientific article increased with historical time. Considerable upward deviations exist, however, for the publications during the 1940s, which might be attributable, in part, to the limited number of items for which, thus far, the retrieval has been completed. After a greater number of reference cards have

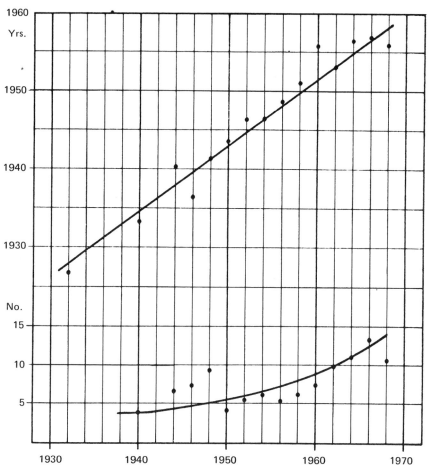

Figure 22. Average number and years of publications cited (ordinate) as a function of historical time (abscissa).

been analyzed, these data points might follow a more consistent trends and might be interpreted with greater confidence.

In comparison, the results on the changes in the average citation span already show at this stage of analysis a highly consistent upward trend. As the number of references increases with historical time, the period covered by these references increases as well. Thus, contrary to my expectations, authors have not necessarily changed their citation habits. Certainly modern authors have not become more contemporaneous in their orientation than former scholars. Most likely, the increase in citation span has to be attributed to the historical growth of the repertoire (represented by our card file) from which authors can select their references. Former scholars had

Table 5. Number of Authors, Number of References, Average Number of References per Author, and Average Year of Reference as a Function of Time

Year	Number of authors	Number of references	Average references	Year of references
1968–69	7	73	10.4	1955.9
1966–67	10	130	13.0	1957.1
1964–65	16	171	10.7	1956.2
1962–63	29	287	9.9	1953.3
1960–61	37	272	7.4	1955.9
1958–59	38	250	6.6	1950.7
1956–57	32	167	5.2	1948.5
1954–55	30	183	6.1	1946.9
1952–53	23	130	5.6	1946.3
1950–51	15	66	4.4	1944.0
1948–49	5	48	9.6	1941.4
1946–47	4	30	7.5	1936.3
1944–45	4	29	7.2	1940.1
1942–43	0	0	0	—
1940–41	4	16	4.0	1933.4

only a few relevant items to choose from; a modern writer can select from a total file of 4,310 items.

The data points in the upper section of Figure 22 fall closely upon a straight line represented by the following regression equation:

$$y = .89x + 208.43$$

The corresponding correlation coefficient equals .98. According to this equation, the citation lag equaled about eight years in 1960; that is, the references cited in articles published in 1960, on the average, had appeared in 1952. In 1940, the citation lag was only five years.

By extrapolating the equation down to the intersect with the major diagonal of the system of coordinates (i.e., to the intersect with a line that originates at the year zero and has a slope of 1.0), it is possible to determine that point in time at which a writer in psychological gerontology would refer only to contemporaneous authors, most likely to himself. This point occurs in 1895 and can be considered as the origin or zero-point of psychological gerontology. Searching through the few publications of the corresponding decade, we find the following entries:

Richardson, B. W. (1891)
Savage, G. H. (1893)
Scott, C. A. (1896)

Galton collected his psychometric data at the World's Health Exhibit in 1885. However, these records were not thoroughly analyzed until the 1920s (Elderton *et al.,* 1928; Ruger and Stoessiger, 1927).

The retrieval analysis can be compared to the study of genealogies. If we were to enumerate the number of ancestors of a present-day individual, we would, after a few generations, exhaust the number of all persons living at that period in history; the present-day individual, theoretically, would be a descendant of all the persons living a few hundred years ago (root structure). Conversely, if we choose one individual living about 800 years ago and determine the number of his present-day descendants for the case of two surviving offspring per generation, this number would exceed the world population of 3 billion (branch structure). This example demonstrates that neither the root structure nor the branch structure is sufficient, when taken alone, to describe the system of intergenerational relationships. We know, for instance, that a considerable degree of intermarriage must exist that, when going backward in time, converts divergent roots into convergent branches and generates a network of relationships closely similar to our retrieval system. The various references converge upon node points and thus prevent an exponential increase in the number of articles cited as we go backward in time. Rather, they generate a steady condition, which has already been demonstrated in the upper part of Figure 21.

Discussion

At the present time, my analysis is far from complete. It needs to be extended by emphasizing topics other than those of intellectual achievements. Through such extensions, it would be possible to determine how many of the previous studies have become obsolete or have never entered into close and repeated connections with the mainstream of publications in psychological gerontology. In particular, it would be possible to determine how many of the 77% unaccounted publications would enter into the retrieval system. In order to maximize the possibility for inclusion, additional lead articles that are as divergent from one another as conceivable should be chosen.

But even if our retrieval system had been extended in such a manner, it is well possible that some of the remaining publications, although insufficiently connected with the mainstream of psychological gerontology, represent significant topics of inquiry. All that we learn from the present type of analysis is that, thus far, they have not been recognized as important issues. Intuitively we might be convinced that, indeed, lack of recognition rather than irrelevance of the topics is often the prevailing condition that determines success in psychological gerontology as well as in psychology in general. All too often our activities and, more important, the recognition of these activities are guided by the well-established and documented trends in a given field; all too rarely are we sensitive enough to detect newly emergent trends and to support them intellectually, financially, and through editorial decisions.

In order to identify such innovative activities at early dates, it remains necessary, at the present time, to retreat from our quantitative study to approaches analyzing these issues in a more traditional manner. By inspection and evaluation of the existing literature and by comparing it with the area of psychology in general and with developmental psychology in particular, we might detect new trends, as well as identify "underdeveloped" and "overdeveloped" areas. Through additional quantitative studies of the type presented here, we might eventually succeed in deriving such decisions from a base that is open to public inspection.

In order to achieve such a goal, our procedures need to be extended and more sophisticated methods for their analysis and models for their interpretation have to be developed. The planning involved in such a task would also force us to perform the analysis in a prospective manner. Our reference system would have to be supplemented as soon as new material appears in print rather than several years after its publication and by means of retrospective retrievals. Such an approach requires a new sense of history. As forcefully emphasized by Lynd (1968), history for all too long has led us to contemplate about the past but has done little to guide us into the future. Historical studies as described and envisaged here would lead us in this direction.

QUALITATIVE ANALYSIS

Our quantitative analysis of the history of psychological gerontology can be regarded as an effort in futility. It represents both another addition to the legion of studies (4,310 of which were entered into our reference file), and it demonstrates that the vast majority of these studies represent little more than an enormous waste of our efforts (77% of which were never retrieved through our analysis and another large percentage of which never appeared in print in the first place, being rejected for publication by the journal editors). How do we prevent this pollution from spreading any further? How can we make our human and scientific efforts more meaningful and efficient?

Numerous people and organizations have become deeply concerned about these problems. Not all of them are ready to admit, however, that any solution has to revolutionize the very basis of knowledge and science. Most of them still believe that with increased efforts and with the allocation of additional funds the problems can be resolved. In contrast to such optimistic views, I am convinced that basic reformulations are necessary in our concepts of knowledge and science, research and theory, education and implementation, and generally in our view of the individual, society, and their development.

Criteria for Knowledge

Despite the enormous increase in research output and despite our pride in the advancement of knowledge (superficially seen as the result of this increase), our concepts of research and theory have not advanced beyond viewpoints of the 19th century. As implied by most contributors to the discussion of communication in psychology in the April 1971 issue of *The American Psychologist* (Garvey and Griffith, 1971), we firmly believe that each of the many studies contributes at least a small bit to our stock of knowledge and thereby strips nature of another secret. These efforts are called the collection of facts and we wait patiently for some exceptional scientists to put these "facts" together and, thereby, "discover" another "law of nature." As clearly realized by the more thoughtful scholars, such a naive and mechanistic viewpoint is not only inadequate for the behavioral sciences but for all other disciplines as well. The prevailing conditions have been summarized by Heisenberg (1952);

> Thus was formed the solid framework of classical physics, and thus arose the conception of a material world in time and space comparable to a machine which, once set in motion, continues to run, governed by immutable laws. The fact that this machine as well as the whole of science were themselves only products of the human mind appeared irrelevant and of no consequence for an understanding of nature. (p. 79)

The naive fact-finding attitude does not come to grips with the interaction of scientific advancements and the growth of society. Progress in knowledge and science is always co-determined by the nonscientific conditions and demands of the society in which they develop. Society, in turn, will be modified by the scientific progress made. By disregarding or rejecting these nonscientific influences, psychologists have remained safely hidden in their ivory towers and have escaped to the perceptual–structural criteria of knowledge (see chap. 6). "Truth" has been regarded as dependent upon the degree to which sensory impressions (both of the common sense and scientific–observational type) match or are congruent with systematic and, perhaps, formal models. By demonstrating such isomorphism, we continue to believe that we are describing and explaining nature as it "really is." Little do we recognize that both our observations as well as the theoretical models proposed are selectively dependent upon social, economic, and political conditions of the society in which we happen to live. Since considerations like these are outwardly rejected by most present-day psychologists, further development of our conceptualizations has been prevented and we have remained unable to discuss these issues in a systematic manner. At the same time, however, we do not hesitate to indoctrinate our students with our biased viewpoints, and it is only the new cohort of students that shows a growing sense of uneasiness in regard to our conceptions.

Goals of Higher Education

Students of psychology, upon entering university programs, are explicitly or implicitly forced to engage in research activities and to acquire sets of inappropriate techniques, for example, statistical techniques of parametric types. These activities may not be damaging as long as they are regarded as tasks, almost in a therapeutic sense, that provide the individual with opportunities for gaining scientific insights and human understanding (of course, the latter might be achieved more readily by sending the student into a school, into a home for the aged, or into a ghetto). These tasks can be harmful, however, if they induce upon the student the same attitude toward science that I have criticized, that is, the conviction that his activities are not merely of educational benefit for the student himself, but that they also contribute to the growing stock of scientific knowledge.

Perhaps students are selectively attracted to the behavioral sciences because of their perference for such a mentality. Certainly this attitude is reinforced throughout undergraduate and graduate education. At least from the time of their admission and continuing throughout their whole academic careers, most psychologists seem to retain this attitude. The outcome is the enormous mass of research, compounded by rejection rates of up to 80% with which editors of leading psychological journals, with an ambivalent feeling of despair and pride, turn down the reports of the activities submitted to them—despair because with a brief notice they might destroy the efforts and hopes of another individual, and pride because the high rejection rate signals to them the exceptional attraction of their journal, the astounding activities of the field, and the high standards presumably attained. To the present author, however, these conditions, much like a continuing unemployment rate of up to 10% in the wealthiest nation on earth, indicate some very basic fallacies in the system of scientific activities that can be corrected only through major changes in our conceptualization of sciences and implemented through major modifications of our system of higher education.

Such modifications ought to be brought about by an emphasis on cooperation rather than competition between individuals, on quality rather than quantity of scientific products, and on integrative–structured rather than specialized–isolated achievements. Instead of setting each student and each scholar on his own track, they should be induced at the undergraduate and graduate levels to engage in group efforts, not in order to increase their productivity further but to direct them toward integration of efforts and to reduce the mass of separate contributions. Additional emphasis should be given to the reanalysis and reinterpretation of previous data, surveys of the literature, and historical studies.

As implied in these suggestions, advances in knowledge are not so much dependent upon the accumulation of additional data but upon the success of organizing those already available. As proposed by Looft (1971), a better psychology should be generated, but not a "psychology of more." Such a goal is not reached by inducing an overcompetitive attitude upon the young scholar but rather by fostering a contemplative reflective orientation. Competition does not assist but rather destroys thinking and merely represents an external, regulating condition that serves as a poor substitute for internal motivation.

Use of Technology

Within the established quarters of the behavioral and social sciences, my suggestions about undergraduate and graduate education might appear as antiscientific. By emphasizing the quality and integration of achievements rather than by evaluating progress through the number of studies produced, I do not want to deny, however, the usefulness of data collection. Indeed, the quantitative exploration of the history of psychological gerontology may serve as a demonstration of how such comparisons can assist us in our tasks of achieving a fuller integration of research information and quick decisions regarding future directions.

The present study represents a limited exploration of determinants and processes in the growth of sciences. For several years such explorations have been demanded by Birren (1961) and have been made possible through the systematic work by Shock (1951, 1957). This study is comparable to the well-known investigations by Asimov (1963), Garfield et al. (1964), Price (1965), Xhignesse and Osgood (1967), and Garvey and Griffith (1971). These investigators have provided descriptive information on the growth of scientific disciplines as well as theoretical models that would allow for predictions and, thus, assist in reaching reasonable decisions. In general, these models further our conceptualization and understanding of the growth of social systems.

In the preceding section, a reduction in research output for the sake of structural integrations was advocated. Such a reorientation has to be implemented through changes in the approach to and in the goals of higher education. In the present section, I am proposing the application of theories and techniques developed through research on computerized retrieval methods and on models of changing social systems. Such applications aim at coping more efficiently with the information overload existing in most scientific disciplines, such as in psychological gerontology. The research and the models may enable us to develop a more rigorous form of conceptualization, to gain an understanding of the dynamics of growing scientific disciplines, and, concretely, of newly emerging trends, of needs for consolidating different coexisting branches, or of splitting apart others that are, as yet, insufficiently differentiated.

Undoubtedly, the techniques for which these investigations of scientific information retrieval have become known do not solve the problems intrinsic to our rapidly expanding scientific disciplines. They may enable us, however, much like the recording devices for air or water pollution, to recognize points of saturation or catastrophe. The solutions for these problems, have to come through reorientations of the participating scientists and through reevaluations of our scientific discipline leading to a new concept of the individual, society, and their development.

Model of Man and Society

Traditionally, behavioral scientists have been bound to a conceptual model in which both the organism and the environment are regarded as passive. This model is the heritage of the sensualistic, elementaristic, and associationist tradition of British philosophy and has been most clearly preserved in studies of verbal learning and behaviorism. As a theory of the individual, society, and their development, such a model is as insufficient as the modified version proposed by Skinner in which the experimenter actively manipulates and shapes the course of the individual's development. Since, in this modified version, the organism remains to be regarded as passive, and since the activities of the experimenter are arbitrary and do not reflect the cultural–historical directions of society, this modification is as insufficient as in the model of the passive organism in a passive environment.

It is the outstanding achievement of Piaget, followed by Chomsky, to have returned activity to its origin, namely, to the organism. Learning and development are no longer considered as being brought about by the organism's exposure to and accumulation of bits and pieces of information and habits, but the organism is seen as actively and selectively exploring his or her environmental possibilities. While the organism thus learns only what he or she explores, this interpretation fails to consider that the environment as well consists of individuals continuously interacting with the developing organism in an active manner. To Piaget and especially to Chomsky, the environment merely provides the necessary material from which the individual can make his selection; the environment does not impose its information on the organism.

Psychological gerontologists would have much to learn from Piaget and Chomsky because the idea of an active, aging individual has not yet attained a respectable place in our thinking. But even more important, psychological gerontologists would have much to learn from Soviet psychology, where, for the first time, the sociocultural environment is also being considered as an active force in the individual's development.

The dialectical psychology initiated by Vygotsky (1929, 1962) and brought to its fruition by S. L. Rubinstein (see Payne, 1968), considers both the organism and the environment as active participants in a process of changes. Psychic activities or behavior are the outcome of two interaction processes: one relating them to the internal biochemical processes, the other to external cultural processes. The analysis of the first interaction process relies on Pavlov's work on the first signaling system. The development of such a system of nervous activities does not emerge in a social vacuum, however. In the ontogenetic sense, it occurs for a particular individual in a particular social–educational setting; in the phylogenetic sense, Pavlov's theory is itself the product of a particular society in a particular cultural–historical setting. The psychic activities developing in the organism will change the cultural–historical conditions as much as cultural–historical developments will change the psychic activities of the individual. These changes characterize the second interaction system.

Since the cultural–historical conditions are the product of continuing efforts by generations and generations of individuals, it is not surprising that in his own development, an individual is bound to generate products essentially similar to those generated in society, for example, cognitive or syntactic structures. In other words, the problem of nature versus nurture does not exist; ontogenetic and phylogenetic progressions converge. Similarly, the problem of consciousness versus behavior (mind–body) does not exist. Both are constructs emerging through the two types of interactions; one is founded in external cultural–historical conditions, the other in internal biochemical conditions. Only in the mechanistic or idealistic views of Western philosophy do these two constructs appear as separate entities; that is, they appear as behavior if the first system is emphasized at the expense of the second, and as consciousness if the reverse reasoning is applied.

Finally, behavior and consciousness, as seen from such a dialectical view, are psychic activities that are not only being changed by biochemical and cultural–historical conditions but that, in turn, might change both these conditions. This conclusion indicates far-reaching revisions, namely, the rejection of naive realism and of scientific fatalism that is insensitive to social issues and problems. Knowledge and science not only rely on sensory–structural truth criteria but also on those of social actions and consequences. If it were possible to conceptualize this problem distinctly, and if it could be applied to psychological gerontology successfully, then knowledge would be attained in the true and only sense of the word.

CONCLUSIONS

The results of this study lead to the following recommendations:

1. Deemphasize the ceaseless accumulation of research data that are more important for the competitive success of individuals than for the growth of knowledge, science, and society. Emphasize integrative and historical perspectives rather than the collection of bits and pieces of research guided by a naive fact-finding attitude.

2. Implement these changes through an overhaul of our system of higher education. Rather than creating overambitious, competitive young scientists, often arrogant and elitist in their thinking, foster an attitude of cooperation and sensitivity toward scientific issues, social problems, and people.

3. In order to cope with the present-day scientific pollution, make maximum use of modern technologies and models of the growth of science and society. Apply these tools for the benefit of scientific disciplines and so-

ciety rather than having the fate of their participating members determined by and subordinated to the advances of these technologies.

4. In order to achieve such intellectual control, formulate a model of man in which his dialectical developmental interdependence with the changing society is emphasized. Such a model overcomes the naive fact-finding orientation, the mechanistic reductionism, the static dichotomization into nature—nurture and body—mind, and the view of man and of society as passive aggregates shaped by blind external forces.

CHAPTER 14

The Recall of Events from the
Individual and Collective Past

Recent studies in life-span developmental psychology (Baltes *et al.*, 1970; Riegel and Riegel, 1972; Schaie and Strother, 1968a, 1968b), related to explorations in the sociology of generational shifts (Bengtson and Black, 1973; Riley, Johnson, and Foner, 1972; Ryder, 1965), have explicated the confounded changes in the individual and in society. These advances have been made possible through the elaboration of developmental research designs (Baltes, 1968; Schaie, 1965, 1970). Primarily, the psychological studies have focused upon formal explorations and not upon the underlying sociohistorical processes that, in principle, were recognized as influencing the growth of the individual. The sociology of generational shifts, on the other hand, directed its attention toward these sociohistorical processes but did not explore their impact upon the development of the individual. The following four studies investigate the interactions between individual–psychological and cultural–sociological changes. In particular, I apply the paradigm of developmental psychology to the study of history and the paradigm of historical inquiries to the study of the growing individual.

On the basis of mutual adaptations of the paradigms of psychological development and history, the following four studies explore ways in which psychological methods may aid in reconstructing the history of individuals

The original article was published under the title, "The recall of historical events," Behavioral Science, 1973, 18, 354–363. A number of pages are taken from "Time and change in the development of the individual and society," in H. W. Reese (Ed.) Advances in child development and behavior, vol. 7, New York: Academic Press, 1973, pp. 81–113 (see chap. 5).

and societies and, thereby, widen our developmental and historical interpretations. The first study reports on the free recall of persons (relatives, friends, acquaintances) and compares the data with potential changes in social contingencies in the life of individuals. The second study extends these comparisons to three different age groups of recalling subjects. In the third study, subjects recollect the names of historical figures (politicians, scientists, artists). These data will be compared with interpretations of the course of political–intellectual history. In the fourth study, a report (recall) of the history of psychology by one eminent historian of the behavioral sciences, Professor E. G. Boring, will be analyzed and compared with the results of the first three studies. While none of our experiments provides definite answers to the many problems raised, it allows us to cast these problems into a more rigorous analytical framework than hitherto possible.

THE INDIVIDUAL AND HIS PAST

Procedures

Undergraduate students in psychology at the University of Michigan, 18 males and 8 females, ranging in age from 19 to 25 years (average age 20.8 years), wrote down as many names of persons they had met during their lifetime (relatives, friends, acquaintances) as they could recall during a 6-minute period. Subjects marked the end of each 1-minute interval by a line and were allowed to use any abbreviations as long as they were able to identify the persons thus denoted. After the completion of the task, subjects indicated the year they had met each of the persons reported for the first time and marked, if listed, their own mothers, fathers, sisters, and brothers. Furthermore, they recorded their sex, birthdates, the years they had attended various types of schools, and the names and years of birth of their sisters and brothers.

Results

Figure 23 shows the average number of persons recalled as a function of successive school years. Since subjects differed in age, school age rather than chronological age was used in this comparison. In a few cases some years had to be discarded, especially between high school and college but, by and large, the 26 records could be aligned without any difficulties within an age span of 21 years.

The results resemble a serial position curve in which the serial order

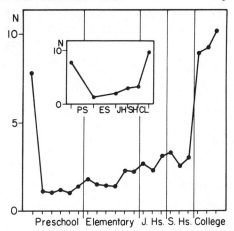

Figure 23. Average number of persons recalled as a function of time (in school years) of first acquaintance.

represents the subjects' school age. Recency had a strong effect, i.e., persons met late in life were recalled much more often than those met earlier. A primacy effect was also revealed, i.e., persons met during the first year of life were recalled more often then those met during the intermediate years.

In analyzing recall strategies, two possibilities were studied: clustering and recapitulation (and its counterpart, regression). *Clustering* was determined by enumerating the differences in years of adjacently recalled persons. A zero-difference represents the strongest clustering and means that the two persons recalled were met within the same year. A total of 768 zero-differences were observed. The largest observed difference equaled 21 years but occurred only three times. If there had been perfect zero-clustering, i.e., if all persons met within specific years were recalled within separate blocks, the total possible number of zero-differences would amount to the total number of responses, 1,813, minus the average age of subjects, 21, minus 1. (The latter figure, 20, represents the average number of transitions from year to year in the average length of the subject's life.) The number of observed over the number of possible zero-differences was found to be 43.9%. If, on the other hand, the recall of the 1,813 persons had been completely random, there would be $1,813^2 = 3,286,969$ possible combinations of names and $\Sigma a_i^2 = 275,354$ zero-differences, whereby a equals the average number of persons recalled within year i. Dividing the latter figure by the former indicated that 8.6% zero-differences could have occurred by chance combination. Since the observed percentage of 43.9 was far above this figure, a strong clustering effect by years of acquaintance was confirmed.

The *recapitulation* strategy (and its counterpart, the regression strategy)

Table 6. Average Number of Persons and of Historical Figures Recalled and Median Years They Were Met for the First Time or Made Their Major Contributions, Listed for 6 Successive Minutes of Recall

Minute:	1st	2nd	3rd	4th	5th	6th
Persons	18.6	11.8	11.3	12.0	11.4	11.4
Years	1962	1962	1964	1962	1964	1963
Historical figures	12.8	8.1	7.7	7.4	7.2	6.4
Years	1840	1860	1850	1888	1825	1918

was tested by computing the median years of first acquaintance for the persons recalled in the successive six minutes of the recall period. As shown in Table 6, the median years for the first two minutes were low, but the changes thereafter are rather irregular and were found to be insignificant. Therefore, neither the recapitulation nor the regression strategy prevailed. However, some support for this hypothesis came from an analysis of the recall of members of the immediate family; altogether 73.1% of the subjects listed their parents. Always, either both or neither of the parents were recalled. Since the mother (or the father) appeared as the first response 19.2%, and during the first minute (including the first response) 53.8% of the time, whereas only 19.3% listed a parent's name during the remaining five minutes, support for a limited version of the recapitulation hypothesis was provided. Apparently, subjects used this strategy at the very beginning of the task but soon after began to rely on clustering as an aid for recall. In addition, large sex differences were observed. Boys recalled their parents 83.3% of the time but girls only 50.0%. The girls always named the mother first (100%); the boys chose randomly the mother (53.3%) or the father (46.7%) as the first parent recalled. Siblings were named 90.0% by boys and 85.7% by girls.

Discussion

The results of Figure 23 led to a hypothetical reconstruction of the conditions under which individuals grow up. Two parameters were considered: The rate of physical–psychological mobility, α_i, with which an individual explores environmental possibilities; and the increases in the environmental potential, a_i, denoted by the number of new persons that enter into the life of an individual at various times.

As shown in Figure 24, an individual, born at time t_0, is being exposed to a social environment with a_0 persons (parents, siblings, friends,

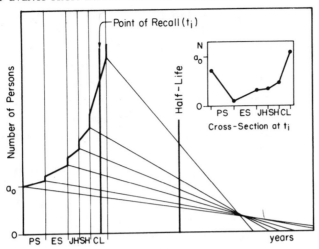

Figure 24. Model of the expansion of the social environment during school years and of the recall of persons during the life span.

neighbors). During the early years the rate of physical–psychological mobility, α_0, will be small. The individual is bound to the immediate environment of his home. During the following years, when the child is entering the various types of school, successive expansions occur. Instead of staying close to home, the child explores the block, visits his schoolmates, travels through the neighborhood, the town, and the country. While, thus, the rate of mobility increases with age (α_1 to α_n), also the opportunity for social interaction expands in ever bigger steps (a_1 to a_n). At first, in the nursery or kindergarten, the child is with few other children. The group size increases from the elementary to the junior and senior high school. He or she enters the college with several hundred or thousands of other freshmen all of whom he or she can, potentially, meet.

Figure 24 depicts the changes in the social possibilities of what one might call the official child regulated by educational policies and laws. Aside from this role, the growing individual is exposed to various other social contingencies. He or she might engage, for instance, in religious, political, recreational, and occupational activities. Each of these settings provides for other partially independent expansions. In conjunction, these settings will smoothen the step-wise curve of Figure 24 and are likely to transform it into an exponential function, $y = 2^x + a_0$, which has been suggested as one potential model for historical growth, the branch structure model (see chap. 4).

My discussion of the environmental potential for social interactions, at this moment does not consider factors that restrict further growths during adulthood and old age. However, an interpretation of the recall process of Study I has to emphasize that the experience of any event or person is subject to forgetting. Utilizing one of the simplest interpretations possible, I propose that the decay of memory will be linear and that at a particular point in time the number of persons recalled will amount to 50% of those encountered at any point earlier in life. This point, measured in years, might be called the "half-life" of the specific experience to be recalled.

Figure 24 shows several forgetting lines originating at those points in time at which individuals enter new educational settings. Extrapolating these lines beyond the "half-life" provides for an inference congruent with "Ribot's law," which states that items learned last during the period of growth are forgotten first; childhood experiences are best retained, adulthood experiences the least. More important for our present considerations, the free recall task can be represented by the cross-section at t_i, indicated by a heavy vertical line in Figure 24. If we plot in a noncumulative manner the average numbers of persons predicted to be recalled by our subjects at t_i, we obtain the curve shown in the upper section of Figure 24. This curve is very similar in form to the empirical data plotted in the upper section of Figure 23.

Undoubtedly my model oversimplifies the growth of the social interaction potential and, especially, the forgetting process. For a more sophisticated model we might substitute the forgetting lines by Ebbinghaus's forgetting curves, or replace our second stipulation on the half-life of experiences by the notion that only those persons will be retained in memory who are being "related" to other persons encountered earlier and already incorporated into the structure of personal memory of an individual. The later a person enters into such structure, the less likely it will be that his or her name becomes intimately connected. For instance, the members of the immediate family enter early and over a long period of time into the cognitive–social structure of the subject; later in life, for instance during the college years, hundreds of persons may enter but only very few will become intimately connected to the structure and are introduced, for instance, to the long-term friends of the family of the subject. While the analysis of clustering and the specific version of the recapitulation hypothesis provides some supportive evidence, supplementary information on the social interactions at various developmental levels, for instance, through sociometric studies, would be desirable.

My discussion served the purpose of contrasting subjective, retrospective recall data with those obtained from "objective" inquiries into social contingencies and their changes with the age of subjects. The suggested mechanisms for forgetting and retrieval, together with the interpretations on the changes of the social environment with the age of subjects, seem to predict the observed recall data surprisingly well. Therefore, it seems justified to make some comparisons between the flow of psychological and chronological time. Such an analysis will be based on the results from a study in which three different age groups were engaged in the same task described above.

AGE DIFFERENCES IN THE RECALL
OF PAST EVENTS

Procedure

Each of twenty subjects from three consecutive generations wrote down as many names of persons as they could recall during a 10-minute session. Most members of the youngest group (average age = 23.1 years) belonged to the same kin; the middle group (average age = 50.0 years) included their parents, aunts, and uncles; the oldest group (average age = 73.3 years) included their grandparents, grandaunts, and grandundun cles. Increasingly, from the youngest to the oldest generation, the groups had to be supplemented by persons unrelated to the kin. After the completion of the recall task, subjects listed behind each name the years they had met these persons for the first time.

Results

The results are shown in Figure 25. Here, the ordinate indicates the number of persons recalled. The abscissa indicates the years these persons were met for the first time. Since the average ages of the three groups were related in ratios of about 1:2:3, the scales were compressed accordingly. Thus, along the abscissa, three different age scales are used.

Discussion

As in the preceding study, the youngest group (III) shows a very strong recency effect and a less strong primacy effect; the curve is J-shaped and the data points are almost bisected by the influence of these two factors. The middle-aged group (II) reveals a strong recency effect but the

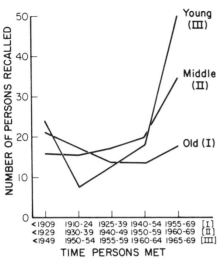

Figure 25. Average number of persons recalled by three age groups plotted against time of first acquaintance.

primacy effect has disappeared; the curve has the shape of a boomerang. For the oldest group (I), the primacy effect reappears slightly, while the recency effect has almost disappeared; the curve resembles a straight line. Thus, in their retrospective perception the oldest subjects attend to all five time periods most evenly; the names of persons recalled are almost equally spread over the full age range. The retrospections of the middle-aged group as well as those of the youngest group are dominated by persons recently met. The youngest group also pays considerable attention to persons encountered very early in life.

According to these results, retrospective perception varies with age. If we consider the number of persons recalled per chronological time period as an index for the intensity of time experience, we would have to conclude that for the young and the middle-aged subjects psychological time flows faster the closer the period recalled is to the time of testing. The farther back in time these subjects go in their search, the more often events and persons seem to have faded away. The oldest subjects, however, live more intensely with their past; recently met persons are of lesser significance. Young subjects, finally, split their attention between the very early and the very late periods of their lives. The intermediate years are experiences with low intensity; times seems to flow slower here.

All these interpretations are based upon subjective recall scores. Since the number of persons recalled is also a function of the number of persons met, and since this number might vary systematically with the age of subjects, the present data and interpretations need to be supplemented by "objective" records of changes in the social environment over the life span.

The resulting interpretations show how one might reconstruct the cognitive–social development of an individual and match it against his recall of past events. In the following study I will extend this comparison to the study of historical growth.

THE PERCEPTION OF HISTORICAL LEAPS

Procedure

Sixteen undergraduate students in psychology at the University of Michigan wrote down as many names of historical figures (politicians, scientists, artists) as they could recall during a six-minute period. Subjects marked the end of each minute by a line. An advanced graduate student in psychology, in cooperation with the author, assigned a most characteristic historical date to each person listed. In the case of political leaders, this would represent the midpoint of their service in public office; in the case of artists and scientists, it would, usually, represent the midpoint of their active careers.

Results

When the average number of persons recalled was plotted against historical time a strong recency effect was observed (see Figure 26). As shown in Table 6, subjects produce many more names of personal acquaintances (reported in the first study) than of historical figures (reported in the present study). There is also a continuous decline in output in the present task whereas in the former task subjects produce many more names during the first minute of recall (18.6) but remain at a constant, though lower, level during the remaining five minutes of the task.

Discussion

The recall of historical figures differs from the recall of personal acquaintances in several ways.

First, there is no zero point in the historical time-scale corresponding to the birth of the recalling subject. Subsequently, no primacy but only a recency effect was produced.

Second, the unusually high occurrence of George Washington's name during the first minute of recall (68.7%) or as the very first response (43.7%) suggests the prevalence of the specific recapitulation strategy. Sub-

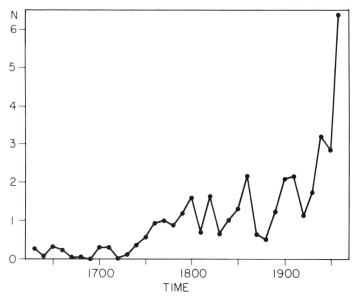

Figure 26. Average number of historical figures recalled as a function of the historical time during which they lived.

jects start out with what they consider to be the earliest historical figure but, then, progress rapidly toward the most recent days and research within the contemporary cluster of persons.

Third, the span of history covers, of course, a much longer time period than the life of any individual. Moreover, an individual will become acquainted with these historical figures during a few short sessions only, extending in the present American high school or college system over a few hours of lecturing and reading. Despite the scarcity of exposure, the progression is likely to proceed in the natural forward order of time; i.e., the early events are presented first in books or lectures. Teachers will disregard, however, large historical sections both because of lack of time and lack of knowledge. As shown in Table 6, subjects do not recapitulate history in the recall task except for the high occurrence of George Washington's name as an early response. The median historical times for the successive six minutes of recall were not found to be significantly different.

Fourth, as the accumulation of names at the time of the American Revolution may have already suggested, politicians, historians, and teachers seem to chop the stream of historical events into didactic chunks. In particular, they seem to prefer what may be called a catastrophe theory of history. As shown in Figure 26, large numbers of names are accumulated at the times of major wars: The War for Independence, the Civil War, the Spanish-American War, World War I, and World War II. However, this statement on the normative effects of historical teaching is not meant to be unreasonably critical; after all, students of developmental psychology are subjected to similar treatment when they are exposed to the all-too-popular stage theories of growth. At this time, very few psychologists have seriously questioned the logic and the methodological basis of such interpretations (see Beilin, 1969; Flavell, 1971; Van den Daele, 1969; see also chap. 5).

Fifth, my last comments raise questions about the accuracy with which our recall data, as well as books, treatises, and teaching by historians, represent "objectively" the sequence of historical events. Do these events occur in leaps and bounds as our data reveal and as—presumably—history is being written and taught, or does history represent a smooth and gradual process of change? Are there historical "mutations" or does *natura non facit saltus?* These questions lead, on the one hand, to the subsequent study in which the report by a single historian is being analyzed. On the other hand, they suggest the reconstruction of history in a manner similar to that of the social–environmental contingencies surrounding the growing individual. Such reconstructions, eventually, may make a precise analysis of the historical recall processes possible.

Similar to the shift from school type to school type and similar to the growth in physical–psychological mobility of the child, shown in Figure 24, history has been regarded as a stepwise progression through social systems of every increasing size, a_i, and with every increasing communicative mobility, α_i. Perhaps the first increase in the modern Western world occurred during the vast migrations at the end of the Roman Empire, the next during the opening of the sea trade in the north by the Hanseatic League and in the Mediterranean during the Crusades, the next during the worldwide explorations by the Spaniards and Portugese, the next during the colonization by Britain and France. As the size of the system for social and economic exchanges increase, the speed of traveling and exchanges grew as well through inventions and technical improvements (Rashevsky, 1968). But this development is not restricted to physical and political modes. It encompasses intellectual and cultural growth as well. As this author has suggested in chapters 4 and 5, the growth of knowledge in a society in general, and the history of a science in particular, can be successfully explained by models of information exchange that are based on the same assumptions as those implied in Figure 24. Similar proposals have been made by other authors (Goffman, 1966; Kochen, 1969; Rashevsky, 1968).

HISTORIANS ARE KINDER TO THE FEW

Procedure

In my last study, the report (recall) of historical figures in psychology by only one person, the late Professor E. G. Boring, is presented. For each decade I recorded the names of all psychologists who appeared at least on eight pages of his *History of Experimental Psychology* (1957). From the total list of 106 names I had to omit seven, being unable to determine their years of birth and death.

Results

As shown in Figure 27, there is a rapid increase with historical time in the number of persons named, reaching its peak at 1880. The decline thereafter is due to the recency of events in reference to the time at which this history was written (before 1929). Also, if I had lowered the criterion and had included persons whose names appear on fewer than eight pages, a continued increase in the number of psychologists, at least up to 1910, would have resulted.

As also shown in Figure 27, the average number of pages devoted to the different persons is bimodal with one broad peak between 1630 and

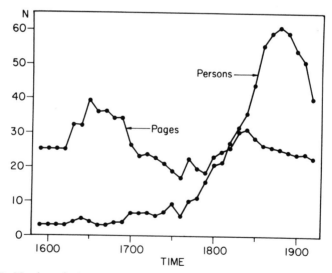

Figure 27. Number of scientists appearing on at least eight pages in Boring's book and average number of pages devoted to them, plotted against historical time.

1690 and a second between 1830 and 1850. Apparently two historical subareas are represented in Boring's book. For further clarification, I asked three staff members in psychology to categorize the 99 persons as being primarily psychologists, philosophers, physiologists, or natural scientists. Obtaining sufficiently high rater agreements (89%, 92%, and 95%), I plotted separately the number of scientists per historical time units omitting the few (eight) natural scientists.

As shown in Figure 28, philosophy reveals an early, slow, and long-lasting growth, followed by physiology with a higher rate of expansion and a sharp peak at around 1850. Psychology shows a very sharp and large increase during all of the 19th century, a development that has been well documented through other sources. Such a result had to be expected for a book on the history of psychology. However, the number of pages that the author devoted to the various individuals is surprising. As shown in Figure 29, there is a rapid and rather steady decline in the number of pages assigned to both the psychologists and philosophers of the more recent days, physiologists being less affected in this regard.

Discussion

Contrary to our intuition that history would require an increasing degree of chronological condensation the farther one looks back in time, historians such as Professor Boring expand the past over the present and thus provide us with counterintuitive descriptions. In writing history, *the*

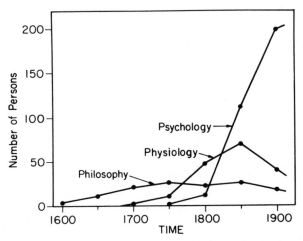

Figure 28. Average number of psychologists, physiologists, and philosophers appearing on at least eight pages in Boring's book, plotted against historical time.

234

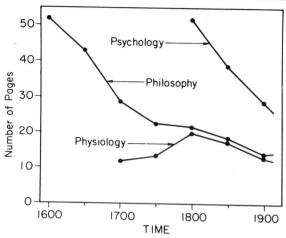

Figure 29. Average number of pages devoted to psychologists, physiologists, and philosophers appearing on at least eight pages in Boring's book, plotted against historical time.

fewer contemporaries there are, the more attention the historians will give to them. If we denote the average number of pages per scientists by y, and the average number of scientists per decade by x, the following linear equations express this inverse relationship:

Psychology: $y = 53.19 - .12x$
Philosophy: $y = 59.07 - 1.53x$

While the difference in the additive constants is small (Boring devotes between 53 and 59 pages to a person who has no competitors within his decade), the large slope factor for the philosophers indicates a relatively stronger emphasis upon the very early historical figures. In psychology, scientists from different time periods are treated more equally but, still, the early few receive greater attention than the late many.

CONCLUSIONS

In trying to consolidate the different types of studies and the different results reported, the following conclusions are suggested:

First, the recall of persons by students and the writing of history by an expert are not as far apart as it might appear. Not only the clinicians but most psychologists consider the early years in life as the most formative ones. Persons encountered during this time, such as parents and siblings, impose the most significant influence upon the individual. It is all but reasonable to expect that the development of a social system, such as a science, is determined by similar conditions.

Subsequently, historians pay greater attention to the few early than to the many late scientists. To be a late scientist places a different burden on the individual than that placed on an early scientist. It may selectively require a different type of a person. As the frequent mentioning of George Washington seems to indicate, similar selective attention is given to the early political figures, at least when these are instrumental at a time of a sharp revolutionary segmentation.

Second, as much as the clinical psychologist will try to make a patient aware of his problems in order to resolve them, so must the writer of a history apprehend the processes that determine the interactions between the social contingencies and the generative, intellectual mobility of the historical persons. Thus far, both the historians as well as the behavioral and social scientists have paid insufficient attention to such an analysis. In this vein, I discussed some theoretical models of these historical processes (Goffman, 1966; Kochen, 1969; Rashevsky, 1968; see also chaps. 4 and 6). The present research describes possibilities for operationalizations and empirical investigations.

Third, both psychological and historical development, when reviewed by the individual, progress in leaps. These perceptions contrast sharply with the idea of continuity in the individual's life and gradual changes in history, often connected with the optimism of political and scientific utopia. Many natural scientists have thought that "nature itself" would eventually provide the answer in this controversy and would inform us whether Cuvier and, more recently, Velikovsky (1955) with their catastrophe theory of the organisms and the world are correct, or whether we should look to Lyell and the common astronomer with their gradualism and conservative, nonrevolutionary conception of history. As I have tried to show, however, (see chaps. 7 and 8), these two views represent different forms of interpretation rather than properties of "nature," which, moreover, are dependent on economic and political ideologies. In particular, interpretations within the framework of qualitative revolutionary leaps have been preferred within the mercantilistic systems of the Continent, whereas those of quantitative gradual changes have been dominant within the capitalistic systems of Britain and the United States. A third interpretation, representing the dialectical interactions between changing outer and inner conditions, has emerged in the socialistic countries and is summarized in the following conclusion.

Fourth, history is regarded by many as a field providing rather "irrelevant" information at the time of contemporary troubles. While this criticism is justified if we were to continue to look at history in the traditional idiographic manner and, thus, with the traditional, selective biases, history can also be looked upon "through mathematical formalism" (Rashevsky, 1968) or in much the same way as we ought to look upon the paradigm of modern developmental sciences, namely, as a system in which inner biological and outer sociological forces are in developmental, dialectical interactions. Perceived in this manner, history may tell us how our present-day establishment of the behavioral sciences, created through the efforts and insights of individuals, fostered through the power of laboratories and institutions, and degenerated under the control of editorial offices and granting agencies, attained both its present functional strength and structural incompetence. History is relevant in delineating the interacting forces that determine the growth of a social system such as a science, emphasizing the creation, access, and control of the means for communication and of the basis for production.

CHAPTER 15

On the Psychology of Development and History

Developmental psychologists have rarely explored the retrospective memories and prospective hopes that each of us brings to life when we think about our own pasts and future deeds. Instead, developmental psychologists have preferred to study abstract performances, attitudes, or behaviors that, more likely than not, are of little concern to the individual who is constantly reviewing his or her own growth of activities, change of situations, and plans for tomorrow. Developmental psychologists have failed to recognize that most objectified performances and products are experientially empty for the individual. They disregarded that any individual, here and now, lives with these experiences at all times, caring little about his or her performance and behavior unless they are understood within the context of the experienced past.

Historians, on the other hand, rely on recollections of the interpreted past. Of course, their attempts are much more systematic than those of individuals who are casually retrieving their experiences. The historian will utilize whatever means available, e.g., archives, books, treatises, documents, and advice by other experts, in order to reconstruct the past as accurately and comprehensively as possible. While the historian attempts to improve the precision of a report, these efforts are hampered because the events to be reconstructed and interpreted are rarely experienced by the historian personally but are made known to him or her through the mediation of other historians. The source material may have been transmitted over long chains that threaten the authenticity of the reports to the same extent in which the abstractness of psychological variables distorts the meaningfulness of developmental interpretations.

Having thus contrasted the approach used by historians with that preferred by developmental psychologists, we ought to recognize that transgressions have been made and combinations have been sought. Historians have encouraged the use, whenever possible, of objectified data as collected during past historical periods by archivists and actuaries. The historical methodology, on the other hand, has been extensively applied in clinical studies and treatments. In particular, psychoanalytical explorations attempt to reconstruct a person's life in order to detect major choice points at which fateful turns were taken and to thereby enable the patient to reprocess his or her life in a different and more successful manner (see Erikson, 1968; Riegel, 1973b; Wyatt, 1962, 1963). By restricting the analyses to particular cases, these explorations lack cross-individual and cross-social systematizations that behavioral and social scientists are aiming for. My own inquiries into the individual and collective past attempt to reach such levels of generality.

DEVELOPMENTAL RECOLLECTIONS

The method on which much of the following interpretations are to be based consists in asking persons, usually in groups, to write down past events or, in the cases reported in Chapter 14, the names of all persons (relatives, friends, acquaintances) that they can remember within a time period of six or ten minutes. At the end of this task, subjects are instructed to go once more through their lists and to indicate after each name the approximate year they met that person for the first time. Also some additional information on the subject's background and development is obtained.

The results demonstrate some conceptual differences between the studies of developmental psychology and history. For the psychologist they raise questions on how the individuals came to recollect the particular names that they listed and not those connected with other, for example, the intermediate periods of their lives. In other words, the psychologists will ask for explanations of the particular outcome of the descriptive data. In order to provide such explanations, they will have to compare the "subjective" recall data with the "objective" changes in the individuals' sociophysical environments.

With additional efforts some of these explanations can be provided. For instance, one could tabulate on the basis of other sources than the individuals' recollections, the names of persons who entered into their lives and co-existed with them in their sociophysical environment. One could obtain this information by asking, for example, their friends and relatives; we could look into former school records or listings of tenants and home owners in the neighborhood; one could study census statistics about various age groups and records about school sizes in various locations of the country.

Dependent upon the desired precision, one could obtain listings of these "objective" conditions that, as most would maintain, made the individuals' experiences and, subsequently, their recollections possible. Further analysis—indeed, the main task for psychologists—consists of determining the degree of congruence and the reasons for any incongruence between these "objective" data and the individuals' recollections. In such an analysis all of the traditional psychological factors would have to be introduced one after another: recognition, storage, recall, attention, attitude, motivation, social relevance, etc.

While I do not wish to elaborate the psychological determinants that transform and explain the relationships between the "objective" records and the individuals' recollections, we should take notice that with sufficient persistence these transformation matrices could be successfully derived. The prerequisite for their analysis would be information about the expansion of the sociophysical environments of the developing individuals and not only an inventory taken at one time. For example, such information would include the number and names of those persons appearing in the environment and potentially interacting with the recollecting individual. If we want to be most precise, we could plan such a listing in a longitudinal manner by selecting a group of individuals and recording the changes in their sociophysical environments before we ask them, at a later time, to recollect these events.

HISTORICAL RECOLLECTIONS

In contrast to psychology, the derivation of transformation matrices in historical studies is either not possible at all or only in a very limited sense. The events and the time periods that most historians explore lie far back in the past. Objectified documentation is available on a selective basis only and in most cases has passed through the hands of many generations of intervening and interfering participants. If the methods and data of developmental psychologists could help us to explore the transformational processes through which information is changed and could help us to reconstruct those portions that might have been lost in the course of their transformations, important inferences about the process and fallacies of historical reconstruction might be drawn. Some of these implications have been discussed in recent attempts to develop quantitative or qualitative models of development and history (see Flavell, 1971; Goffman, 1966; Kochen, 1969; Rashevsky, 1968; Riegel, 1969, 1972; Van den Daele, 1969). Instead of describing these possibilities in abstract terms, the following supplementary study demonstrates some of the problems that need to be clarified.

We asked three groups of students—freshmen, seniors, and graduates—to write down in 10 minutes the names of historical figures influential in military, political, or government affairs. The results, shown in Figure 30, reveal some striking similarities but also some important differences from those on the recall of personal acquaintances presented in chapter 14. First, we find again a strong recency effect by obtaining the names of a large number of political figures who entered history less than a few months prior to the study. Second, the primacy effect was as negligible as in the former study. The earliest accumulation of names occurred again for the time of the American Revolution, most notably because of the frequent listing of George Washington. The absence of a steep early ac-

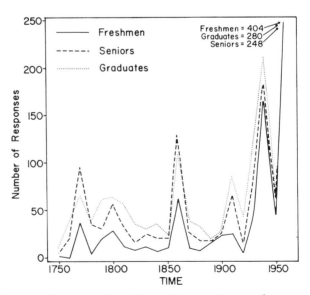

Figure 30. Number of persons influential in political, military, and governmental affairs named by three groups of 30 students each during 10-minute periods.

cumulation is due to the lack of a historical initiation or zero point comparable to the birth of the recalling subject. Third, again sharp spikes occurred, the first representing the time of the American Revolution, the others coinciding regularly with major catastrophes, the outbreaks of wars. It is this issue that attracted my further attention.

For further explorations I compared, first, the records of the students by their degrees of education and, presumably, their historical knowledge, i.e., freshmen, seniors, and graduates. I expected that the more advanced students would show the spiking effect less strongly and would fill the gaps between the spikes more evenly with the names of historical figures not engaged in warfare and uprisings. Unfortunately, this expectation was not clearly confirmed. Although the spikes of the graduate students' records are less marked, and although one of the most formative periods in American history, the period at the beginning of the 19th century, is more evenly filled with names of historical figures, the differences among the student groups were not strong enough to provide convincing support for our expectation.

Next I asked two other groups of students to list important persons in the areas of music, literature, and painting, hoping that I would obtain a similar distribution of names over historical time as observed for the political leaders shifted, however, by ½ phase. In other words, I expected the peaks of the former task to coincide with the valleys of the present task. As shown in Figure 31, these expectations were again not clearly confirmed. When inspecting the distributions of the names of musicians and painters, distinct peaks were observed for historical periods intermediate between wars, i.e., 1870, 1880, and 1920, thus confirming the distributional shift interpretation. For writers, however, large accumulations of names occur at 1810, 1860, and 1940, i.e., at periods of military instability. Of course, the latter group includes political and historical writers whose activities might coincide with periods of tension and wars. Moreover, many of the different painters, musicians, and writers are from countries other than the United States and their activities extend beyond the national boundaries. At least in regard to the wars of the 19th century, they are less clearly influenced by the disturbances and changes in priorities brought about in this country.

After my first two attempts provided some suggestions but no definite conclusions regarding either selective biases in the recollection of historical names as a function of educational levels or the distributional shift as a function of military–political versus artistic–scientific dominations, I finally analyzed the most likely source of these biases, namely, the professional

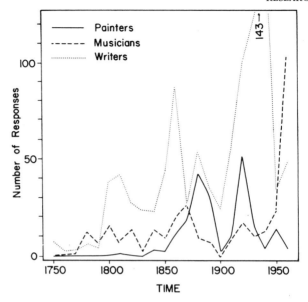

Figure 31. Number of persons influential in painting, music, and literature named by 30 seniors during a 10-minute period.

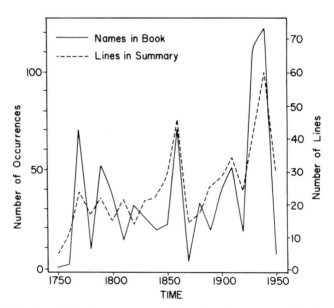

Figure 32. Number of lines in a summary and number of names appearing in a book on American history.

writing in political history. The results of Figure 32 were obtained from an analysis of an advanced high school book, A *History of the United States,* by Alden and Magenis (1962).

Figure 32 shows the number of lines given in a summary of historical events to each of the decades after 1750 as well as the number of pages greater than two on which the names of particular historical figures appeared according to the index of the book. The results show more clearly than the listing of the names by the students that the dominant emphasis given by the writers of this book relates to military interventions and wars, rather than to contributions in arts, sciences, education, and welfare. Very marked spikes are observed for the time of the American Revolution, the Civil War, and World War I and II.

HISTORICAL INTERPRETATIONS

My comparisons, as incomplete as they may be at the present time, reveal some of the general problems of historical inquiry. History is always perceived and interpreted history. As Leopold von Ranke (1885) stated many years ago: "Do we ever know in history, how it really was?" Let us consider the famous example of Caesar crossing the Rubicon during his march on Rome in the year 49 B.C. This event might have been quite accurately reported. After all, if a few days earlier Caesar was found to the north of the river and a few days later to the south he could not have avoided the crossing unless he made a swing around it either far to the west or to the east through the Adriatic. But regardless of how accurately the "facts" were recorded, their description by itself is insufficient to give them the status of an historical event. Only the interpretation of these steps by the historical perceiver, who views them as leading to civil war and to the downfall of the earlier form of Roman government, transforms these "facts" into historical events. Perhaps Caesar himself was aware of the potential interpretation; perhaps later admirers projected this interpretation into the insignificant need of passing a small river in order to reach the destination, while Caesar himself remained unaware of the potential implications of this event; perhaps the crossing was glorified in much the same way in which Washington's crossing of the Delaware, at a time when his army was in anything but a superb state, was glorified in the famous painting.

Our inability to learn "how it really was in history" should disturb us as little as our failure, according to Kant, to recognize "the thing as such." As shown in Figure 33, "history as it really was" is hidden behind a series

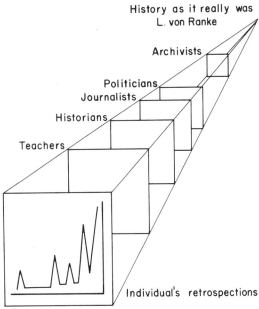

Figure 33. Representation of historical schemata of interpretations.

of interpretive filters provided through the selective preservation of information by archivists, the insufficient scrutiny of scholars, the driving brevity of teachers, and the unchallengeable apathy of students. But even if we were able to look behind all of these filters, we would not find what we were hoping for because the events themselves, in their numerousness and in their details, such as all those involved in the crossing of the Rubicon, are uninteresting to the observer. They are without historical meaning.

Denoting these interpretations as selective filters is misleading, however. A filter presupposes something behind it, something that is being filtered but recognized in some of its grosser features. But all that we will find behind an historical filter is another filter and another filter. It might be better, therefore, to compare these selective interpretations with a Sudarium, for example, with the holy veil of Saint Veronica, which when laid upon the face of the dying Christ preserved his image forever. Every interpretation derived by looking at or looking through the Sudarium, thereafter, imposed the image of Christ upon the events under concern. Of course, the "holy handkerchiefs" that modern interpreters of history provide do not impose Christ's image any longer, but that created by the cold sweat of dying soldiers of senseless wars.

Our discussion of filters and Sudaria makes us aware of two alternative views of history. The first insists upon the need for recognizing the "facts" behind historical interpretations. This view I will call objectivistic. It aims for and depends upon "the historical thing as such," which—it is insisted—makes historical interpretations possible at all. Filters select essential issues from unessential details. The other interpretation, which I shall call constructivistic, is exclusively concerned with the interpreting Sudaria and their relationships to one another. The systematic study of their transformations and of the invariant properties sustaining these transformations would represent a most advanced study of history or rather of the "science of the science of history," of metahistory.

DEVELOPMENTAL SCIENCE AS ACTION

With the recognition of the constructivistic viewpoint, we apprehend the future dimensionality of history. As already observed in the introduction, the retrospective report of development by an individual is always directed by and includes wishes, expectations, and hope. Similar implications for historical changes have been demonstrated in the studies described above. If these show that our interpretations of history are dominated by apocalyptic views, emphasizing warfares and catastrophes at the expense of welfare, arts, and sciences, we have also gained insights and access to alternative concepts. By exploring these options, by discussing them with our students, and by presenting them to a larger audience in the form of essays or books, we generate and implement a new Sudarium, a new interpretation of history, a new concept of man and his development. As emphatically claimed by Staughton Lynd (1968), the recognition of new interpretations and the awareness of former viewpoints should lead us to implementation or enactment of history. The historian does and should participate in creating history.

Not surprisingly, few developmental psychologists have shown any appreciation of the constructive character of knowledge. Like the former-day historians they have continued to restrict their task to the description of "development as it really is." Endless and mostly futile efforts have been invested in the refinement of methodologies and the increasing abstractness of theoretical constructs. Little did developmental psychologists apprehend that the most important part of their investigations ought to be the changes in experienced, lived, and directive development both from an individual and societal point of view but not the mere description of objectified performances across chronological ages.

For all too long did psychologists commit themselves to a belief in fixed capacities, such as general intelligence. This view, which has been refuted by J. McV. Hunt (1961), did not even take developmental changes into account. Developmental psychologists did not keep us waiting, however. Soon, they began to promote their view of a fixed developmental order that was thought of as lying underneath all observable changes and was to be detected, like a universal law, through increasingly refined methodologies and controls. This viewpoint, too, is now being replaced, at least among the students of a life-span developmental psychology, by investigations that take both the development of the individual and that of the society into account. The perspective of earlier scholars was that individuals were developing in a fixed social environment if not in a social vacuum.

But these approaches would be as futile as the earlier simplistic investigations, if they were again leading us to search for stable trends or universal developmental "laws," now not only residing inside the organism but in the social surroundings as well. Decisive advancement will only come when the sources and determinants of development are sought in the interactions between inner and outer processes. As the organism explores the world through his activities he, at the same time, generates the world in which he grows. These outer conditions, which in their totality have been created through the ceaseless efforts of mankind, in turn, impose themselves upon the organism. Development consists of dialectical interactions leading to the emergence and continuous change of inner and outer structures in mutual determination.

It is at this point where my concluding remarks link up with the introduction to this book. As much as the acquisition of advanced historical awareness begins to change history itself, so will an awareness of one's own development change the course of this development. Rather than apprehending our societal origin and our cultural history by the products generated, we ought to appreciate history by the activities that force it into new directions. Development of the individual, likewise, should no longer be apprehended by the products left behind, such as achievements and test scores, but by the critical awareness of past experiences that remain with the individuals and direct them toward their future. What we desire is neither a history of past failures, i.e., catastrophes, nor a developmental psychology of petrified performances, i.e., test records, but a science of the development of the individual and society based upon lived experiences and directed actions.

References

Aebli, H. *Didactique psychologique: Application à la didactique de la psychologique de Jean Piaget.* Neuchâtel: Delachaux and Niestlé, 1951. (Psychologische Didaktik. Stuttgart: Klett, 1962).

Alden, J. R., and Magenis, A. *A history of the United States.* New York: American Book, 1962.

Allport, G. W. *Personality: A psychological interpretation.* New York: Holt, 1937.

Anderson, J. E. *The psychology of development and personal adjustment.* New York: Holt, Rinehart and Winston, 1949.

Asimov, I. *The genetic code.* New York: New American Library, 1963.

Avenarius, R. Bemerkungen zum Begriff des Gegenstandes der Psychologie. *Vierteljahresschrift für wissenschaftliche Philosophie und Soziologie,* 1894, *18,* 137–161; 1895, *19,* 1–18.

Balance, W. The Grundzüge revisited: A review for contemporary psychology. Paper presented at the 81st Annual Convention of the American Psychological Association, Montreal, 1973.

Baltes, P. B. Longitudinal and cross-sectional sequences in the study of age and generation effects. *Human Development,* 1968, *11,* 145–171.

Baltes, P. B., Baltes, M. M., and Reinert, G. The relationship between time of measurement and age in cognitive development of children: An application of cross-sectional sequences. *Human Development,* 1970, *11,* 145–171.

Baltes, P. B., and Nesselroade, J. R. The developmental analysis of individual differences on multiple measures. In J. R. Nesselroade and H. W. Reese (Eds.), *Life-span developmental psychology: Methodological issues.* New York: Academic Press, 1973, pp. 219–251.

Barker, R. G., and Wright, H. F. Psychological ecology and the problem of psycho-social development. *Child Development,* 1949, *20,* 131–143.

Beard, A. *A history of business.* Ann Arbor: University of Michigan Press, 1962.

Beilin, H. Developmental stages and developmental processes. Paper presented at the Conference on Ordinal Scales of Cognitive Development. Monterey, Calif.: California Test Bureau, 1969.

Benedict, R. *Patterns of culture.* Boston: Houghton-Mifflin, 1934.

Bengtson, V. L., and Black, K. D. Intergenerational relations and continuities in socialization. In P. B. Baltes and K. W. Schaie (Eds.), *Life-span developmental psychology: Personality and socialization.* New York: Academic Press, 1973, pp. 208–234.

Berlyne, D. E. Recent developments in Piaget's work. *British Journal of Educational Psychology,* 1957, *27,* 1–12.

Berlyne, D. E. *Aesthetics and psychobiology.* New York: Appleton-Century-Crofts, 1971.

Birren, J. E. Age changes in speed of simple responses and perception and their significance for complex behavior. In *Old age in the modern world.* Edinburgh: Livingstone, 1955, pp. 235–247.

Birren, J. E. (Ed.) *Handbook of aging and the individual: Psychological and biological aspects.* Chicago: University of Chicago Press, 1959.

Birren, J. E. A brief history of the psychology of aging. *Gerontologist,* 1961, *1,* 69–77, 127–134.

Birren, J. E., and Botwinick, J. The relation of writing speed to age and to the senile psychoses. *Journal of Consultant Psychology,* 1951, *15,* 243–249.

Blondel, C. *Introduction à la psychologie collective.* Paris: Colin, 1928.

Bloomfield, J. *Language.* New York: Holt Co., 1933.

Blum, J. E., Jarvik, L. F., and Clark, E. T. Rate of change on selective tests of intelligence; a twenty-year longitudinal study of aging. *Journal of Gerontology,* 1970, *25,* 171–176.

Blumenthal, A. *Language and psychology.* New York: Wiley, 1970.

Boll, J. J. The input and output of 22 psychological periodicals: A study of bibliographical coverage. Unpublished manuscript, University of Illinois, Urbana, Ill., 1952.

Boring, E. G. *A history of experimental psychology* (2nd ed.). New York: Appleton-Century-Crofts, 1957.

Boring, E. G., and Boring, M. D. Masters and pupils among the American psychologists. *American Journal of Psychology,* 1948, *61,* 527–534.

Bousfield, W. A., and Sedgewick, C. H. W. An analysis of sequences of restricted associative responses. *Journal of General Psychology,* 1944, *30,* 149–165.

Brandenburg, G. C., and Brandenburg, J. Language development during the fourth year: The conversation. *Pedagogical Seminar,* 1919, *26,* 27–40.

Brentano, F. von. *Psychologie vom empirischen Standpunkt.* Leipzig: Meiner, 1874.

Bringmann, W. The background: Wundt at Heidelberg. Paper presented at the 81st Annual Convention of the American Psychological Association, Montreal, 1973.

Brown, R. *Words and things.* Glencoe, Ill.: Free Press, 1958.

Bruner, J. S. The course of cognitive growth. *American Psychologist,* 1964, *19,* 1–15.

Bruner, J. S. *Toward a theory of instruction.* Cambridge: Harvard University Press, 1966.

Brunswik, E. *Systematic and representative design of psychological experiments.* Berkeley: University of California Press, 1949.

Bühler, K. *Sprachtheorie.* Jena: Fischer, 1934.

Cardno, J. A. The network of reference: Comparison in the history of psychology. *Journal of Genetic Psychology,* 1963, *68,* 141–156.

Carnap, R. *Der logische Aufbau der Welt.* Hamburg: Meiner, 1928. (Logical structure of the world. Berkeley: University of California Press, 1967.)

Carroll, J. B. Diversity of vocabulary and the harmonic series law of word-frequency distribution. *Psychological Records,* 1938, *2,* 279–386.

Cassirer, E. *Substanzbegriff und Funktionsbegriff*. Berlin: B. Cassirer, 1910. (Substance and function and Einstein's theory of relativity. Chicago: Open Court, 1923).

Chamberlain, H. S. *Die Grundlagen des 19. Jahrhunderts*. München: Bruckmann, 1909. (The foundations of the 19th century. London: Lane, 1910).

Charles, D. C. Historical antecedenty of life-span developmental psychology. In L. R. Goulet and P. B. Baltes (Eds.), *Life-span developmental psychology: Research and theory*. New York: Academic Press, 1970, pp. 23–52.

Chomsky, N. *Syntactic structures*. The Hague: Mouton, 1957.

Chomsky, N. Review of B. F. Skinner's *Verbal behavior*. *Language*, 1959, *35*, 26–58.

Chomsky, N. *Aspects of the theory of syntax*. Cambridge, Mass.: MIT Press, 1965.

Chomsky, N. *Language and mind*. New York: Harcourt, Brace & World, 1968.

Chotlos, J. W. Studies in language behavior: IV. A statistical and comparative analysis of individual written language samples. *Psychological Monographs*, 1944, *56*, 75–111.

Cipolla, C. M. *Money, prices, and civilization in the Mediterranean world*. Princeton, N.J.: Princeton University Press, 1956.

Coombs, C. H. *Theory of data*. New York: Wiley, 1964.

Curtis, H. J. Biological mechanisms underlying the aging process. *Science*, 1963, *141*, 686–694.

Darwin, C. *On the origin of species by means of natural selection, or, the preservation of favored races in the struggle for life*. London: Murray, 1859.

Dekekind, R. *Was sind und was sollen Zahlen?* (*II Aufl.*) Braunschweig: Vieweg, 1893. (Essays on the meaning of numbers. Chicago: Open Court Publications, 1924.)

Dewey, J. The reflex-arc concept in psychology. *Psychological Review*, 1896, *3*, 357–370.

Dilthey, W. Ideen über eine beschreibende und zergliedernde Psychologie. *Sitzungsberiohte der Königlichen, Preussischen Akademie der Wissenschaften*, Berlin, 1894.

Duckett, E. S., *Carolingian portraits*. Ann Arbor, Mich.: University of Michigan Press, 1962.

Durkheim, E. *Les formes élémentaires de la vie réligieuse*. Paris: Alcan, 1912. (The elementary forms of religious life, a study in religious sociology. New York: Macmillan, 1915).

Durkheim, E., and Mauss, M. De quelques formes primitives de classification. *L'Annés Sociologique*, 1903, *6*, 1–72.

Ebbinghaus, H. *Über das Gedächtnis*. Leipzig: Duncker und Humblot, 1885.

Ehrenfels, C. von. Über Gestaltqualtäten. *Vierteljahresschrift für wissenschaftliche Philosophie*, 1890, *14*, 249.

Elderton, E. M., Moul, M., and Page, E. M. On the growth curves of certain characters in women and the interrelationship of these characters. *Annals Eugenics*, 1928, *3*, 277–335.

Erikson, E. H. *Young man Luther*. New York: Norton, 1958.

Erikson, E. H. *Identity, youth and crisis*. New York, Norton, 1968.

Flavell, J. H. *The developmental psychology of Jean Piaget*. New York: Van Nostrand, 1963.

Flavell, J. H. Stage related properties of cognitive development. *Cognitive Psychology*, 1971, *2*, 421–453.

Frazer, J. G. *The golden bough*. London: MacMillan, 1890.

Frege, G. *Grundgesetze der Arithmetik*. Jena: Pohle, 1903. (The basic laws of arithmetic. Berkeley, Calif.: University of California Press, 1964).

Furth, H. G. *Piaget for teachers*. Englewood Cliffs, N.J.: Prentice-Hall, 1970.

Gaettens, R. *Inflationen*. München: Pflaum, 1955.

Galton, F. *Hereditary genius: An inquiry into its laws and consequences*. London: Macmillan, 1869.

Galton, F. *Inquiries into human faculty and its development*. London: Macmillan, 1883.

Garfield, E. Primordial concepts, citation indexing and historio-bibliography. *Journal of Library History*, 1967, *2*, 235–249.

Garfield, E., Sher, I. H., and Torpie, R. J. *The use of citation data in writing the history of science*. Philadelphia, PA.,: Institute Scientific Information, Inc., 1964.

Garvey, W. D., and Griffith, B. G. Scientific communication: Its role in the conduct of research and creation of knowledge. *American Psychologist*, 1971, *26*, 349–362.

Giorgi, A. Psychology: A human science. *Social Research*, 1969, *36*, 412–432.

Gobineau, J. A. *Essai sur l'inégalité des races humaines*. (5th ed.) Paris: Firmin-Didot, 1884. (The inequality of human races. London: Heinemann, 1915).

Goffman, W. Mathematical approach to the spread of scientific ideas—the history of mast cell research. *Nature*, 1966, *212*, 449–452.

Groffmann, K. J. Life-span developmental psychology in Germany: Past and present. In L. R. Goulet and P. B. Baltes (Eds.), *Life-span developmental psychology: Research and theory*. New York: Academic Press, 1970, pp. 53–68.

Halbwachs, M. *Les cadres sociaux de la mémoire*. Paris: F. Alcan, 1925.

Halbwachs, M. La psychologie collective d'aprés C. Blondel. *Revue philosophique de la France et de l'étranger*, 1929, *54*, 444–456.

Halbwachs, M. *La mémoire collective*. Paris: Presses Universitaires de France, 1950.

Hall, G. S. *Adolescence*. New York: Appleton, 1904.

Hall, W. E., and Robinson, F. P. The role of reading and life activity in a rural community. *Journal of Applied Psychology*, 1942, *26*, 530–542.

Harary, F., Norman, R. Z., and Cartwright, D. *Structural models*. New York: Wiley, 1965.

Hay, D. *The medieval centuries*. London: Methuen, 1964.

Heisenberg, W. *Philosophic problems of nuclear science*. New York: Pantheon, 1952.

Henle, M. (Ed.) *The selected papers of Wolfgang Köhler*. New York: Liveright, 1972.

Herdan, G. *Type-token mathematics: A textbook of mathematical linguistics*. The Hague: Mouton, 1960.

Herodotus (Translated by A. D. Godley). London: Heinemann, 1931.

Hobbes, T. *Elementa philosophica de cive*. Amsterdam: Elzevirium, 1669.

Hölder, O. Die Axiome der Quantität und die Lehre vom Mass. *Berichte der Sächsischen Gesellschaft der Wissenschaften, Leipzig, mathematische-physikalische Klasse*, 1901, *53*, 1–64.

Holzkamp, K. Wissenschaftstheoretische Voraussetzungen kritisch-emanzipatorischer Psychologie: Teil I. *Zeitschrift für Sozialpsychologie*, 1970, *1*, 5–21.

Holzkamp, K. *Kritische Psychologie*. Frankfurt/M.: Fischer, 1972.

Horvath, W. J. Jig-saw puzzle solving as a stochastic process. *MHRI research memorandum*, University of Michigan, 1963.

Hull, C. L. *Principles of behavior*. New York: Appleton-Century-Crofts, 1943.

Hunt, J. McV. *Intelligence and experience*. New York: Ronald Press, 1961.

Hyatt, A. Genesis of the Arietidae. *Smithsonian contributions to knowledge*, 1890, *26*, (673), 1–21.

Jacobi, J. S. *The psychology of C. G. Jung*, (6th ed.). New Haven: Yale University Press, 1962.

James, W. *The principles of psychology*. New York: Holt, 1890.

Jensen, A. R. How much can we boost IQ and scholastic achievement? *Harvard Educational Review*, 1969, *39*, 1–123.

Jesperson, O. *Analytic syntax*. London: Allen and Unwin, 1937.

Johnson, S. C. Hierarchical clustering schemes. *Psychometrika*, 1967, *32*, 241–254.

Kantor, J. R. *Interbehavioral psychology*. Granville, OH: Principia Press, 1959.

Kessler, M. M. Biographic coupling between scientific papers. *American Documentation*, 1963, *14*, 10–25.

Kochen, M. Stability in the growth of knowledge. *American Documentation*, 1969, *20*, 186–197.

Koga, Y., and Morant, G. M. On the degree of association between reaction times in the case of different senses. *Biometrika*, 1923, *15*, 355–359.

Köhler, W. *Die physischen Gestalten in Ruhe und im stationären Zustand*. Braunschweig: Vieweg, 1920.

Krüger, F., and Spearman, C. Die Korrelation zwischen verschiedenen geistigen Fähigkeiten. *Zeitschrift für Psychologie*, 1907, *44*, 50–114.

Kuhn, T. S. *The structure of scientific revolutions*. Chicago: University of Chicago Press, 1962.

Labov, W. The study of language in its social context. *Studium Generale*, 1970, *23*, 30–87.

Lamb, S. M. Prolegomena to a theory of phonology. *Language*, 1966, *42*, 536–573.

Lazarus, M., and Steinthal, H. (Eds.) *Zeitschrift für Volkerpsychologie und Sprachwissenschaften*, 1859–1890, 1–20.

Leach, E. *Claude Lévi-Strauss*. New York: Viking Press, 1970.

Lehman, H. C. *Age and achievement*. Princeton: Princeton University Press, 1953.

Lehman, H. C. The creative production rates of present versus past generations of scientists. *Journal of Gerontology*, 1962, *17*, 409–417.

Lenin, V. L. *What is to be done*. New York: International Publishers, 1929(a).

Lenin, V. L. *Philosophical notebook* (Collected Works, Vol. 29) New York: International Publishers, 1929(b).

Lenneberg, E. *The biological basis of language*. New York: Wiley, 1967.

Lévi-Strauss, C. *Anthropologie structurale*. Paris: Plon, 1958. (Structural anthropology. New York: Basic Books, 1963).

Lévy-Bruhl, L. *La mentalité primitive*. Paris: Presses Universitaires de France, 1922. (Primitive mentality. New York: Macmillan, 1923).

Lewin, K. Gesetz und Experiment in der Psychologie. *Symposion*, 1927, *1*, 375–421.

Lewin, K. *Principles of topological psychology*. New York: McGraw-Hill, 1936.

Lewin, K. Behavior and development as a function of total situation. In L. Carmichael (Ed.), *Manual of child psychology* (2nd ed.). New York: Wiley, 1954, pp. 492–630.

Link, H. C., and Hopf, H. A. *People and books*. New York: Book Manufacturing Institute, 1946.

Looft, W. R. The psychology of more. *American Psychologist*, 1971, *26*, 561–565.

Lynd, S. Historical past and existential present. In T. Roszak (Ed.), *The dissenting academy*. New York: Pantheon Books, 1968, pp. 101–109.

Mach, E. *Analyse der Empfindungen und des Verhältnis des Psychischen zum Physischen*. Jena: Fischer, 1886. (The analysis of sensations, and the relation of the physical to the psychial. New York: Dover, 1959).

Malinowski, B. The problem of meaning in primitive languages. Supplement I. In C. K.

Ogden and I. A. Richards (Eds.), *The meaning of meaning.* New York: Harcourt and Brace, 1923, pp. 296–336.

Malinowski, B. *Myth in primitive society.* London: Kegan, 1926.

Marshall, M. E. Gustav Fechner, Mises, and the comparative anatomy of angels. *Journal of the History of the Behavioral Sciences,* 1969, *5,* 39–58.

Marx, K. *Lohnarbeit und Kapital.* Berlin: Vorwärts Verlag, 1891. (Wage-labor and capital. Chicago: Kerr, 1948.)

Marx, K. *Capital, a critical analysis of capitalistic production.* Moscow: Foreign Languages Publishing House, 1954. (Das Kapital, Kritik der politischen Oekonomie. Hamburg: Meissner, 1890–1894.)

McCarthy, D. Language development in children. In L. Carmichael (Ed.), *Manual of child psychology* (2nd ed.). New York: Wiley, 1954, pp. 492–630.

McCullers, J. C. G. Stanley Hall's conception of mental development and some indications of its influence on developmental psychology. *American Psychologist,* 1969, *24,* 1109–1114.

McLaughlin, G. H. Psycho-logic: A possible alternative to Piaget's formulation. *British Journal of Educational Psychology,* 1963, *33,* 61–67.

McNeill, D. On theories of language acquisition. In T. R. Dixon and D. L. Horton (Eds.), *Verbal behavior and general behavior theory.* New York: Prentice-Hall, 1968, pp. 406–420.

McNeill, D. The development of language. In P. H. Mussen (Ed.), *Carmichael's manual of child psychology.* New York: Wiley, 1970, pp. 1061–1161.

Meacham, J. A. The development of memory abilities in the individual and society. *Human Development,* 1972, *15,* 205–228.

Mead, G. H. *Mind, self, and society.* Chicago: Chicago University Press, 1934.

Merleau-Ponty, M. *The structure of behavior.* Boston: Beacon, 1963.

Moscati, S. *Ancient Semitic civilizations.* London, Elek, 1957.

Munnichs, J. M. A. A short history of psycho-gerontology. *Human Development,* 1966, *9,* 230–245.

Mussen, P. H. (Ed.) *Carmichael's manual of child psychology* (2 vols.) (3rd. ed.) New York: Wiley, 1970.

Neary, J. A scientist's variations on a disturbing racial theme. *Life,* 1970, *68,* (22) 64.

Neill, A. S. *Summerhill: A radical approach to child rearing.* New York: Hart, 1960.

Nesselroade, J. R., and Baltes, P. B. Adolescent personality development and historical changes: 1970–1972. *Monographs of the Society for Research in Child Development,* 1974, *39,* No. 154.

Nestle, W. *Vom Mythos zum Logos.* Stuttgart: Kröner, 1940.

Nietzsche, R. W. *Die Geburt der Tragödie.* Stuttgart: Kröner, 1872. (The birth of tragedy. New York: Doubleday, 1956.)

Norderskiöld, E. *The history of biology: A survey.* New York: Knopf, 1928.

Osgood, C. E., Suci, G. J., and Tannenbaum, P. H. *The measurement of meaning.* Urbana: University of Illinois Press, 1957.

Osgood, C. E., and Wilson, K. V. *Some terms and associated measures for talking about human communication.* Urbana: University of Illinois, Institute of Communication Research, 1961.

Parkinson, C. N. *Parkinson's law or the rising pyramid.* Boston: Houghton-Mifflin, 1957.

Payne, T. R. *S. L. Rubinstein and the philosophical foundations of the Soviet psychology.* New York: Humanities Press, 1968.

Pearsons, K. On the laws of inheritance of man. *Biometrika*, 1904, *3*, 131–190.

Piaget, J. *Le langage et la pensée chez l'enfant*. Neuchatel: Delachaux & Niestlé, 1923. (The language and thought of the child. New York: Harcourt & Brace, 1926).

Piaget, J. *Le jugement et le raisonnement chez l'enfant*. Neuchatel: Delachaux and Niestlé, 1924. (Judgement and reasoning in the child. New York: Harcourt & Brace, 1928).

Piaget, J. Logique génétique et sociologie. *Revue philosophique de la France et de l'étranger*, 1928, *53*, 167–205.

Piaget, J. *Introduction a l'épistémologie génétique*. (3 vols.). Paris: Presses Universitaires de France, 1950.

Piaget, J. *The origins of intelligence in children*. New York: Norton, 1963.

Piaget, J. Explanation in psychology and psychophysiological parallelism. In P. Fraisse and J. Piaget (Eds.), *Experimental psychology: Its scope and method*. (Vol. I), New York: Basic Books, 1968, pp. 153–191.

Piaget, J. *Structuralism*. New York: Basic Books, 1970.

Pirenne, H. *Mohammed and Charlemagne*, New York: Norton, 1939.

Platt, J. What we must do. *Science*, 1969, *166*, 1115–1121.

Pledge, H. T. *Science since 1500; a short history of mathematics, physics, chemistry, and biology*. New York: Philosophical Library, 1947.

Poincaré, H. *Wissenschaft und Hypothese*. Leipzig: Lindemann, 1902. (Science and hypothesis. New York: Dover, 1952).

Pressey, S. L., and Pressey, L. C. *Pressey diagnostic reading test, grades 3–9, Form A*. Bloomington: Public School Publications Co. (undated).

Price, de Solla, D. J. *Science since Babylon*. New Haven: Yale University Press, 1961.

Price, de Solla, D. J. Networks of scientific papers. *Science*, 1965 *149*, 510–515.

Rader, W. T. and O'Conner, J. Percentiles for men in ideaphoria, Work-sample 161, Based on 33,007 cases. *Technical Report Number 625*, Boston: Human Engineering Lab., Inc., 1957.

Rader, W. T., and O'Conner, J. Percentiles for women in ideaphoria, Work-sample 161, Based on 10,127 cases. *Technical Report Number 635*. Boston: Human Engineering Lab., Inc., 1959.

Ranke, L. von. *Geschichte der romanischen und germanischen Völker von 1494 bis 1514* (3. Aufl.). Leipzig: Duncker and Humblot, 1885.

Raphelson, A. C. *Psychology at the University of Michigan: 1852–1950*. (Mimeographed Report) Department of Psychology, University of Michigan Flint College, 1968.

Rapoport, A., Rapoport, A., Livant, W. P., and Boyd, J. A. A study of lexical graphs. *Foundations of Language*, 1966, *2*, 269–286.

Rashevsky, N. *Looking at history through mathematics*. Cambridge, Mass.: MIT Press, 1968.

Raven, J. C. The comparative assessment of intellectual ability. *British Journal of Psychology*, 1948, *39*, 12–19.

Reese, H. and Overton, W. F. Models of development and theories of development. In L. R. Goulet and P. B. Baltes (Eds.), *Life-span developmental psychology: Research and theory*. New York: Academic Press, 1970, pp. 115–145.

Reinert, G. Comparative factor analytic studies of intelligence throughout the human lifespan. In L. R. Goulet and P. B. Baltes (Eds.), *Life-span developmental psychology: Research and theory*. New York: Academic Press, 1970, pp. 467–484.

Richardson, B. W. Memory as a test of age. *Asclepiad*, 1891, *8*, 230–232.

Riegel, K. F. Die Bedeutung der Statistik für das psychologische Experiment. *Psychologische Beiträge*, 1958, *3*, 595–618. (a)

Riegel, K. F. Ergebnisse und Probleme der psychologischen Alternsforschung: Teil I–III. *Vita Humana,* 1958, *1,* 52–64, 111–127, 204–243; 1959, *2,* 213–237. (b)

Riegel, K. F. Age and cultural differences as determinants of word associations: Suggestions for their analysis. *Psychological Reports,* 1965, *16,* 75–78. (a)

Riegel, K. F. Speed of verbal performance as a function of age and set: A review of issues and data. In A. T. Welford and J. E. Birren (Eds.), *Behavior, aging and the nervous system.* Springfield, Ill.: Thomas, 1965, pp. 150–190. (b)

Riegel, K. F. Development of language: Suggestions for a verbal fallout model. *Human Development,* 1966, *9,* 97–120.

Riegel, K. F. Some theoretical considerations of bilingual development. *Psychological Bulletin,* 1968, *70,* 647–670. (a)

Riegel, K. F. Untersuchungen sprachlicher Leistungen und ihrer Veränderungen. *Zeitschrift für allgemeine und angewandte Psychologie.* 1968, *15,* 649–692. (b)

Riegel, K. F. History as a nomothetic science: Some generalizations from theories and research in developmental psychology. *Journal of Social Issues,* 1969, *25,* 99–127.

Riegel, K. F. A structural, developmental analysis of the Department of Psychology at the University of Michigan. *Human Development,* 1970, *13,* 269–279. (a)

Riegel, K. F. Relational interpretation of the language acquisition process. In G. B. Flores d'Arcais and W. J. M. Levelt (Eds.), *Advances in psycholinguistics.* Amsterdam: North-Holland, 1970, pp. 224–236. (b)

Riegel, K. F. The language acquisition process: A reinterpretation of selected research findings. In L. R. Goulet and P. B. Baltes (Eds.), *Life-span developmental psychology: Theory and research.* New York: Academic Press, 1970, pp. 357–399. (c)

Riegel, K. F. The influence of economic and political ideologies upon the development of developmental psychology. *Psychological Bulletin,* 1972, *78,* 129–144.

Riegel, K. F. Cardinal Chomsky's Platonic revival movement or linguistics out of HIS mind: A rejoinder to Professor Weimer's paper. *American Psychologist,* 1973, *28,* 1013–1016. (a)

Riegel, K. F. Developmental psychology and society: Some historical and ethical considerations. In J. R. Nesselroade and H. W. Reese (Eds.), *Life-span developmental psychology: Methodological issues.* New York: Academic Press, 1973, pp. 1–23. (b)

Riegel, K. F. Dialectic operations: The final period of cognitive development. *Human Development,* 1973, *16,* 346–370. (c)

Riegel, K. F. The recall of historical events. *Behavioral Science,* 1973, *18,* 354–363. (d)

Riegel, K. F. Time and change in the development of the individual and society. In H. W. Reese (Ed.), *Advances in child development and behavior,* vol. 7. New York: Academic Press, 1973. (e)

Riegel, K. F. Adult life crises: Toward a dialectic theory of development. In N. Datan and L. H. Ginsberg (Eds.), *Life-span developmental psychology: Normative life crises.* New York: Academic Press, 1975, pp. 97–124. (a)

Riegel, K. F. From traits and equilibrium toward developmental dialectics. In W. J. Arnold and J. K. Cole (Eds.), *1974–75 Nebraska symposium on motivation.* Lincoln: University of Nebraska Press, 1975. (b) (in press).

Riegel, K. F. Semantic basis of language: Language as labor. In K. F. Riegel and G. C. Rosenwald (Eds.), *Structure and transformation: Developmental and historical aspects.* New York: Wiley, 1975, pp. 167–192. (c)

Riegel, K. F. Structure and transformation in modern intellectual history. In K. F. Riegel and G. C. Rosenwald (Eds.), *Structure and transformation: Developmental and historical aspects*. New York: Wiley, 1975, pp. 3–24. (d)

Riegel, K. F. (Ed.) *The development of dialectical operations*. Basel: Karger, 1975. (e)

Riegel, K. F. The dialectics of human development. *American Psychologist*, 1976. (a) (in press).

Riegel, K. F. The dialectics of time. In N. Datan and H. W. Reese (Eds.), *Life-span developmental psychology: Dialectical perspectives on experimental research*. New York: Academic Press, 1976. (b) (in press).

Riegel, K. F., and Birren, J. E. Age differences in verbal associations. *Journal of General Psychology*, 1966, *108*, 153–170.

Riegel, K. F. and Riegel, R. M. An investigation into denotative aspects of word meaning. *Language and Speech*, 1963, *6*, 5–21.

Riegel, K. F. and Riegel, R. M. Changes in associative behavior during later years of life: A cross-sectional analysis. *Vita Humana*, 1964, *7*, 1–32.

Riegel, K. F., and Riegel, R. M. Vorschläge zu einer statistischen Interpretation von Alternsveränderungen sprachlicher Leistungen. In F. P. Hardesty and K. Eyferth (Eds.), *Forderungen an die Psychologie*. Bern: Huber, 1965, pp. 87–105.

Riegel, K. F. and Riegel, R. M. Development, drop, and death. *Developmental Psychology*, 1972, *6*, 306–319.

Riegel, K. F., Riegel, R. M., and Meyer, G. A study of the drop-out rates in longitudinal research on aging and the prediction of death. *Journal of Personality and Social Psychology*. 1967, *4*, 342–348.

Riley, M. W., Johnson, W., and Foner, A. (Eds.), *Aging and society, Vol. 3: A sociology of age stratification*. New York: Russell Sage Foundation, 1972.

Rousseau, J. J. *Si le rétablissement des sciences et des arts a contribué à épurer les moeurs*. Dijon, France: L'Académie Dijon, 1750. (Republished: The miscellaneous works of Mr. J. J. Rousseau. London: Becket and De Hondt, 1767.)

Rousseau, J. J. *Emile ou de l'éducation*. LeHaye: J. Néaulme, 1762. (Emile or education. New York: Dutton, 1950).

Rubinstein, S. L. *Grundlagen der allgemeinen Psychologie*. Berlin: Volk und Wissen, 1958.

Rubinstein, S. L. *Principien und Wege der Entwicklung der Psychologie*. Berlin: Akademie Verlag, 1963.

Ruckmick, C. A. The use of the term *function* in English textbooks of psychology. *American Journal of Psychology*, 1911, *24*, 99–123.

Ruger, H. A., and Stoessiger, B. On the growth curves of certain characteristics in man (males). *Annals of Eugenics*. 1927, *2*, 76–111.

Russell, B. *The principles of mathematics*. Cambridge, England: Cambridge University Press, 1903.

Ryder, N. The cohort as a concept in the study of social changes. *American Sociological Review*, 1965, *30*, 843–861.

Salton, G. Information dissemination and automatic information systems. *Proceedings Institute of Electrical Engineers*, 1966, *54*, 1663–1678.

Saussure, de F. *Cours de linguistique generale*. Paris: Payot, 1916. (Course in general linguistics. New York: McGraw-Hill, 1966.)

Savage, G. H. Symptoms of mental dissolution. *Transactions of the Medical Society* (London), 1893, *16*, 252–263.

Schaie, K. W. A general model for the study of developmental problems. *Psychological Bulletin*, 1965, *64*, 92–108.

Schaie, K. W. A reinterpretation of age-related changes in cognitive structure and functioning. In L. R. Goulet and P. B. Baltes (Eds.), *Life-span developmental psychology: Research and theory.* New York: Academic Press, 1970, pp. 486–508.

Schaie, K. W. Limitations on the generalizability of growth curves of intelligence. *Human Development,* 1972, *15,* 141–152.

Schaie, K. W., and Strother, C. R. The cross-sequential study of age changes in cognitive behavior. *Psychological Bulletin,* 1968, *70,* 671–680. (a)

Schaie, K. W., and Strother, C. R. The effects of time and cohort differences on the interpretation of age changes in cognitive behavior. *Multivariate Behavior Research,* 1968, *3,* 259–293. (b)

Scott, C. A. Old age and death. *American Journal of Psychology,* 1896, *8,* 67–122.

Shock, N. W. *A classified bibliography of gerontology.* Stanford, Calif.: Stanford University Press, 1951, Supplement One, 1957.

Skinner, B. F. *Walden Two.* New York: Macmillan, 1948.

Smith, M. E. Linguistic constancy in individuals when long periods of time are covered and different types of material are sampled. *Journal of General Psychology,* 1955, *53,* 109–143.

Smith, M. E. The application of some measures of language behavior and tension to the letters written by a woman at each decade of her life from 49 to 89 years of age. *Journal of General Psychology,* 1957, *57,* 289–295.

Smith, N. W. Some background considerations to the development of Greek psychology. Unpublished manuscript, Department of Psychology, State University of New York, Plattsburgh, 1970.

Society for the Psychological Study of Social Issues [SPSSI]. Statement by SPSSI on current IQ controversy: Heredity versus environment. *American Psychologist,* 1969, *24,* 1039–1040.

Spencer, H. *The principles of psychology,* vol. I. New York: Appleton, 1897.

Spengler, O. *Der Untergang des Abendlandes.* München: Beck, 1918–1922. (The decline of the West. New York: Knopf, 1946.)

Spranger, E. *Lebensformen: Geisteswissenschaftliche Psychologie und Ethik der Persönlichkeit.* (4. Aufl.) Halle/Saale: M. Niemeyer, 1924.

Stern, W. *Die differentielle Psychologie in ihren methodischen Grundlagen.* (2. Aufl.) Leipzig: Barth, 1921.

Stern, W. *Allgemeine Psychologie auf personalistischer Grundlage.* Den Haag: Nijhoff, 1935. (General psychology from the personalistic standpoint. New York: Macmillan, 1938.)

Stevens, S. S. Mathematics, measurement, and psychophysics. In S. S. Stevens (Ed.), *Handbook of experimental psychology.* New York: Wiley, 1951, pp. 1–49.

Strehler, B. L. *Time, cells and aging.* New York: Academic Press, 1962.

Sumner, W. G. *Social Darwinism.* Englewood Cliffs, N.J.: Prentice-Hall, 1963.

Titchener, E. G. The postulates of a structural psychology. *Philosophical Review,* 1898, *7,* 449–465.

Tuddenham, R. D. Soldier intelligence in World Wars I and II. *American Psychologist,* 1948, *3,* 149–159.

Tukey, J. W. Keeping research in contact with the literature: Citation indices and beyond. *Journal of Chemical Documentation,* 1962, *2,* 34–37.

Uexküll, J. J. von. *Umwelt und Innenwelt der Thiere.* Berlin: Springer, 1909.

Van den Daele, L. D. Qualitative models in developmental analysis. *Developmental Psychology,* 1969, *1,* 303–310.

Velikovsky, I. *Earth in upheaval*. New York: Doubleday, 1955.

Vygotsky, L. S. The problem of cultural development of the child. *Journal of Genetic Psychology*, 1929, *36*, 415–434.

Vygotsky, L. S. *Thought and language*. Cambridge, Mass.: MIT Press, 1962.

Wechsler, D. *Wechsler intelligence scale for children*. New York: Psychological Corporation, 1949.

Wechsler, D. *Manual for the Wechsler adult intelligence scale*. New York: Psychological Corporation, 1955.

Wechsler, D. *The measurement and appraisal of adult intelligence*. Baltimore: Williams and Wilkins, 1958.

Werner, H. *Einführung in die Entwicklungspsychologie*. Leipzig: Barth, 1926. (Comparative psychology of mental development. New York: Follett, 1948.)

Wesley, F. Masters and pupils among the German psychologists. *Journal of the History of the Behavioral Sciences*, 1965, *1*, 252–258.

Wesley, F., and Hurtig, M. Masters and pupils among French psychologists. *Journal of the History of the Behavioral Sciences*, 1970, *5*, 320–325.

Wilden, A. *System and structure: Essays in communication and exchange*. London: Tavistock, 1972.

Wills, A. R. An investigation of the relationship between rate and quality of handwriting in primary school. *British Journal of Educational Psychology*, 1938, *8*, 229–236.

Windelband, W. *Geschichte und Naturwissenschaft*. Strassburg: Heitz, 1894.

Witte, W. Transposition als Schlüsselprinzip. In F. Weinhandl (Ed.), *Gestalthaftes Sehen*. Darmstadt: Wissenschaftliche Buchgesellschaft, 1960, pp. 406–412.

Woodward, W. R. Fechner's Panpsychism: A scientific solution of the mind–body problem. *Journal of the History of the Behavioral Sciences*, 1972, *8*, 367–386.

Wozniak, R. H. Verbal regulation of motor behavior: Soviet research and non-Soviet replication. *Human Development*, 1972, *15*, 13–57.

Wozniak, R. H. Dialecticism and structuralism: The philosophical foundation of Soviet psychology and Piagetian cognitive developmental theory. In K. F. Riegel and G. C. Rosenwald (Eds.), *Structure and transformation: Developmental and historical aspects*. New York: Wiley, 1975, pp. 25–47.

Wyatt, F. A psychologist looks at history. *Journal of Social Issues*, 1962, *16*, 182–190.

Wyatt, F. The reconstruction of the individual and collective past. In R. W. White (Ed.), *The study of lives*. New York: Appleton-Century-Crofts, 1963, pp. 304–320.

Xhignesse, L. V., and Osgood, C. E. Bibliographical citation characteristics of the psychology networks in 1950 and in 1960. *American Psychologist*, 1967, *22*, 778–791.

Zipf, G. K. *Human behavior and the principle of least effort*. Cambridge, Mass.: Addison-Wesley, 1949.

Index

DATE DUE